AGENTS OF EMPIRE:
BRITISH FEMALE MIGRATION
TO CANADA AND AUSTRALIA, 1860s–1930

The period between the 1860s and the 1920s witnessed a wave of female migration from Britain to Canada and Australia, much of which was managed by women. *Agents of Empire* explores the work of the women who promoted, managed, and ultimately transformed single British women's experiences of migration.

Lisa Chilton examines the origins of women-run female emigration societies through various aspects of their work and the responses they received from emigrants and settled colonists. Working in the face of apathy in the community, resistance by other (usually male) managers of imperial migration, and agency exerted by the women they sought to manage, the emigrators endeavoured to maintain control over the field until government agencies took it over in the aftermath of the First World War.

Agents of Empire highlights the aims and methods behind the emigrators' work, as well as the implications and ramifications of their long-term engagement with this imperialistic feminizing project. Chilton provides tremendous insight into the struggle for control of female migration and female migrants, adding an important dimension to the study of gender, migration, and empire.

(Studies in Gender and History)

LISA CHILTON is an assistant professor in the Department of History at the University of Prince Edward Island.

STUDIES IN GENDER AND HISTORY

General Editors: Franca Iacovetta and Karen Dubinsky

AGENTS OF EMPIRE

British Female Migration to Canada and Australia, 1860s–1930

Lisa Chilton

UNIVERSITY OF TORONTO PRESS
Toronto Buffalo London

ISBN 978-0-8020-9274-8 (cloth)
ISBN 978-0-8020-9474-2 (paper)

∞

Printed on acid-free paper

Library and Archives Canada Cataloguing in Publication

Chilton, Lisa
  Agents of empire : British female migration to Canada and Australia,
  1860s–1930 / Lisa Chilton.

  Includes bibliographical references and index.
  ISBN 978-0-8020-9274-8 (bound)
  ISBN 978-0-8020-9474-2 (pbk.)

  1. Women immigrants – Canada – Social conditions – 19th century.
  2. Women immigrants – Canada – Social conditions – 20th century.
  3. Women immigrants – Australia – Social conditions – 19th century.
  4. Women immigrants – Australia – Social conditions – 20th century.
  5. Women – Great Britain – Social conditions – 19th century.
  6. Women – Great Britain – Social conditions – 20th century.
  7. Canada – Emigration and immigration – History – 19th century.
  8. Canada – Emigration and immigration – History – 20th century.
  9. Australia – Emigration and immigration – History – 19th century.
  10. Australia – Emigration and immigration – History – 20th century.
  I. Title

JV7224.c55 2007   305.48'821071   c2006-906423-7

University of Toronto Press acknowledges the financial assistance to its
publishing program of the Canada Council for the Arts and the Ontario
Arts Council.

This book has been published with the help of a grant from the Canadian
Federation for the Humanities and Social Sciences, through the Aid to
Scholarly Publications Programme, using funds provided by the Social
Sciences and Humanities Research Council of Canada.

University of Toronto Press acknowledges the financial support for its
publishing activities of the Government of Canada through the Book
Publishing Industry Development Program (BPIDP).

Contents

Illustrations follow page 54.

Acknowledgments

A large number of friends and acquaintances have contributed to the production of this book by sharing their knowledge of potentially useful primary and secondary sources, and through their suggestions about how I might push my analysis further. The knowledge and practical assistance of archivists on three continents have enriched this work. I would especially like to thank Richard Summerell at the Australian Archives in Canberra, and Anne Monk at the Girls' Friendly Society Archives in London, who made my work at these archives particularly pleasant. Kathryn McPherson, my PhD supervisor, and Bettina Bradbury and Nick Rogers, my thesis committee members at York University, provided me with a wealth of inspiration, support, and practical guidance at key points of this study's development. Jim Hammerton gave me extensive, invaluable commentary on the completed PhD dissertation in the capacity of external examiner. I am grateful to the members of the York University Women's History Reading Group, who commented upon material from several of my chapters during my time at York University. Intellectually and socially, I benefited greatly from these meetings. Of this group, I would especially like to thank Magda Fahrni, Amanda Glazbeek, Laila Haidarali, Molly Ladd-Taylor, Liz Millward, Kato Perdue, and Adele Perry. I would like to thank Seth Koven and Lynn Hollen Lees, both of whom welcomed me into their academic community during my year as a Visiting Scholar at the University of Pennsylvania, as well as other members of the Delaware Valley British History Study Group for their comments on an early version of chapter 2. My colleagues at my new academic home in the history department at the University of Prince Edward Island have provided me with a wonderfully supportive environment in which to revise my dissertation for publication. *Agents of Empire* benefited from the generosity of the University of Toronto Press's anonymous reviewers, all of whom combined positive encouragement with excellent critical commentary. As the Studies in Gender and History series editor, Karen Dubinsky has been both supportive and inspirational, while Jill McConkey, the book's editor, has made the process of publishing this book a pleasure. I would also like to give special thanks to Bill Jones and Michele Langfield, both of whom have been generous with their work, their insights, and their friendship.

Various members of my family helped me to bring this book to fruition. Dawn and Tony Newton and Wendell White welcomed me into their homes for long visits during my research time spent in Australia, and Anton Sternberg and Bruce Newton provided me with comfortable homes and great companionship in London while researching there. Jim and Michele Moran supported and encouraged me at all points of my academic development. My parents, Erica and Patrick Chilton, provided a deep well of energy and confidence upon which I drew freely in times of need. Finally, I would like to thank Camille Soucie and James Moran for their endless enthusiasm, patience, and emotional and practical support while I worked on this project. The writing of this book would not have been nearly as enjoyable without their involvement.

Abbreviations

BLFES	British Ladies Female Emigrant Society
BWEA	British Women's Emigration Association
CIL	Colonial Intelligence League
FMCES	Female Middle-Class Emigration Society
GFS	Girls' Friendly Society
NSL	New Settlers' League
SACS	South African Colonisation Society
SOSBW	Society for the Oversea Settlement of British Women
SPCK	Society for Promoting Christian Knowledge
TAS	Travellers' Aid Society
WES	Women's Emigration Society
WNIS	Women's National Immigration Society
WPIS	Women's Protective Immigration Society
YWCA	Young Women's Christian Association

AGENTS OF EMPIRE:
BRITISH FEMALE MIGRATION
TO CANADA AND AUSTRALIA, 1860s–1930

Introduction

The Paris International Exhibition of 1900 was anticipated with great excitement by 'leading' men and women around the world. Since the Great Exhibition in London in 1851, these events had gained a reputation as fantastic cultural events, at which history and the future, cosmopolitan urban society and 'exotic' colonized peoples, agricultural science and industrial innovations were brought together to illustrate Western society's forward march of progress. International exhibitions were competitive events, where representatives of participating countries endeavoured to reveal to observers (at the exhibition and back home) their nations' various assets. As the exhibition that would usher in a new century, the Paris exhibition was seen as a particularly important event in which to take part.

In the lead-up to the exhibition at Paris, members of the National Council of Women of Canada (NCWC) mobilized to ensure that Canada's women would be appropriately represented in their nation's display. The outcome of their meetings with Sydney Fisher, the minister of agriculture, who was responsible for the Canadian exhibit, was that the Canadian government would sponsor the publication of a book by the NCWC on Canadian women. *Women of Canada: Their Life and Work* was designed to communicate to a large international audience 'some idea of the happiness, freedom and richness of opportunity enjoyed by the women living under the beneficent sway of "Our Lady of the Sunshine and of the Snows."'[1] The book's essays offered its readers information on a wide array of subjects relating to women's position in Canada, including their history, their legal and political status, their paid work experiences, their education, their involvement with international organizations, and their engagement with charities and reform work. The closing section of the book comprised two sections: 'one on Immigration, the other on Indian women.' According to Julia Drummond (one of the book's authors), the pairing of these topics was conscious; it allowed the study to close with 'an invitation to the women of the old world, and a backward glance at the first women of the new.' Reflecting upon the significance of Canadian women's position, as illustrated in the pairing of these two subjects, Drummond noted, 'It was a good world in those early days, when the Indian women gathered in the harvest and sang their hymn of praise to the sun, or gave their voice to the councils of war. It is a better world now; for the Sun-god still shines as it did of old; the land is peopled by the children of two races who came hither from the old world and share under one flag the privileges of a great Empire.'[2]

Drummond's introduction to *Women of Canada* encapsulates a set of assumptions that underlay the construction of the NCWC's study, as well as much of the work that the organization's members performed for the good of their country on a voluntary basis. In spite of much evidence to the contrary (even contained within the book itself), Canada's aboriginal peoples are largely assumed to be a disappearing race, Canada's population is understood to be the offspring of two founding peoples (French and English), and the country's inhabitants are imagined as united in their appreciation of their privileged status as members of the British Empire. In Drummond's essay it is also made clear that Canada will achieve great things in the future because of the energetic involvement of its educated women. '[This] book goes forth from the women of Canada that it may tell something of the building up of this youngest of the nations,' Drummond writes. It tells how, 'not alone by material prosperity, but also by "the power of intellect and knowledge, the power of beauty, the power of social life and manners," and, above all, by "the power of conduct," it is growing to its full share.'[3]

Thinking about the international context within which the NCWC produced its *Women of Canada* study adds layers of meaning to this very interesting piece of work. The book was created at the height of the 'Scramble for Africa,' and during the unexpectedly long and internationally unpopular Anglo-Boer War. It was published just as New Zealand and Australia were gaining independent national status, and at a point when Canadians (like Australians) were engaged in heated debates about what sorts of ethnic/racial groups should be encouraged (or allowed) to immigrate. It was also written in a period of polarized opinion regarding women's rights with respect to suffrage and the professions.

Women of Canada reveals assumptions and concerns that were shared by large numbers of women (and men) throughout the British Empire at the turn of the twentieth century. Confidence in the need for the carefully managed migration of single British women to colonial destinations played an important role in these individuals' shared understandings. In public discourses of white superiority in colonial contexts, women – as mothers of the race and as keepers of the home – carried the burden and the honour of appropriately acculturating colonials and colonized peoples.[4] In Canada and in Australia, as in New Zealand, South Africa, Rhodesia (Zimbabwe), India, and a host of other colonies, understanding of femininity, domesticity, civilization, and British culture were inextricably intertwined.

Yet female migrants were not motivated, first and foremost, by these sorts of considerations,[5] nor were the immigration-sponsoring colonial and dominion governments. As Jan Gothard points out, government officials in Australia (as elsewhere within the British Empire) noted the 'civilizing' and 'settling' effects of women's integration into male-dominated, frontier communities, and they were concerned about increasing the white population of Australia through reproduction. But colonial governments' financial support of single women's immigration had far more to do with single women's domestic labour capacity than with any of these other factors. Gothard reminds us that 'the ninety thousand or more single working-class women who migrated to the Australian colonies under government assistance schemes in the second half of the nineteenth century did so as paid domestic workers.' Australian governments' assisted immigration policies related 'single mindedly' to women's productive labour.[6]

Studies of women, gender, and empire have proliferated in the past two decades. Whereas even twenty years ago historians of the British empire were not particularly interested in women – as imperialists, as emigrants, or as colonized persons – or in theorizing about the gendered nature of imperialism, an impressive number of recent studies of the empire and imperialism have made women or gender a central focus of concern.[7] The work of Adele Perry, Ann McClintock, Antoinette Burton, Margaret Strobel, Mary Louise Pratt, Ruth Frankenberg, and the authors of *Creating a Nation, 1788–1990*, to name only a few, has fundamentally altered our understanding of the relationships between colonizers and colonized, while it has transformed our sense of nation building and national identity.[8] Indeed, as recent debates about the publication of the *Oxford History of the British Empire* and David Canna-

dine's *Ornamentalism* clearly illustrate, it is no longer acceptable to publish histories that purport to be survey studies of the British Empire that
do not adequately take into account colonizing and colonized women.[9]

A logical result of the increased interest by academics in subjects relating to women, gender, and empire has been a substantial increase in
attention to the experiences, identities, and roles of the thousands of
single British women who emigrated to the colonies and dominions during the nineteenth and early twentieth centuries. For a full decade,
James Hammerton's *Emigrant Gentlewomen: Genteel Poverty and Female Emigration, 1830–1914*, published in 1979, was the only book-length, theoret-
ically engaged study of British female emigration.[10] Since the late 1980s,
a large number of books, dissertations, and articles dealing solely with
this subject have been produced.[11] Although Hammerton's early work is
still influential in this field,[12] the types of questions that historians have
raised about the nature and meanings of imperial female migration,
and the ways in which they have attempted to answer those questions,
have changed considerably since its publication. Questions pertaining
to the identities of the emigrants, their emigrators, and the communities into which the migrants settled have become central to the field.
These questions revolve around concepts of 'whiteness,' nation, empire,
class, and culture, and how these concepts intersected with and were
moulded by gender relations. Similarly, questions concerning women's
agency and the practice of power in the imperial context have shaped
the way this field has evolved.[13]

If historians of British women's emigration have effectively taken up
some of the 'hotter' questions currently circulating in the 'gender and
imperialism' field of history, they have been relatively slow to adopt
some of the themes and methods coming out of the larger field of
migration history. With few exceptions, historians who have written
about imperial female migration have chosen to focus upon the migration of British women to specific colonial destinations. Where more
than one destination has been examined, little has been made of this
fact. Comparative analysis has been, at best, a side comment in most of
the recent literature in this field.[14] Likewise, transnational histories of
British female migration still remain to be written. According to Christiane Harzig, transnational histories of migration abandon the traditional analysis of migration as occurring 'along the push-pull paradigm,
by which people moved from one place (culture/region of origin) to
another place (receiving culture).' 'The process was seen as linear,'
Harzig writes: 'one-directional, with a beginning in one culture and an

end in another.' In this scenario, 'the migrant tried to insert him/herself into one new culture, creating a hyphenated identity, bicultural at the most.'[15] Increasingly, researchers are rethinking migration history in terms of a more complicated set of alliances, experiences, power structures, and cultural identities. Now that a relatively large body of secondary literature on British female migration is available, excellent transnational studies in migration history, such as Donna Gabaccia's *Italy's Many Diasporas*,[16] will no doubt stimulate new and interesting ways of approaching the history of British women's migration.

Agents of Empire does not set out to do for British women what Gabaccia has done for Italians. It is by no means a transnational study in the way that *Italy's Many Diasporas* is. But as with Gabaccia's work, the value of transnational studies – like the value of comparative studies – will be clearly evident in this book. By looking at British women's migration in various national and international contexts over a substantial period of time, and by working through the interactions of interested parties in Britain, Canada, and Australia around the subject of female migrants, this study provides insights into the gendered politics of imperial migration that would not have been possible through a more geographically limited study of British women's migration.

During the late nineteenth and early twentieth centuries, British women migrated to a large number of destinations, both within and outside of the British Empire. This study of imperial migration might easily have focused upon migration to southern Africa, New Zealand, or even the less popular destinations of India or the West Indies. I decided that Canada and Australia would be my destination case studies for two compelling reasons: both of these destinations consistently received large numbers of single female migrants between the middle of the nineteenth century and 1930; and they were the two destinations that were compared to each other most explicitly throughout the period under study. There are other reasons why Canada and Australia make interesting comparisons. For example, they offered significantly different destinations for single women: Canada was of the northern hemisphere, cold, and relatively close at hand; Australia was of the southern hemisphere, hot, and the other side of the world from Britain. Their governments also differed in their responses to immigration as a whole, and to the work of British female emigrators specifically.

The people at the centre of this book are the British, Canadian, and Australian women who promoted, managed, and transformed imperial migration between the middle of the nineteenth century and 1930; an

imperial network of female emigrators who had in common their affilia-
tion (in one way or another) with a limited number of well-respected,
long-lasting British female emigration societies. *Agents of Empire* is about
how these women endeavoured (usually together, though sometimes in
opposition to each other) to gain control over this field of work in the
face of apathy in the community, resistance by other (usually male)
managers of imperial migration, and agency exerted by the women they
sought to manage. It is about the aims and methods behind these emigrators' work, as well as the implications and ramifications of their long-
term engagement with this imperialistic feminizing project.

In *Agents of Empire*, emigrants feature first and foremost as the objects
of attention by emigrators and state representatives. The core of my discussion about emigrant women relates to emigrants' collective public
identities, and how and why these changed over time. The identities of
single female emigrants were contested terrain during the late nineteenth and early twentieth centuries. Various interest groups battled to
reformulate and control these identities in their efforts to implement
their own imperial migration agendas. At the heart of this study, then, is
this struggle for the control of public images of female migration and
female migrants, and what an analysis of this struggle tells us about gender, migration, and empire.

Agents of Empire is organized temporally and thematically. On a basic
level, this study moves from the early nineteenth century, when female
migration was largely unmanaged – and certainly not managed by female
emigrators – to the end of the 1920s and the onset of the Great Depression. Thematically, this book moves from an exploration of the origins of
women-run female emigration societies, through various aspects of the
emigrators' work and the responses that it received from emigrants and
settled colonists, to the post–First World War period, when government
agencies throughout the British Empire took over this field of work,
absorbing the voluntary female emigration societies in the process.

Chapter 1 examines the nature and composition of British female
emigration societies, from their origins in the mid-nineteenth century. I
review the extensive practical work of middle-class women, in conjunction with the financial, political, and ideological support of elite women,
that determined that these societies would gain a niche of strategic
importance within the world of imperial female migration. Chapters 2
and 3 explore two aspects of British women's emigration work in greater
detail. Chapter 2 focuses upon the period of most intense concern
about the white slave trade. It shows how the women who worked with

female emigrants in the 1880s and thereafter manipulated and re-fashioned contemporary discourses of sexual danger to serve their own emigration-management agendas. Chapter 3 also addresses the period of emigration management that began in earnest in the 1880s. In this chapter, however, it is the promotion of female imperialism to prospective middle-class emigrants rather than the promotion of the female emigrators themselves that is of primary interest.

In chapter 4, I turn away from this focus on emigrators to examine more closely the relationship between emigrators and emigrants as seen through an analysis of emigrants' writings and actions. Specifically, this chapter assesses emigrants' responses to the emigrators and their paid helpers. It begins with the now standard assumption that female emigrators were oppressive/repressive in their efforts to control single female emigrants. It then moves on to explore instances where emigrants chose to embrace, rather than reject or merely tolerate, the female emigration project. Chapter 5 examines the work performed by emigrators who were based in Canada and Australia rather than in Britain. Here, the negotiations that surrounded the reception of single female immigrants in the colonies and dominions are at the centre of analysis. The immigration (as opposed to the emigration) context is also explored in chapter 6. In this final chapter I move to the end of the period covered by this book – the late 1920s – to a case study of female migration as it was managed by male government administrators after governments in Britain, Australia, and Canada had effectively absorbed the female emigration societies into state administrations. This study of the importation of British domestic servants to Australia's purpose-built capital city, Canberra, highlights the extent to which British female emigrants continued to be the focus of competing social and political agendas through the 1920s, while it emphasizes the differences between the management of female migration by women and by men.

An interconnected set of arguments runs through this book. The first is that starting at the middle of the nineteenth century, women of middle- and upper-class backgrounds sought to transform female migration. They aimed to increase female emigration to imperial destinations; they worked to improve the 'types' of women who were settling in the colonies; and they endeavoured to make single women's migration safe and respectable. Central to this transformation process was the emigrators' assumption that it could only occur if directed by themselves. In other words, the transformation of female migration was designed to go hand in hand with the empowerment of the female emigrators.

Second, *Agents of Empire* argues that by the turn of the century these emigrators had achieved a significant amount of success in their efforts to influence prospective emigrants, the members of the various publics, and government bodies concerning female emigrants and their needs. It is clear that the female emigration societies' management and promotion of imperial migration stimulated some women to emigrate who might otherwise have stayed in Britain. Likewise, their enthusiastic promotion of British imperial over American or other non-imperial destinations affected some women's decisions about where to go. Between 1884 and 1916, at least 22,482 women emigrated to imperial destinations through the auspices of the British Women's Emigration Association (BWEA) and the South African Colonisation Society (SACS). As Marjory Harper notes, this figure underestimates the number of women who used the services of female emigration societies, as it does not take into account the women who emigrated with the Colonial Intelligence League (CIL) or the many local emigration societies working within Britain. Large numbers of women were aided in one way or another by the emigration societies and affiliated organizations, though they never actually emigrated with the societies' parties.[17] The annual numbers of letters written in response to queries by prospective emigrants and their friends by the secretaries of these organizations were regularly noted in the societies' annual reports. These numbers were always far in excess of the number of women who actually emigrated. Moreover, emigrators like Ellen Joyce and Adelaide Ross, who also worked extensively with church and local emigration societies, were involved in the management of the migration of much larger numbers of people than would be evident from the female emigration societies' statistics. Hundreds of people were managed, directed, and advised in emigration matters by these two women alone. Between the mid-nineteenth century and the depression of the 1930s, British, Canadian, and Australian governments became increasingly interested in the supervision and regulation of single women in transit. The facts that matrons became standard features on government-sponsored emigrant ships, and that the involvement of female emigrators fundamentally affected government policies relating to female migration in Britain, Canada, and Australia, provide further testament to the emigration societies' success beyond their own ability to control the emigration of a large number of single women.[18]

The third set of arguments relates to current debates about women's agency and access to power during the late nineteenth and early twentieth centuries. Historians of women have worked over the past couple of decades to re-evaluate the relationship between women's engagement with formal politics and their ability to effect social and political change.[19] This book enters the debate about women and power with an illustration of how, in a period that was marked by numerous rebuttals of women's attempts to gain suffrage, a great number of women armed with determination, some social connections, and the necessary social and managerial skills were able to carve out for themselves positions of authority and power in the imperial context. As James Hammerton has suggested, the emigrators' 'strategic placement of women at the centre of a male enterprise on a world scale was empowering both for promoters and emigrants.'[20] For the emigrators, there was little ambiguity about the benefits of holding a position of influence within the politically charged system of empire management. The emigrators' work gave these women valuable knowledge, skills, social connections, and confidence. For emigrant women, the female emigration societies' successes of the late nineteenth and early twentieth centuries were more of a mixed blessing. Emigrators purposely infantilized young single women, stripping them of the right to look after themselves during the processes of migration and settlement. At the same time, the emigrators' various programs were designed to make female emigrants more competent and confident. Regardless of whether or not the emigrants had imperialistic ambitions, they were directed to consider themselves part of a serious social mission. They were encouraged to believe that it fell to them to elevate whole societies. The emigrators simultaneously sought to empower and disempower emigrant women. The emigrants themselves regularly demonstrated their disinterest in playing the emigrators' games strictly according to the emigrators' rules.

If the emigrators' project contained mixed meanings for the emigrant women, it is clear that the same could not be said for the aboriginal inhabitants or the 'other'-raced residents of Canada and Australia. The emigrators' efforts to domesticate the dominions entailed a firm assertion of British superiority over all other peoples. The emigrators were explicit about the fact that the migration of single British women of the right sort was about transforming 'frontier' spaces; about colonizing and reforming the 'uncivilized' inhabitants of the empire's relatively unsettled regions. Yet with only a very few, unobtrusive exceptions, the people most obviously targeted by these colonizing missions are not named in the emigrators' official records. What did the emigrators think about the non-British populations that inhabited the areas within which their emigrants would settle? How did the emigrant women themselves feel about their new aboriginal, Métis, Asian, East European, or, in the case of Canada, French-speaking neighbours? We can make educated guesses about likely answers to these questions – after all, there is now a rich and growing body of literature on this subject.[21] But it is possible to learn very little on this subject from the voluminous primary sources that were created by these emigration societies, for on this front they are silent. How can this be? A central mandate of these societies was to educate prospective emigrants about the colonies. Why would a subject that would clearly be of significant interest to the women who would settle in the Canadian West and the Australian Outback (the emigrators' favoured destinations) be ignored? As in Drummond's sleight of hand in her turn-of-the-century introduction to *Women of Canada*, the emigrators and their emigrant correspondents literally wrote other racial and ethnic groups out of the colonial setting, their unsettling presence in the colonies symbolically denied. The emigrators' colonizing project thus became, at least rhetorically, a program to manage settlers of British origin.[22]

Finally, this book argues that the gains that the emigrators had made for themselves in the imperial management of female migration were undermined in the period after the First World War, as independent initiative was replaced by state bureaucracy. For most of the century before the war, the British government was content to leave the work of promoting, advising, and protecting British emigrant women to colonial governments, philanthropic societies, and the various individuals and organizations for whom emigration formed a business interest.[23] Towards the end of the First World War, opinions within the British government changed. The Colonial Office began to make serious overtures towards an official partnership with voluntary female emigration societies – a move that had been encouraged, tentatively, by female emigrators for some time. In answer to the Colonial Office's strong encouragement, the female emigration societies amalgamated in 1917. In 1919, the resulting Joint Council of Women's Emigration Societies was made an official part of British state bureaucracy in the form of the Society for the Oversea Settlement of British Women (SOSBW). With this shift from more or less independent voluntary organizations to state-directed agencies, the work of female emigrators became increasingly tied to government agendas and bureaucracies.[24]

Within Canada and within Australia, roughly similar patterns emerged over the late nineteenth and early twentieth centuries. But while the larger picture of increasing state control over recruitment, migration, and reception applied to Britain, Canada, and Australia alike, there were marked differences in how the processes and politics behind these transformations played out. For example, there were significant differences between how Canada and Australia dealt with female migration, the most obvious being that Canadian immigration was managed federally, while the Australian colonies/states continued to manage their own programs until 1920. Women's voluntary work relating to female immigrants was supported earlier and more thoroughly in Canada than it was in Australia, where tensions between women's organizations and state officials were more regularly on public display. There were also notable differences between the British emigrators' experiences of the transition from independent work to management by the state and those of women working in the dominions. From at least the middle of the nineteenth century, colonial governments were more concerned than British governments about the 'quality' of immigrants in general, and about the morality and protection of immigrant women in particular. One result of this concern was that, unlike in Britain, Canadian and Australian governments periodically funded or otherwise supported women's organizations that were willing to recruit and chaperone female emigrants out of Britain, or to provide reception and aftercare services for new immigrants in the dominions, in the decades before the Great War. Canada and Australia were also similar in their increasing independence from British imperial agendas during the late nineteenth and early twentieth centuries. The investment of state power into the newly minted SOSBW and its affiliates in Canada and Australia came at the price of the women emigrators' autonomy. As the dominions' governments increasingly removed themselves from British control, the emigrators' loss of control over international female migration was even more clearly evident in Britain than in the dominions.

To make these arguments, this book draws on a wide range of archival sources produced by the British female emigration societies, and by British, Canadian, and Australian individuals, private organizations, and government bodies. The study begins with an examination of British emigrators and their emigration agendas through a reinterpretation of a group of sources that have been used extensively by historians of female migration. These sources are the annual reports, minutes, and various publications of the key British female emigration societies of the second half of the nineteenth century through the 1920s,[25] as well as the papers of three other organizations that worked closely with the female emigration societies during the late nineteenth and early twentieth centuries. These are the Girls' Friendly Society, the Society for Promoting Christian Knowledge, and the Travellers' Aid Society.

In reading these sources I have been sensitive to the fact that they offer a reflection both of the day-to-day business of female emigration societies' work and of the public face that the emigrators gave to that work. These documents provide valuable information concerning the projects designed and implemented by the emigrators and they provide valuable insights into how the emigrators divided up the labour that these projects demanded. But it is clear that none of the sources created by the emigration societies can be read as 'clean' evidence of the emigrators' motivations, attitudes, and ambitions. Even the unpublished minutes of meetings of these emigration societies were created with an eye to the possibilities of future readers. They were carefully worded, then edited, recounts of the meetings' events, with the bits and pieces of information that a historian might particularly wish to find left out. The works that were created for the purpose of communicating with a wider, public audience were even more self-consciously produced. They are works of propaganda that reveal much about the methods that the emigrators used to influence how their readers understood British female migration. They are less useful as a gauge of the actual success rate of the emigrators' efforts.

The key women in the female emigration societies were avid and effective self-promoters. They published their opinions widely in British and dominion newspapers, and they were enthusiastic contributors to their own societies' publications. I have been unable to find statistics on the circulation of the *Imperial Colonist*, the official organ of the dominant female emigration societies, but it is evident that copies of this journal were distributed throughout the empire. Beyond whatever readership subscribed to the journal, a wide range of women and men would have had access to issues owing to the way in which they were circulated. Copies of the *Imperial Colonist* were left in the lobbies of immigrant hostels, and they were parcelled up and sent to lonely women living on isolated homesteads. In response, emigrants from Canada, Australia, New Zealand, South Africa, and Rhodesia regularly sent letters and articles to the editor of this journal with the intention of having their views on life in the dominions published. Likewise, the societies' annual reports were circulated around the empire. The women who ran these organizations regularly quoted from or referred to information and opinions communicated in the annual reports of other, affiliated associations. Government officials also received copies of the annual reports of women's organizations that dealt with female migrants   and they considered them worthy of archival space.

In order to gain an understanding of the relationships that were forged between British emigrators and Canadian and Australian emigrators (or immigrators), I have also examined primary material generated by men and women working in the colonial contexts. These sources include published and unpublished papers produced by Canadian and Australian branches of the Girls' Friendly Society and the Travellers' Aid Society, as well as the papers of colonial female emigration and imperial societies that claimed ties with the British organizations. These Canadian and Australian organizations include the Victoria League, the British Immigration League, the Country Women's Association, the New Settlers' League, the Imperial Order Daughters of the Empire, the Young Women's Christian Association, the (Canadian) Women's Protective Immigration Society, and the Canadian and Australian Councils of Women. The papers produced by various local committees of women who managed female immigrant homes and reception programs have also been examined. Likewise, government files containing correspondence between state officials in Canada and in Australia relating specifically to female immigration have been analysed.

I have endeavoured to cast as broad a geographic net as possible in my study of Canadian and Australian immigrant reception. As a result, with the exception of the case study featured in chapter 6, specific colonial organizations, immigration projects, and women's hostels have not been explored in depth. The variety of sources that might have been used in this sort of a comparative project is boundless. In my selection of sources, I have gravitated towards those documents that touch upon the relationships that were established between the emigrators and the various agencies, organizations, and individuals with whom they interacted in the interests of facilitating imperial female migration. Thus, the Australian and Canadian government-generated files that I have used here are those that hold correspondence between private bodies and government agents, reports and commentaries on immigrants and on the management of migration, and petitions for reforms and for new migration initiatives.

A Note on Terminology

I have chosen to refer to the women who managed single female migration as *emigrators*, with Janice Gothard's discussion of this term in mind:

'"To emigrate" is commonly an intransitive verb: "she emigrates"; "they emigrate." However, in the language of nineteenth century female emigration it was frequently transitive: e.g. "they emigrated the women." Thus "emigrating" becomes something which is "done" to someone else. The *Oxford Dictionary* attributes an early usage of the term in this manner to Maria Rye ... The term "emigrate" used in this way denotes the taking away of agency from the people who were "emigrated"; they became the objects of the action, rather than its subjects.'[26] I use this term to refer to women who worked with emigrants in Britain, as well as women who worked at immigrant reception in Canada and Australia. I consciously use the terms 'emigrator' rather than 'immigrator,' and 'emigrant' rather than 'immigrant,' to signify the migration managers' interest in the female migrants' British origins.

Throughout the text, I tend to use '*British*' rather than 'English,' and '*Britain*' rather than 'England,' even though most of the emigrators were clearly anglophiles who assumed that their work related to English imperialism. I do so because the female emigration societies that are studied here were British organizations, with representatives working in Wales, Scotland, and Ireland, as well as overseas. The emigrants who were managed by these emigrators were also not just English, and even those who departed from England's shores were often Irish women who had moved to England before departing overseas.

I use the term '*colonies*' to refer to Canada, Australia, and their provinces and states when discussing these locations as understood by British emigrators. Technically, 'dominions' would work better for most of this period, for most of these areas, and I try to make use of this term whenever it clearly makes more sense to do so. But there are no derivatives of 'dominion' to compare with those of colony: colonial, colonist, and colonize – terms that were used liberally by the emigrators. Newfoundland, Nova Scotia, New Brunswick, Prince Edward Island, Ontario, and Quebec gained responsible government in the 1840s and 1850s. The Canadian nation was formed at Confederation in 1867, with Manitoba and British Columbia added in 1870 and 1871, and Saskatchewan and Alberta in 1905. In Australia, New South Wales, Victoria, South Australia, and Tasmania gained responsible government in 1854, with Western Australia separating into its own state with responsible government in 1890. The Australian states confederated in 1901.

'With This Sign I Conquer':
Middle-Class Female Emigrators and
the Management of Imperial Migration

In Mary Heath-Stubbs's official history of the Girls' Friendly Society (GFS), published in 1925 to mark the society's golden anniversary, there is a striking visual representation of the relationships between the women who promoted and facilitated female emigration during the late nineteenth and early twentieth centuries and the British Empire (see figure 1 in the illustration section). The image is dominated by a carefully staged photograph of Ellen Joyce, who was the head of the GFS's Emigration Department and a key member of the British Women's Emigration Association (BWEA) for over forty years. In this photograph Joyce appears confident and competent. She is sitting at her desk, holding a letter she was reading when the photographer happened upon her. Undoubtedly, it is correspondence pertaining to female migration. Upon her chest are pinned the symbols of her country's and her empire's appreciation of her work. As the caption below the photograph points out, Joyce is a Lady of the Order of St John of Jerusalem and Commander of the British Empire.[1]

The photograph of Joyce is at the bottom of the page. Above the photograph is a map of the world – a reminder of the British Empire, and of British women's responsibilities and opportunities beyond their own shores. At the top of the page is a crossed anchor, an image 'used in the [GFS] Emigration Department under which the Joyce Parties were recognized all over the world.'[2] Because it was used by emigrators with solid reputations and recognised authority, this symbol served as an 'open sesame' for young women at their ports of destination. Female migrants who affixed the anchor-cross ribbon to their clothing and luggage were assured friendly, hassle-free receptions wherever they went.[3] This symbol was selected by Joyce to identify young women travelling to the colonies in protected female parties. The anchor-cross image had been used by Christians towards the end of the fourth century AD. Joyce chose this symbol because it signified for her some of the most important aspects of her work with female migrants: 'The anchor was especially dear to the hearts of believers; it expressed the hope of reunion; it symbolized to the baptized fortitude under the pains of persecution or martyrdom; it spoke always of stability amid the waves of this troublesome world.'[4]

The combined cross and anchor was a fitting symbol for emigrants on a serious mission: the civilization and feminization of British white-settler societies. It also served as an appropriate reminder of the involvement of women like Joyce in the management and protection of single female emigrants. 'To the outside world it will be the anchor label,' wrote Joyce. '[To] our travellers it will have a deeper significance. The great Roman Emperor, Constantine, who erected a statue of himself in Rome bearing a cross in his right hand, as the representation of the power in which his victories were won, stamped the cross on his medals with the words, "By this sign I conquer."'[5] By the sign of the anchor-cross, the female emigrants sent out with the support and guidance of Joyce and her co-workers within the female emigration societies would conquer their own personal frailties and temptations while raising their colonial host societies to a higher level of civilization.

The timing of the creation of this 1925 GFS celebration of women-centred emigration is ironically significant. Stubbs's history highlights a period when female emigrators were at the height of their power. But by the book's publication in the mid-1920s, female migration promoted, directed, and protected by all-women organizations was a thing of the past. In the aftermath of the First World War, the various organizations that had been involved in the management of single female migration combined and reorganized themselves to work with the British government as a semi-official arm of the Colonial Office. A closer relationship with the state had been desired by the women who ran the female emigration societies – although they had envisioned a relationship on different terms to those that were ultimately established.[6] The female emigration societies' increased collaboration with the British government in the post-war period was evidently good for some of the women who were involved in this work. A small number became career civil servants. But the loss of autonomy also meant the loss of control. The female emigration societies' incorporation into state structure spelled the end of an era of women's separate visions and agendas.

This chapter introduces Ellen Joyce and the numerous other women who carved out a field of stimulating, empowering work for themselves from the largely unregulated mess of British emigration that had existed at the middle of the nineteenth century.[7] It will trace the transformation of female emigration work from a relatively disreputable occupation to one that attracted royal patronage and a wide range of eminently respectable women who were willing to dedicate their time and money to the cause. It will review the process by which the migration of single women came to be dominated by the visions and agendas of a network of imperially minded women, at the centre of which was the BWEA and its offspring, the South African Colonisation Society (SACS) and the Colonial Intelligence League (CIL). Three arguments are central to this chapter. The first is that the efforts of middle-class women were critical to the successes of female emigration societies of the late nineteenth and early twentieth centuries. Although the contacts, social and political skills, and financial involvement of elite women were of invaluable service to these emigration societies, the driving force behind them was their middle-class membership. The second argument that I make here – an argument that is further elaborated in chapter 3 – is that the women who worked within the female emigration societies consciously and aggressively struggled to turn their societies into powerful institutions for the management of imperial female migration. They strategized, politicked, manipulated, and sweet-talked themselves into positions of moral authority and managerial power. Third, I argue that the relationships that were forged between the elite and middle-class members of these female emigration societies were fundamental to the consolidation of their own gendered class identities.

In her study *Edwardian Ladies and Imperial Power*, Julia Bush argues that 'female imperialism was dominated by a relatively small and close-knit leadership group' of elite women.[8] The success of women-run imperial organizations, she writes, 'depended upon the gendered upper-class skills which Society fostered.'[9] Bush bases her assessment of the role of these women upon a detailed examination of the involvement of upper-class women in Edwardian women's imperialist organizations – some of which were female emigration societies. As Bush shows, women connected to Britain's aristocratic elite were highly visible, influential members of female emigration societies during the Edwardian period. The increasingly imperialist nature of female emigration work at the end of the nineteenth century had attracted a large number of elite women to the female emigration cause. Around the turn of the century, women such as Lady Grey and Lady Knightley of Fawsley and members of the Balfour and Grosvenor families became personally involved in the work of the BWEA, the SACS, and the CIL. Not only did these women promote female emigration to the dominions through their published writing, their speeches, and their behind-the-scenes lobbying, but they also sat on committees where the societies' decisions were made.

But even during the Edwardian period, at the height of elite women's involvement in female emigration societies, the daily workings of these organizations were not controlled by upper-class women to the extent that is suggested in Bush's study. Moreover, as the following review of the history of female migration in the decades before the end of the nineteenth century reveals, it was largely the efforts of middle-class women that nurtured female emigration societies into internationally respected organizations with which many of the empire's most privileged women would enthusiastically become associated.

The popularity of imperial female migration as a cause at the turn of the twentieth century is striking when contrasted with the state of the field only half a century earlier. According to the standards of late-nineteenth-century female emigrators, the emigration of women from Britain to the colonies was largely unmanaged before the 1880s. Most of the philanthropists and parish authorities who worked at facilitating British female emigration in the first half of the nineteenth century did so as part of their larger projects to remove a wide range of impoverished individuals and families from state assistance programs, or from estates undergoing processes of reform.[10] These emigrators devoted little attention to issues of emigrant selection and care.[11] In the colonies, these British-funded emigration projects were derisively labelled 'shovelling out paupers.'[12]

When small groups of British reformers began to focus more squarely on female migration at mid-century, they were tarred with the same brush as the 'pauper' emigrators. As a result, they regularly came under attack in the press for their work. They were depicted as either naive and inept or immoral. Likewise, the women who emigrated under these charitable schemes were abused in newspaper reports. They were portrayed as women devoid of feminine virtues, and lacking the most basic domestic skills – women corrupted by the emigration experience, and themselves corrupting influences in their host societies.[13]

At mid-century, concerns regarding security and reputation limited the number of women who would have considered emigrating without family on their own initiative.[14] Those single women who did wish to emigrate seldom had the financial resources to fund their own emigration.

This was especially the case for the more expensive, distant colonial destinations, where subsidies and loans offered by governments and philanthropic emigration societies were essential for most women's emigration.[15] Even in Canada, where the cost of transportation was significantly lower, women frequently required help to find the money needed to emigrate. For these reasons, single women were a small minority of the emigrants who settled in the colonies at this time.[16] By the end of the nineteenth century, however, female migration had been revolutionized. An international network of women worked to promote and support the migration of single women. This network of women was well respected, and their services were used extensively by colonial governments. Canadian and Australian governments frequently relied upon voluntary women's organizations to welcome and house immigrants, and government bodies sought their advice on matters of policy.[17]

In short, the context into which middle-class British women inserted themselves when they began to take an interest in problems of female migration in the 1840s and 1850s was steeped in a history of underfunded and poorly managed immigration projects, unhappy emigrants and colonials, and negative press coverage. Those women who felt compelled to get involved in migration work at this time were motivated by an urgent sense of the need for reforms in shipping conditions and colonial reception for single women.[18] These early reformers of female migration were philanthropists who sought to improve conditions where they considered that the most basic of necessities for a 'civilized' existence were absent. Central to their reform work was the desire to make the emigration experience more respectable.

Over the course of the second half of the nineteenth century, middle-class women became increasingly enthusiastic about promoting and managing female migration, and more and more upper-class women were convinced to subsidize this work. This broad-based increase in interest had much to do with the fact that the reputation of female emigrators and their work had improved greatly during this period. By the 1880s, the stigma that had been attached to female emigrants and emigration projects had effectively been eroded. Two factors influenced this change. First, starting in the middle of the century, high-profile, publicity-conscious emigrators endeavoured to make the public aware of the virtues of sensitively managed migration. Of the mid-century propagandists for this cause, Caroline Chisholm was the most effective. In the late 1840s, Chisholm, supported by Lord Shaftesbury and Charles Dickens among others, successfully wooed the press and popular opinion with the image of 'respectable' female migration.[19] By the 1860s, a number of women had taken up their pens in support of imperial female migration. Of these the most conspicuous was Maria Rye, whose combative style brought much attention to this subject.[20]

The second factor that contributed to the altered image of female emigration was the successful separation of emigration from charity work.[21] By the end of the nineteenth century, the desire to give impoverished single women a new start in life was of relatively little importance to female emigration societies. Rather, female emigrators had become concerned about overseeing the emigration of women who they felt would be of most benefit to the colonies and to the empire, and about protecting female emigrants during their journey. Again, the origins of this understanding of female emigration may be found in the work of Caroline Chisholm. As she put it, 'Neither the Government nor the parishes can give us a sound and satisfactory system of Colonization; they may give us convict emigration; exile emigration; paupering or Government emigration, but they cannot give us a wholesome system of national colonization.'[22] According to Chisholm, only well-organized, voluntary bodies of high-minded citizens – citizens who would not be influenced by the 'wrong' sort of motives – could manage imperial migration in a manner that would benefit the health and welfare of both emigrants and their new communities. Although Chisholm was very much a philanthropist, driven to this work by her religious convictions, her desire to manage single female migration had as much to do with protecting Australian society from the effects of mismanaged (or unmanaged) migration as it did with the urge to offer needy single women a new start. As the various Australian colonial governments became more assertive about the needs of their people over those of Britain, this sort of perspective gained extensive support. It became less possible for Britons to see emigration to their colonies as an ideal solution to problem populations at home, and more imperative that emigrators promote their work with this colonial perspective in mind.

While the work of Caroline Chisholm and others[23] at mid-century helped to separate emigration out from charity work, the establishment of the Female Middle-Class Emigration Society in 1862 further separated emigration work from charity work by introducing a feminist perspective. The FMCES was a well-publicized philanthropic venture with an avowedly feminist agenda. Its supporters included some of Britain's most outspoken feminists.[24] In contrast to Chisholm, Maria Rye and Jane Lewin (the two women at the centre of the FMCES) did not believe that woman's natural place was in the home as wife and mother. Whereas Chisholm was motivated by a desire to see the formation of happy families in the Australian outback, these women argued that emigration would provide middle-class women with a range of work opportunities that were not available in the male-privileged, over-peopled British context. In the relatively sparsely populated, less rigidly conservative colonies, they argued, intelligent, resourceful women would be able to carve out stimulating, economically independent lives.[25] In practice the FMCES scheme failed to live up to the hopes of its originators. The reports sent back to the society by its emigrants were not as positive as had been anticipated, and its base of funding and number of workers remained cripplingly small. But the legacy of the FMCES's commitment to making emigration a field of work by women for women survived this society's demise. After the formation of the FMCES, emigration societies dealing solely with single women would play a key role in the management of female migration.

The fact that female emigration had been transformed into a relatively respectable sphere of work for social reformers who desired to further the interests of women was clearly a factor in its increased popularity. Of at least equal significance was the fact that female migration came to be associated with women's imperialist efforts.[26] The female emigration promoters of the late nineteenth century emphasized in their published writing and in their speeches that the settlement of large numbers of carefully selected British women in the colonies was of paramount importance to the future of the empire. As Bush has shown, the imperialist fervour of the late Victorian period ensured that this sort of promotion of the female emigration project would find an interested audience.[27] In the emigrators' literature, the association of imperialism and female migration was heightened during the aftermath of the Boer War, when it became obvious to many observers that South Africa could be won by war, only to be lost through a failure to assert cultural imperialism.[28] When the BWEA subcommittee charged with overseeing emigration to southern Africa branched off to form the SACS in 1902, the urgency of South Africa's political position, combined with the popularity of imperial female migration among the philanthropic elite, ensured that the SACS would be an unusually well-supported women's organization.[29] The enthusiasm for female emigration generated by the turn-of-the-century passion for imperialism supported the BWEA and its affiliated female emigration societies right through the difficult years of the First World War.[30]

By the end of the nineteenth century, emigration promotion had lost its tenuous status as a worthy field of work for socially conscious women and had emerged as an exceptionally popular focus of voluntary effort and patronage. The emigration societies that were founded at mid-century had relied heavily upon the work of energetic individual women for their survival. When Chisholm retired from front-line migration work, her emigration scheme began to dissolve.[31] Similarly, Jane Lewin's work was critical to the survival of the FMCES. When she retired, the society folded.[32] The female emigration society that emerged out of the 1880s was of quite a different stamp. After a couple of relatively ineffective attempts to form solid female emigration societies in the 1870s and early 1880s,[33] the BWEA, which was founded in 1884, emerged as the primary location of women's voluntary endeavours to promote and manage female migration. Unlike its predecessors, this organization was supported by the efforts of a large number of women who were committed to this work.

The popularity of imperial female migration as a cause was not limited to middle-class voluntary workers like Chisholm, Lewin, and Rye. From its foundation, the BWEA had the support of royal patrons.[34] By the end of the century, Princess Alexandra (from 1901, Queen Alexandra) was the BWEA's patron. The female emigration societies working in the 1850s, 1860s, and 1870s had also boasted the support of aristocratic patrons, but they would not have had a chance of attracting Queen Alexandra, the princesses, and the large number of aristocrats who followed in their wake. The patronage of this class of women provided the cause with influence and glamour that middle-class women could not hope to secure through their work alone. By the early twentieth century, the BWEA and its affiliated societies shared members with most of the other notable women's organizations of the period.[35]

The increased interest of elite women in supporting female emigration societies at the end of the century was matched by an increased desire by these women to become personally involved in the management of female emigration. The representatives of elite society who had linked their names with female emigration projects from the 1840s through the 1870s had generally limited their support to financial patronage and to promotion of the cause in government and elite circles.[36] By the turn of the century, aristocratic enthusiasts had become interested in undertaking certain aspects of the association's work themselves. A review of the publications and committee minutes produced by the BWEA and associated organizations reveals a solid representation of elite women in positions of managerial prominence.

But even at the height of their involvement, the work that elite women performed for these societies was generally limited to promoting the cause, formal and informal networking, and participation on committees. Although this sort of involvement was crucial to the emigration societies' public image and power, in reality it formed only a part of the work that the members of these organizations performed. It was the middle-class volunteers and working- or lower-middle-class paid employees of these organizations who performed most of the day-to-day tasks that were critical to the effective operation of their emigration programs. As the experienced, insightful workers at the centre of an international system of migration management, these women played a key role in how female emigration societies were perceived by prospective emigrants, members of the public, and government administrators. The skills, insights, and social connections that these middle-class women brought to their work were fundamental to their societies' strength and longevity.

For the elite women who devoted time and money to the female emigration societies, single female migration was but one of a number of causes that vied for their attention. As Bush's study shows, these were women who associated themselves with a variety of imperialist organizations, to say nothing of their other spheres of political and philanthropic engagement.[37] Although many of the middle-class women who joined the BWEA, the SACS, and the CIL also gave this work only partial attention, there were a significant number of women of this class for whom this was their life's work. The investment of self into these organizations was considerable for some middle-class members. The careers of three women who began their voluntary work with female emigrants in the 1870s and 1880s are instructive. As members of the BWEA and a host of associated organizations, Ellen Joyce, Adelaide Ross, and Grace Lefroy served as non-profit emigrators for many years. Joyce, who was introduced at the beginning of this chapter, began her career as a promoter and manager of female emigration in her early fifties. By her death in 1924 she had dedicated at least forty-two years of her life to this work.[38] Ross and Lefroy were involved in emigration work for at least thirty-five years each.[39] Joyce, Ross, and Lefroy were not unique in the length and degree of their dedication to the work of promoting emigration and protecting female emigrants. There were a significant number of women of this class who chose to embrace female emigration work as a voluntary career.[40]

An examination of the careers of Joyce, Ross, and Lefroy provides a good sense of the range of work this class of member performed and of the meaning that this work held for them. Of these three women, Joyce was the most prominent. She was an exceptionally ambitious, energetic, competent, and politically astute individual who quickly carved out leadership positions as the head of the GFS's Emigration Department and within the BWEA. Joyce worked hard at promoting female emigration, the associations with which she was connected, and herself. Her management style was typically domineering.[41] Ross and Lefroy seem to have been uninterested in gaining for themselves the sort of power and authority that were so central to Joyce's engagement with emigration work. Unlike Joyce, neither of these women celebrated her own worth in her published writing. Ross was clearly well respected by other men and women working in the field, but she never became a recognized authority on female migration as Joyce did. She appears to have enjoyed making promotional speeches, and she published the odd piece of writing on aspects of the BWEA's work about which she had the most knowledge, but she seems to have been content to take a low-profile position within the association as an organizer and as an archivist of material relating to organized imperial migration.[42] Lefroy was even less interested in cultivating a position of authority for herself than was Ross. Consequently, her contribution to the management of female migration has received less notice. In the histories of female emigrators and their work, Lefroy is among a great number of middle-class women who have received barely a mention.[43]

Joyce, Ross, and Lefroy had in common their lengthy careers as emigrators of single women. They also had in common close ties to the Anglican church, pro-empire attitudes, and a belief in women's special place in society.[44] Joyce and Ross were the wives, then widows, of Anglican clergymen. Lefroy, who never married, was a clergyman's daughter. Although ties with the Church of England were certainly not mandatory for membership in the female emigration societies of the late nineteenth century, a high percentage of such women were associated with this church. The sense of a religious and cultural mission was central to how they understood their own roles as emigrators. In their published writing they made it clear that they believed that women of their class were duty bound to guide their sisters of a lower class through the migration process. As Joyce put it in an essay aimed at middle-class philanthropists rather than prospective emigrants, '[We] shall have their pitiable, spoilt, joyless lives on our consciences if we do not [help them to emigrate].'[45] By working as emigrators, she argued, women of her class could ensure that other women, whose special skills and talents had gone unappreciated in Britain, would find their true value. Religion, imperialism, and a desire to perform women's work for women were combined in these individuals to form a potent sense of social duty.

Elite women brought their knowledge of British and imperial political affairs, useful social connections with politicians and government administrators, and the glamour of their own social status to the BWEA and its affiliated organizations. Middle-class women like Joyce, Ross, and Lefroy brought experience they had gained through previous philanthropic and reform ventures, the sympathy and interest of other philanthropists and reformers, and, most important, their own dedicated labour to the cause. It is unclear what experience and connections Lefroy brought to her female emigration work,[46] but we do know that Ross and Joyce came to the BWEA with a wealth of resources upon which they could draw. Both had had years of involvement with working-class and destitute men and women before their work with the female emigration societies. Joyce's earlier philanthropic work had included helping the working-class men and women of her own community, Winchester, who had fallen upon hard times. Whenever possible, this assistance was provided in the form of Joyce's facilitation of their emigration to the British colonies.[47] As the wife of a Stepney vicar, Adelaide Ross had also gained a wealth of philanthropic experience by the time she took on female emigration work as her primary occupation.[48] Like Joyce, she had overseen the emigration of 'worthy' applicants for aid from her parish.

The experience and insights that women like Ross and Joyce brought to their work with female emigrants was immensely important to the future of the BWEA. So too were the social networks that these women were able to use in their emigration work. Joyce was personally responsible for the involvement of at least three other women (Grace Lefroy, Emily Bromfield, and Louisa Knightley of Fawsley) who went on to play significant roles in female emigration societies. Her position of authority within a network of women's organizations proved to be very useful when the BWEA was trying to consolidate its power at the turn of the century. Joyce was also able to use her contacts within the Anglican Church to further her association's interests. These connections proved to be particularly beneficial at key moments in the early history of the BWEA.[49] Ross also made use of a large circle of friends and associates in promoting the interests of female emigrants. Perhaps of most importance was her ability to interest local clergymen in ministering to all of the groups of women who met in London at the BWEA hostel on their way overseas.[50]

A number of elite women became powerful figures within the BWEA and its sister organizations in the early years of the twentieth century. But the foundation, structure, and early strength of the BWEA were due to Joyce, Ross, Lefroy, and other women of their class. When the short-lived Women's Emigration Society (WES) fell apart in the early 1880s as a result of infighting between the society's patrons and its voluntary workers over who would direct its work,[51] Joyce, Ross, Lefroy, and a number of other like-minded women were on the scene to pick up the pieces and build a new, more cohesive organization. They designed their new emigration society with great care, so as to eliminate the sort of power struggles that had destroyed the WES. They also put a great deal of thought into how best to promote their society to the public. The founding members of the BWEA constructed a purposely gendered identity for the association that disassociated its work from charity. To the public, they presented the BWEA as an organization 'founded by Women for Women.'[52] For women like Ross and Joyce, the GFS – which demanded references concerning the virtue of prospective candidates from employers, community leaders, and clergymen – provided an admirable model for female emigration work.[53] The mechanisms of control implemented by the BWEA to ensure that only virtuous female emigrants would be assisted by the association had much in common with those of the GFS. The 'Regulations for Working Members' that were laid out in the BWEA's annual reports highlighted the association's three core aims:

a) to emigrate only such women and girls as are of good character and capacity;
b) to secure for them proper protection on the voyage, and adequate reception on arrival;
c) and, if possible, not to lose sight of them, for a year or two after emigration.[54]

The terms 'character,' 'capacity,' and 'protection,' as used here, all hold distinctly gendered meanings. Female-centred rather than obviously feminist, this was an organization that would confine its aid to female emigrants of undisputed respectability.

The women who ran the female emigration societies based their demands for state and public recognition of their value to society upon their own reputations as women who would not relax their vigilance about emigrant selection and protection, and who would always keep the best interests of the colonies and of the empire to the fore in their work. They portrayed themselves as migration managers who were scrupulous in their attention to the moral and physical safety of their charges. This image of high-minded feminine morality dominated how they presented themselves and their work. They were fierce about establishing and maintaining images of their societies that emphasized their own reliability and respectability. For women like Joyce, Ross, and Lefroy, the BWEA's reputation was closely allied with their own. 'The weeding out with tender touch of persons who would be sorry failures in the colonies, is no small part of [our] work; but it has to be done, when done, with an unflinching hand,' reads the BWEA's annual report of 1896–7. The ramifications of a failure to do so would be devastating, for if members of the BWEA were to be associated with laxity in this respect, 'we should degrade the standard of our work, and lose our good name for sending suitable women.'[55]

The extent to which Joyce took her work for the BWEA personally is illustrated by how she dealt with the case of a young woman, Sarah Weston, who emigrated with one of the BWEA emigration parties in 1896. When the Canadian minister of the interior contacted Joyce to inform her that he had received negative reports about Weston's suitability as an immigrant, Joyce's response revealed her own sense of hurt pride. She asserted that the person who had informed the minister about Weston had done so with the explicit intention of damaging her reputation. She immediately got in touch with her associates in Montreal in order to determine the validity of the report, and she requested that if Weston was found to be as incapable of supporting herself as had been asserted by her detractor, she should be deported immediately at Joyce's own expense.[56]

The level of irritation expressed by Joyce in this case was unusual, and says much about the problems relating to reception in Montreal that Joyce was dealing with at the time.[57] But her response is typical of how she viewed 'her' emigrants. Like the other women who were dedicated to working for the BWEA and associated societies, Joyce took immense pride in the BWEA's reputation as an organization that would not sacrifice its high moral standards for any other consideration. As Brian Blakely has shown in his article about a scheme to promote female emigration to South Africa in the period after the Anglo-Boer War (1898–

1901), no amount of pressure from the British government could convince the women who ran the SACS to sacrifice their standards in the interest of mass migration.[58] This commitment to sending out only those women whom the emigrators considered to be of good moral and physical health meant that a wide range of prospective emigrants were turned away. No matter how worthy a woman might otherwise be, if she had a 'blemished' history, she was ineligible for their help.[59] This policy was not only the result of their own attitudes and sentiments about who constituted worthy recipients of their aid, but also a carefully constructed strategy to justify the BWEA and affiliated societies' assumption of control over single female migration.

As the following chapters will illustrate, female emigrators like Joyce, Ross, and Lefroy dedicated large amounts of time to their emigration work. The tasks they undertook as members of their emigration associations, and as independent philanthropists for whom emigration was an attractive answer to a range of social ills, were wide ranging. They lobbied for changes to existing laws relating to female migration in Britain and in the colonies and dominions,[60] and worked hard to find work for the women they sent overseas. They raised funds by means of private networking, by public promotion of their various 'pet' projects, and by organizing regular fund-raising events. At the heart of their efforts as emigrators was the mundane work of organizing and overseeing the movement of migrants from their British homes to new homes overseas.

Like their upper-class co-members, Joyce, Ross, and Lefroy contributed an enormous amount of literature to the cause.[61] All three women worked hard to help produce interesting annual reports and journals to promote the work of the BWEA, and the effects of their enthusiasm and energy may be found throughout the periods of their involvement with the association. Joyce was particularly prolific, and the articles she produced were used again and again in different contexts.[62] Lefroy's extensive correspondence with women who had emigrated with the BWEA was regularly plundered for good text for the association's publications. By taking on the roles of creators and editors of the emigration societies' publications, these women shaped how their societies and their own work would be perceived by others. Through the societies' published literature, they were able to disseminate information, ideas, and images of their choosing to an international audience.

By producing and circulating promotional literature, Joyce, Ross, and Lefroy actively promoted female emigration and their own emigration societies. Unlike most of their more privileged sisters, these and other women of their class also furthered the interests of their organizations by personally engaging with prospective emigrants. From the societies' minutes of meetings, annual reports, and other publications comes evidence of these women's daily interactions with the single women who made use of the societies' services. For example, as part of her work as the BWEA's honorary secretary in London, Lefroy interviewed candidates for emigration. She did this at her home until a more suitable space was obtained in 1893 in the BWEA's office in South Kensington. It was also her job to welcome women who came to London to stay at the society's hostel upon their arrival, and to ensure that all was in order for their imminent departure. Ross met regularly with emigrants at the London hostel, where she gave them pep talks and led prayer sessions. She also frequently accompanied them onto their ships to see that they were comfortably settled there before departure. For years Ross ran a clothing donation service from her home for the use of needful emigrants. Her short statements about the desperate need for clothing for women who could not emigrate for want of an outfit appeared regularly in the early issues of the *Imperial Colonist.* In the early years of the BWEA, Joyce's home was used as the organization's central office. In the late nineteenth century Joyce served as both the emigration secretary of the GFS and the central organizing secretary of the BWEA. These two positions ensured that she would correspond with all prospective emigrants going out under the auspices of these societies. Joyce personally checked the references of all candidates for emigration, and made the ultimate decision about who would be accepted, and who would not. Like Ross and Lefroy, Joyce also regularly visited the emigrants' hostels and ships to bid the young women farewell (see figure 2).

Through their personal interaction with female emigrants, these three women, like many others involved in this work, provided the BWEA with a human identity. Even when the core members of the BWEA were dealing with thousands of women's inquiries, problems, and travel plans per year, they continued to give precedence to activities that gave the emigrants the sense that the emigrators really cared about them. By offering the emigrants little gifts to celebrate the momentous occasion of the departure from their homeland, these women aimed to secure for themselves and their organizations loyal supporters with whom future contact would be possible.[63] This personal interaction continued long after the emigrants left Britain's shores. The societies' secretaries sent settled emigrants friendly letters, along with their reminders about the need to return the money loaned to them, and Christmas cards to show their continued interest. These women's commitment to forming personal relationships with the emigrants was informed by their desire to influence the young women's attitudes and future behaviour. The emigrators also maintained ties with 'old emigrants' because they could provide up-to-date information about colonial conditions and because they were often willing to welcome new emigrants.

The women who ran the female emigration societies of the late nineteenth and early twentieth centuries tried to be diligent about providing support only for women who they thought would prove to be assets to their new communities. They were equally careful about the characters and abilities of those women with whom they associated in their emigration work. By the 1890s, not only were there incentives for emigrators to work through organizations that controlled substantial funds and had access to the ears of persons of authority, but the BWEA had become so powerful that it was proving difficult for individual operators to compete.[64] Emigration agents who desired to work in partnership with the BWEA and its sister organizations were not automatically permitted to do so. The credentials of prospective associates were scrutinized and debated before their names could be linked to the BWEA, the SACS, or the CIL. For example, when Miss Wileman publicly indicated her desire to establish her own British women's emigration society – a society that would presumably work in conjunction with the BWEA, the SACS, and the CIL – the women who ran these emigration societies agreed that 'Miss Wileman was not a woman with whom they could cooperate.'[65] The BWEA and associated organizations jealously guarded their increasingly powerful positions as the directors of British female emigration, and worked to undermine the legitimacy of comparatively small operations. The intention to cut out possible competitors from female emigration work was made explicit by the women who organized the amalgamation of the BWEA, the SACS, and the CIL into the Joint Council of Women's Emigration Societies in 1917–18. They believed that the post-war environment would prove to be a fertile context for female emigration, and they wanted to ensure that in this new context they would consolidate rather than have to share the gains they had made in the field over the previous three decades.[66]

The effective promotion of the interests of the emigration societies, like the successful promotion of female emigration, was achieved as a result of careful strategizing by the societies' leading women. Behind closed doors, the management of the female emigration societies' public images was taken very seriously, which meant that silence was regularly practised in spite of the desire to speak out. A letter sent from Ellen Joyce to Adelaide Ross in 1914 illustrates the point that the female emigrators consciously strategized about how, when, and by whom pronouncements about the societies' affairs would be made. Ross had taken it upon herself to publish the exciting news that the Queen had decided that a large donation would be made for the work of the female emigrators. Just in time, Ross's efforts to go public had been discovered. It fell to Joyce to chastise her. 'I do not think that you or I or anyone has been authorised to print a circular about what the Queen has or has not been doing, and especially not one which professes to come from Miss Lefroy at the Office,' Joyce wrote. 'Hardly a post has passed without my being told, cautioned, and warned, that the only notice we must publish or circulate is that provided by Mrs. Harcourt ... and more than that, I have been told officially that if any but the authorised view of the case is put forward that the permission of the Queen to use the money will be withdrawn and we shall lose the grant!!' It was all about politics, Joyce pointed out. If the Labour party were to get hold of the information, a scandal would ensue. 'Government people must be interpreted in their own way,' wrote Joyce, 'unless we want to oppose them and fight them, and then we could say what we liked, but that would not play the game of our women who want outfits.'[67]

The ability of BWEA, SACS, and CIL members to effectively negotiate with male-dominated voluntary associations, Anglican church authorities, government bodies, and the British and colonial publics was central to their successful bids for power as the managers of the imperial migration of women. Upper-class women were able to use their ready access to men in positions of power to further the interests of their female emigration projects. Likewise, the skills and knowledge that elite women learned as a part of their highly privileged education were of great value to the emigration societies.[68] But middle-class members were also key players in their societies' struggles for influence and authority throughout the empire. Middle-class women who performed the daily work of managing the migration of single women were regularly put into positions where their tact or blunt determination could help or hinder their societies' interests. The knowledge that they gained from their managerial work was of enormous value to the societies' committees when hard decisions had to be made about how problems relating to uncooperative government officials or poorly managed colonial reception programs ought to be handled. Moreover, the privilege of having access to men in positions of authority was not monopolized by elite women.

Ellen Joyce's confident assumption that, as an official representative of the BWEA, her opinions ought to be taken seriously by authorities within the Australian and Canadian governments, and within the Anglican Church, is proof that middle-class women could, and did, engage in politics effectively on behalf of their societies.

Historians of philanthropy and social reform in the nineteenth and early twentieth centuries have tended to focus upon the largely middle-class philanthropists who actually performed the philanthropic work, and on the relationships that were established between these philanthropists and the local lower-class or (more recently) the aboriginal, 'colonised,' objects of their attention. This focus has been of particular interest to historians concerned with the formation and evolution of class and race identities. Historians of the middle class have argued that in the late eighteenth and nineteenth centuries, men and women of a similar middling social and economic status came to identify with each other in opposition to men and women of the working class.[69] As historians of British imperialism have shown, a similar process of establishing self in contrast to the 'other' occurred through imperial philanthropic work.[70] Central to this process of class identification was the involvement of members of the middle class in charitable organizations and private philanthropy. In fact, as F.K. Prochaska has pointed out, the association of philanthropic activity with middle-class attitudes and values has come to be assumed.[71]

Historians interested in the relationships between class and gender have also found the history of philanthropy a fruitful area of study. They have shown how an examination of the unpaid work of women who aimed to better the lots of their less fortunate 'brothers and sisters' reveals that such work was fundamental to the emergence and solidification of gendered class identities.[72] Through their philanthropic work, women revealed their own moral superiority and right to authority over the recipients of their benevolence, while affirming and consolidating their own middle-class status. Simultaneously, female philanthropists used their experiences in this field of work to broaden their spheres of influence and to support their arguments for increased power within societies dominated by men.

By the late nineteenth century, the BWEA and affiliated societies were no longer clear-cut examples of philanthropic organizations. The emigrators had worked hard to distance emigration work from pauperism and charity work. By the 1890s, imperialism was a more evident motivation behind the BWEA's work than was philanthropy. Moreover, the class relations and identities established through female emigration management were complicated by the fact that working-class women were not the emigrators' preferred sort of emigrant. In spite of these differences between more traditional philanthropic work and the management of female migration, the work performed by the emigrators informed class and gender relations and identities in many of the ways that have been identified by historians of more obviously mainstream philanthropic organizations.

The middle-class women who worked within the female emigration societies presented themselves as eminently more capable than the less-privileged recipients of their aid. Their superior breeding, schooling, and relative maturity were claimed as credentials to explain why they were so much better qualified to manage all aspects of single women's migration than were the emigrants themselves. They advised emigrants about much more than where to go, what to take, and how to navigate the migration bureaucracy. They also told the women how to behave while in transit, what frame of mind they should develop for life in the colonies, and how to perform as good colonial employees. Women like Ellen Joyce created images of themselves that were steeped in maternalism. Yet it is clear that the younger women who played the symbolic roles of the emigrators' daughters could be unceremoniously stripped of their benefactors' protection if they stepped out of line. For the good of the larger cause, Joyce and others like her were quite willing to sacrifice the interests of young women who made inappropriate choices or who otherwise failed to live up to the emigrators' expectations. Generally, the British-based women's emigration societies were adamantly opposed to the deportation of British female emigrants from the colonies.[73] But as the case of Mary Weston in Montreal, discussed earlier in this chapter, makes clear, deportation could be seen as a viable solution to the emigrators' own problems.

Historians of philanthropy have been most interested in the relationships that were established between the philanthropists and the recipients of their attention.[74] But, as a study of the female emigration societies reveals, the relationships that were forged between the two classes of women who funded and worked for these organizations can also provide interesting material for analysis. Most aspects of the emigration enterprise served to clarify the emigrators' gender and class positions within British society. The dynamics that were established between different classes of women who were members of the emigration societies were no different in this respect. The manner in which the elite and middle-class members of the organizations interacted, and the ways in which these women were presented in the texts that these societies created for public consumption, simultaneously reflected and redefined the class relations between the women involved in single female migration.

Historians of English philanthropy have made it clear that, as much as philanthropic work might have been dominated by the middle class, philanthropy also played an important role in justifying or improving the status of the British aristocracy. Although it might not have added much to most upper-class men and women's self-identities as members of an elite social class, philanthropic work could affect the way they were perceived by members of the classes below them. In his study of the British royalty and philanthropy, Prochaska claims that from the late eighteenth century, the royal family was keenly aware that public displays of charity were valuable correctives to an image of royalty that was too often presented as 'costly and corrupt.'[75] According to Prochaska, 'By the time Queen Victoria ascended the throne, philanthropy had become, if not crucial to the monarchy's survival, extremely useful ... No other role offered such rich returns in publicity and deference for so little effort.'[76] The members of the royal family were not the only members of the aristocracy to be conscious of the role of philanthropy in the formation of a positive upper-class image. As Brian Harrison shows, philanthropists such as Shaftesbury and Gladstone were all too aware that 'aristocratic philanthropy ... provided justification for rank and wealth.'[77] It is evident that philanthropically promoted and managed female emi-gration likewise served as a means by which the aristocracy's privileged position was supported.

The middle-class identity that emerged out of the early nineteenth century was forged, in part, in opposition to images of a profligate aristocracy.[78] But by the end of the nineteenth century, the cultures and attitudes of the upper classes had evolved so that images embraced by upper-class and middle-class women had much in common. At least publicly, the middle-class women who managed female migration from the 1880s had no disdain for the class above them. In the documents created by the female emigration societies there is no indication that the middle-class women who did the daily legwork resented or attempted to diminish the privileges that went along with the patrons' class status. The middle-class women who worked in these organizations were highly conscious of the value of prominent elite women's support for their cause. They saw no benefit in undermining aristocrats' attempts to be seen as good citizens. In fact, they actively enhanced their titled sisters' auras of dignified benevolence. The middle-class members of the BWEA and affiliated societies were complicit in the creation of positive aristocratic identities. In the *Imperial Colonist*, articles about the success of past experiments in migration and updates on the progress of current emigration projects sat comfortably next to detailed accounts of speeches made by elite men and women at meetings held by patrons of the emigration societies. The published accounts of aristocrats' praise about work already performed, and admonishments about the work still needing to be done for the emigration cause, served symbolically to claim for the upper classes the work of the middle-class emigrators. Middle-class women supported these claims. The aristocratic identity that was constructed in female emigration societies' published texts was of serious, sympathetic women who were working hard to solve the problems of the nation and of the empire.

The single women who made use of the services provided by the women's emigration societies would have learned from a variety of sources that they owed gratitude and respect to aristocratic benefactors. The elite women who financed and promoted the work of the emigration societies were regularly highlighted in the emigrators' speeches and publications. Instances of titled women's visits to emigrants' hostels were related in the societies' pamphlets and journals in great detail, along with commentary about the great honour that was thus bestowed upon the emigrant women temporarily residing there. Properties owned by the emigration societies were sometimes named after notable patrons,[79] and signed portraits of the societies' titled patrons and members were given pride of place in emigrant hostels. Most women who emigrated with the help of philanthropic emigration societies would never actually meet any of the societies' elite members. But all they had to do was read one of the societies' magazines or stay in one of the societies' hostels to be reminded that whatever help they had received from the emigration societies had been made possible by the generosity of the empire's leading ladies. Any dissension that might have existed between the upper-class and middle-class members of the female emigration societies was suppressed in published representations of these organizations' activities so that the societies' work would not be undermined. These women's shared understanding of an empire informed by a female imperialist agenda was highlighted. Together, middle-class and elite women worked hard to create an identity for their organizations that revealed the members' mutual supportiveness.

Julia Bush has argued that the organizations run by female imperialists of the Edwardian period were guided by upper-class concerns and ambitions. Yet the evidence that comes out of the female emigration societies reveals a more complicated picture. In part, Bush bases her argument about the significance of elite society for the management of women's imperial projects upon the fact that upper-class women strategized, gossiped, and attempted to win each other over to different perspectives at private, 'exclusive' social engagements.[80] But middle-class women also socialized together outside of their formal emigration-society committee meetings. These social interactions would likewise have been exclusive events, at which strategies were planned and alliances formed. It would be wrong to assume that women like Ellen Joyce, Adelaide Ross, and Grace Lefroy were merely carrying out the programs designed by their elite co-members. The discussions that took place in the meetings of the societies are poorly represented in the meetings' minutes. All the same, it is clear that the upper-class women did not call all the shots. In fact, because of their daily involvement in this work, middle-class women frequently had more to say at committee meetings about what had been going on, and about what future steps ought to be taken, than did the societies' titled members. Sometimes, elite women silenced their middle-class sisters, but sometimes they deferred to the superior knowledge and more forceful opinions of the women who knew the work better. For example, a disagreement concerning whether or not Mrs Walter Browne should be included as a member of the BWEA central committee pitched Ellen Joyce against Lady Grey. In this case, it appears that Joyce's rejection of Browne won the day over Lady Grey's firm support for her inclusion.[81]

Some of the elite women who promoted female emigration were powerful individuals. Female members of the Balfour and Grosvenor families, Lady Knightley of Fawsley, Violet Markham, and Laura Ridding were able to use their own standing in society, along with their relationships with other well-placed men and women, to effect change in whatever fields of work they found of interest.[82] However, most of the emigrators exercised power and authority in this way only as representatives of their emigration societies. Their ability to influence governments and government agents, shipping companies, and potential emigrants was due to their membership within an organization of women who, together, could make a claim for authority based upon their knowledge, insights, experience, and social connections. As managers of female migration, these women established relationships with men and women in social situations widely different to their own on terms that would otherwise not have been possible. Membership within these emigration societies thus played an important role in the definition and playing out of their own visions of their places in Britain and in the larger context of the British Empire. Simultaneously, their work in this field, and the way in which they interpreted their work and its effects, helped to define more than just their own sense of their roles and status in society. Their work and their projections of that work were also instrumental in the definition and confirmation of the relationships among the different classes in Britain, and between Britain and its dominions.

To suggest that middle-class emigrators nurtured their relationships with elite female patrons purely as a strategy to realize their ideals of empire migration would be to underestimate the cultural power wielded by elite women. Nevertheless, a serious analysis of middle-class women's work strongly suggests that women like Ellen Joyce attempted strategically to manipulate the power of elite women just as they did that of male-dominated organizations and state bureaucracies. In fact, when middle-class promoters are situated at the centre of an analysis of single female migration, the image of Ellen Joyce in the official 1925 history of the Girls' Friendly Society gains historical clarity. That image is both a reflection of these women's continuing imperial ambitions and a symbol of their own sense of importance within the processes of migration management and empire building. As the following chapters will show, the power and respect that these women had gained by the beginning of the twentieth century were the results of female migration promoters' ongoing efforts to redefine the single female migrant and the immigration process, to promote a specific understanding of empire and the role of women within it, and to harmonize their own agendas with those of other power brokers of imperial migration.

chapter two

Safe Passage: Narratives of Women in Transit

In their annual report for 1905, the Travellers' Aid Society (TAS) out-lined a 'typical' turn-of-the-century incident. Two young Irish women set out by train for London on the first leg of their journey to Australia. Soon after their departure from Ireland, a man attempted to befriend them. He assured them that if they were not met in London as had been planned, he would help them find suitable overnight accommoda-tion. According to the TAS worker who had been asked to meet them at Euston Station, the stranger made the women anxious by his refusal to accept politely their indications that his company and his assistance were not desired. Upon their arrival at Euston, the TAS worker took control of the situation. She accompanied the young women to a respectable women's hostel, and then met them again the next morning to see them onto their ship. En route to the ship, the stranger reap-peared and treated the young women in a friendly and familiar fashion. The TAS worker informed him that 'the girls were in her charge and did not wish his interference,' whereupon he departed with apologies. To ensure that the stranger would not further annoy the girls while in transit, the TAS worker found a trustworthy fellow passenger who was willing to watch over them. The two young Irish women, understanding that they had been saved from a situation fraught with danger, were 'thoroughly frightened' by the incident, and were 'most grateful for the assistance of the T.A.S.'[1]

By the end of the Victorian era, stories such as this had become part of an identifiable discourse – a 'safe passage' discourse in which the efforts of 'nefarious persons to entrap the ignorant girl of the servant class for the purposes of gain,'[2] were thwarted by older, wiser women, invested with a wealth of moral authority. As in the case related above, the typical story around which this discourse was constructed looked, in many ways, like many other works of melodramatic, romantic, pulp fiction written during this period. The central character was always a young woman who, owing to circumstances that may or may not have been beyond her control, suddenly found herself in a distressing predicament. The climax of the story was reached at the moment of the woman's (or the reader's) most acute distress about her situation. In spite of the fact that the young woman was inevitably poorly equipped to effectively extricate herself from her hazardous position, the story's plot usually ended positively. In such cases, the plot resolved in this way because a hero stepped in at the story's climax to make things right again. But some stories were left open-ended, with the fate of the young woman left up to the imagination of readers who were expected to assume the worst. In such cases, no hero was available, or the hero's guidance had been shunned.

In these narratives, the typecasting of central characters was largely predictable. The woman at the centre of the plot was typically young and naive. Whether she was timid and nervous, or confident and head-strong, she was portrayed as a character in need of support and protection. In spite of what she might have thought, she was clearly incapable of taking care of herself.[3] The stories' villains appeared in a wide range of guises, although they were generally consistent in their masculinity.[4] White slave traders and Mormons, rakes and cads, corrupt employment agents and inept emigration agents – together they provided a mine-field of dangers from which even the best behaved girl might not have escaped.

Where these narratives differed from most other contemporary literary works was in the nature of the stories' heroes. Male figures of authority and lovers proved to be shockingly incapable of guiding and protecting young women. Their priorities were all wrong and their knowledge inadequate for the job of hero. In fact, the most insightful and gallant men in these stories were those who chose to temporarily abdicate their traditional role of protector in favour of those who were more knowledgeable and competent.[5] The void created by the absence of male heroes was confidently filled by well-educated, well-connected, civic-minded women and their carefully trained, paid female helpers.

The safe-passage narratives were published in the annual reports, journals, pamphlets, and lectures of the female emigration societies and affiliated women's organizations. With the exception of the odd fictional tale published in the GFS journals, they were intended to be read as factual. Yet, most of these narratives had been extensively processed by the time they appeared in print. The organizations' editors carefully sorted through the mass of information that reached them on a daily basis, prioritizing some stories over others, and editing out 'superfluous' details and objectionable perspectives. Recounted experiences of single female travellers were seldom published as complete narratives in and of themselves. Rather, stories taken from letters, verbal communications, other publications, and hearsay were dissected and used out of context, along with other story fragments and an overlay of analysis, to make specific points about young women, migration, and problems of safety.

The safe-passage discourse was much more than the sum of the stories of female danger inserted into the journals and annual reports of women's organizations that aimed to protect single women in transit. The stories were supported by the actions of the women who constructed these narratives, and they were augmented by a range of other published bits and pieces that were likewise fashioned for public consumption. The societies' announcements, warnings, obituaries, reports on recent activities, and quotes lifted from thankful letters from girls and their families all served to give credence to the central message behind the narratives – that the moral and physical safety of young women travelling around the empire was in peril wherever the services of qualified female emigrators were not being used.

In this chapter I will argue that the safe passage genre of writing was the purposeful creation of a group of reform-minded women.[6] During the second half of the nineteenth century, a variety of women-run organizations were created or expanded to oversee the safe passage of single women in transit. At the centre of the loosely affiliated organizations were the women's emigration societies, the TAS, the Girls' Friendly Society (GFS), and the Young Women's Christian Association (YWCA). In their efforts to promote and consolidate the successes of their organizations, the societies' members created a body of literature that would publicly further their ambitions. The authors of these texts did not aim to teach young women how to become more adept at looking out for themselves, although this was sometimes a subtext.[7] Rather, the safe-passage narratives were designed to educate and castigate ignorant young women and a scandalously complacent public about the need for more appropriate care and guidance for young female travellers. The safe-passage discourse was designed to show that through their negligence, incompetence, greed, and lust, men had proved themselves unfit for their patriarchal responsibilities, and that only through the use of the emigrators' services could potential disasters be averted.

The women who created the safe-passage narratives were united in their belief that ensuring young women's safety when away from their homes required special efforts on their behalf. Empowered by their membership in national and international women's organizations, they took upon themselves the role of chaperone for girls on the move. Their understanding of 'movement' extended beyond the physical movement of young women by train or by ship. It also included female travellers' movements from job to job, and from one accommodation to another. Through widely disseminated literature and lectures, these authors encouraged young women and their families to use the services that their organizations provided. As dramatic, true accounts of endangered women, the safe-passage narratives worked as part of a discourse that was actively managed by middle- and upper-class women to create a need for travellers' protection and care.

The emigrators' safe-passage narrative had a history that predated the 1880s. Early versions of the narrative may be seen in the literature produced to support the work of the British Ladies Female Emigration Society (BLFES) at mid-century. Yet it was really in the decade of the 1880s, when William Stead and other journalists turned the issue of sexual predation into one of England's most newsworthy social problems, that this literature solidified into a recognizable genre. As Elaine Showalter and others have shown, the sex scandals of the 1880s 'changed the level of public awareness about sexuality and engendered a fierce response in social purity campaigns, a renewed sense of public moral concern, and demands ... for restrictive legislation and censorship.'[8] This altered awareness was both constitutive of, and partly the result of, the emigrators' safe-passage project. As chapter 1 has shown, many of the individuals who got involved in the work to ensure single women's safe passage first became interested in this work in the 1880s. In this decade individual emigrators and failing emigration organizations combined to form new, more powerful organizations to deal with problems of women's safe passage. As the movement to protect young women from the vices of men gained momentum and gelled into concrete, women-centred reform programs, the various fragments of the safe-passage narratives that had been published in separate locations were brought together in the publications of a few, interconnected women-dominated societies.

In *City of Dreadful Delight: Narratives of Sexual Danger in Late-Victorian London*, Judith Walkowitz describes the Jack the Ripper narrative as 'a mythic story of sexual danger' that may be seen as 'part of a formative moment in the production of ... popular narratives of sexual danger.'[9] Her book explores some of the ways in which these narratives of sexual danger were contested and reworked by groups and individuals with different points of view. According to Catherine Stimpson, 'One tool that [Walkowitz's] men and women have for displaying power is some degree of control over the narratives about sex and gender.'[10] An examination of the discourse that was produced by the emigrators who aimed to provide single female migrants with safe passage illustrates that for these women, the extent to which they had control over the production and dissemination of narratives of sexual danger was not only an indication of their place in their society's hierarchy of power, but also a key factor in their successful efforts to increase their access to power. These women used their ability to communicate their version of the sexual danger story to fundamentally alter other women's migration experiences, and to legitimate their claims that women of their class and social backgrounds should have a larger say in the regulation of society – not just in England, or in Britain, but throughout the British Empire.[11]

Although these women would have disagreed with each other on a wide range of social and political issues, they presented a uniformly maternalist solution for problems relating to the movement of young women.[12] Central to the safe-passage project for which these women worked was the assumption that, on account of their gender, age, and class status, responsible female reformers ought to be in charge of matters that directly affected the safety and dignity of all women. They agreed that what was needed to ensure the safety of young women was a greater degree of involvement and control over their movement by older, better-educated women. Convinced that changes in the way single women experienced migration were necessary, they confidently promoted themselves as the only suitably qualified persons to oversee those changes. In spite of the conservative overtones in much of the literature that they produced, the women who became involved in the safe-passage project deviated from conservative understandings of gender relations in their attitudes and expectations concerning their own roles in Britain and the British Empire.

Historians of middle-class women's voluntary efforts during the late nineteenth and early twentieth centuries have illustrated how maternalist politics drove women's reform agendas,[13] and how maternalism was used as a rhetorical strategy in women's search for power and authority.[14] A similar argument is made in this study for the relationship between maternalism and women's work relating to imperial female migration. Through the British Women's Emigration Association (BWEA) and associated organizations, British women's emigration was managed 'by Women for Women.'[15] Maternalist discourses were used both to justify the need for separate facilities and special programs for young, unattached female emigrants, and to legitimate the domination of this field of work by women of more privileged backgrounds. As historians have suggested for other areas of middle-class women's voluntary work, the nature of these women's gendered claims to authority over problems relating to women and children changed during this period. The nature of the claims evolved in response to changing socio-political conditions.[16] But as Angela Woollacott points out, while altering their claims to suit the times, 'middle-class women drew a line of continuity between old and new forms of feminine authority' in which authority was based on class superiority.[17] Right through the 1920s, class-based maternalist arguments were marshalled – albeit in different ways at different times – in favour of the middle-class female emigrators' right to manage the migration of other women.

The authors and editors of safe-passage literature constructed their texts in a social and literary context that provided them with a variety of useful, well-worked themes and narrative structures. The safe-passage narratives relied upon their readers' familiarity with conventional character stereotypes and formulaic dramatic scenarios.[18] They both borrowed from and wrote against other currently circulating bodies of literature. Two competing narrative types are of particular significance for an examination of the safe-passage narratives produced by the emigrators. In the one, central female characters were the largely passive recipients of men's attentions. As predators and protectors, male characters determined the women's fate. This type of narrative dominated the literary scene in which the safe-passage narratives were constructed.[19] The other body of literature against which the emigrators' female philanthropists wrote featured central female characters who were determined to decide their own fates. These characters came to be labelled 'New Women,' and were the self-consciously political creations of feminist authors and their detractors.[20]

Judith Walkowitz and Sally Ledger have explored the ways in which the various characters in the narratives of sexual danger and the New Woman stories were late-Victorian literary constructs, related to, yet significantly different from, the living people they were supposed to represent. The characters produced by the 'safe passage' promoters likewise grew out of their creators' social observations, and were moulded according to their makers' insights, politics, and agendas. The identity given to the single female traveller in these narratives serves as a good example of the emigrators' creative manipulation of the evidence with which they worked on a daily basis. The single British women who emigrated to overseas destinations during the late nineteenth and early twentieth centuries represented a wide range of socio-economic backgrounds, personality types, and life experiences. They were young and middle-aged, healthy and physically incapacitated, poorhouse orphans and independently wealthy adventurers, morally suspect and above reproach.[21] The picture presented by the emigrators allows little of this diversity. In safe-passage stories, female emigrants were typically of the servant class, and from the country or a small town. They were '[girls] leaving sheltered homes, where the lurking evil of the outside world [had] never been even talked of.'[22] Simple and naive, or self-willed and foolish, these young women had not learned the reticence of experienced urbanites, and they lacked the good sense and decorum that belonged to similarly aged women of a better class. As in the case of the two young Irish women emigrating to Australia, young women without a middle-class education were predictably easy prey for criminally minded persons.

The emigrators urged young women to adhere to a strict code of behaviour as the best way to help themselves and those who wished to protect them from danger. In an open letter to young female travellers published in 1885, Lady Grey lectured her readers on their conduct: 'When travelling alone, you cannot be too careful to do what is commonly described as "keeping yourself to yourself."' 'Do not enter into conversation about yourself or your plans with any stranger, man or woman,' she wrote, 'and do not put yourself under an obligation to a stranger; never allow yourself to be treated to any refreshment, either meat or drink ... There should be nothing remarkable in your dress, nothing in look or manner that can call attention to you.' According to Lady Grey, if a girl who has gained unwanted attention examines her own previous conduct, 'she will generally find that some fault or mistake on her own part has led to it, though she may not have been aware that she was doing anything unfitting.' As she advised young women: 'Never forget this one rule: That the greater the *freedom of action* that is allowed to women, the smaller the *freedom of manner* that they should allow to themselves.'[23] To embrace a 'New Woman' identity was to court danger. In these emigrators' literature, the erasure of self was key to a young woman's safety.

In safe-passage narratives, young women's decisions to move could be grudgingly supported or heartily encouraged.[24] Yet, having made the decision to migrate, young women were advised to keep a low profile and leave the management of their movement to the experts. In the stories produced by the female emigration societies, the attempts of young women to carry out their own plans for migration were almost certain to result in unnecessary hardship. GFS publications and the *Imperial Colonist* regularly posted warnings that dire consequences would follow young women's attempts to arrange their own migration. A warning posted in an 1884 edition of the GFS journal *Friendly Work* is consistent in tone with those that would follow in these organizations' publications for several decades:

> ... a most earnest word of caution: *Do not attempt to make your own arrangements* ... NO GIRL SHOULD EMIGRATE UNLESS IT HAS BEEN PLANNED FOR SOME ONE TO EXPECT HER, AND MEET HER WHEN SHE LANDS; ... NONE OF THE SPECIAL ADVANTAGES OFFERED TO G.F.S. MEMBERS CAN BE OBTAINED BY THEM UNLESS THEIR APPLICATIONS FOR EMIGRATION PASS THROUGH MY HANDS, AS APPOINTED CORRESPONDENT FOR THE G.F.S.[25]

Not only were most of the prospective migrants portrayed as woefully ill-informed about their chosen destinations, they were also presented as incapable of managing the most simple tasks involved in executing their plans to move.[26]

The results of improperly managed single female migration were recorded throughout the publications of the organizations that worked at promoting greater safety for women on the move. In these texts the folly of young women's attempts to make their own migration plans was highlighted. The emigrators fumed about emigrants arriving at their destinations in poor health, with no one to meet them, no means of support in sight, no idea of what to expect of the country, and no money in hand. In the opinion of colonial correspondents, a great deal of work was necessary after the fact to ensure that these women were not dragged down into an existence of poverty, vice, and crime as a result of their migration experiences.[27]

Although many young women were clearly repelled by the efforts of the safe-passage providers to ensure their safe passage, others not only made use of these societies' protection but were complicit in the creation of the images of the young female traveller as foolish, incompetent, intimidated, or just plain needy. Published letters to the emigrators and matrons who had provided them with help criticized the actions and attitudes of fellow female travellers who had made a show of themselves. Young emigrants also chronicled their own trepidation about leaving all that was known to them for the uncertainties of a new life overseas. Some of the more timid emigrants admitted that it was unlikely that they would have attempted emigration at all had it not been for the support systems that the emigrators had put in place,[28] and even seasoned travellers periodically wrote thank-you letters that highlighted their own consciousness of the inherent vulnerability of unaccompanied women.[29]

Letters from men were also used in support of the emigrators' representations of young women as subject to a wide range of dangers. Some of the most belittling statements about the inability of young women to effectively look out for themselves were taken from letters written by men. For example, in a letter published by the BWEA under the heading 'A Plea for Protection,' a man indicated his concern about what might happen to his fiancée if she were left to travel without supervision from her home in England to him in Canada. He noted that he had 'seen many girls crossing to their intended husbands, and must say, they were ... running rather wild and making friends with all that cared to approach them.'[30] The emigrators who inserted comments such as this into the publications were careful to emphasize that these girls were not necessarily bad. Rather, they were poorly equipped to make sensible decisions about the company they ought to keep. Unchaperoned women ran the risk of losing their men folk's respect and adoration. Published letters from lovers, brothers, and fathers highlighted the fact that women's reputations were exceptionally vulnerable while women were in transit.

Between the 1840s and the beginning of the First World War, emigrators' representations of young women in their safe-passage literature remained largely unchanged. Throughout this period, 'girls' were portrayed as naive, foolish, easily led astray. Their naivety consistently associated with country simplicity, young women were pictured as befuddled and endangered by urban terrors. This persistent image was inconsistent with the urban origins of most of the women the emigrators dealt with on a daily basis. Nor did it fit well with the very public demands that young women were making on their own behalf during this period.[31] The contradictions between the images of young women promoted by the creators of the safe-passage narratives and the public personas that young women were increasingly embracing were augmented by the experiences of the First World War.[32] In the years around the turn of the century, the authors of the safe-passage narratives had largely managed to ignore or gloss over the more problematic aspects of New Woman attitudes and behaviour. But the increased confidence and independence that came from wartime work and the changed circumstances of the post-war period made avoidance of the issue of young women's desires for freedom from restraint impossible. After the war there was a new tone of defensiveness in the emigrators' efforts to get young women to use their protective services. Those women who continued to push the issue of protection declared that young women still needed, and desired, to be chaperoned. 'The modern girl rather jibs at the offer of protection,' wrote the *Imperial Colonist*'s editor in 1920, '[but] these inexperienced travellers are unaware of the difficulties and risks they may encounter on a long voyage.' According to this author, sensible girls still recognized that inconveniences and dangers could only be avoided by travelling in chaperoned groups.[33] Over the course of the 1920s, fewer and fewer safe-passage stories and warnings found their way into the literature published by these organizations. The protective work of the women's organizations became less prominent, replaced by a greater emphasis upon the convenience, and the social and financial benefits, of travelling with chaperoned parties of female emigrants.

The image of the young woman in transit changed remarkably little between the mid-1800s and the First World War in the emigrators' safe-passage literature. By contrast, the face that these emigrators gave to the danger confronted by female migrants changed considerably over the same period. Male lust was consistently the central element of danger in narratives about unsafe travel, but the form in which this danger was understood to present itself changed significantly. Before the 1880s, emigrators focused largely on the potential for seduction and violence at the hands of individuals and small groups of men who might happen upon the unsuspecting emigrant while she was in transit on land, or of sailors and fellow passengers during ocean passage. From the early 1880s, emigrators who worked with single women in transit increasingly became obsessed with the idea of the white slave trade. They drew extensively from images in the popular press to show that the primary threat to women's safety was not so much the individual male as it was networks of conspirators who desired to profit from the marketability of vulnerable young women.

For several of the organizations that worked to provide young women safe passage, the emergence of the white-slave-trade scare served as a useful justification for their existence. Annual reports of the TAS, the GFS, and the BWEA emphasized that it was a '[small] matter for wonder if [girls] do not escape the evil persons who are on the look-out to entrap inexperience and innocence.'[34] In the safe-passage narratives, the characters of the white-slave-trade villains were left conveniently ambiguous. They were shadowy figures, as befit individuals whose occupations required that they become adept at luring naive young women into their traps. The image of the villain changed according to the context of the story's plot. Villains could be young or they could be much older than the girls they aimed to ensnare. They could appear to be vile and sleazy, charming and disarming, or respectable and dignified. They could even come in the form of a seemingly empathetic woman.[35] Part of the message that the emigrators wished to send about sexual predators was that they could be packaged in any form, and that only a well-trained eye could pick out deception. Without the right sort of protection, young women were easy pickings for the class of villains that plotted their fall.[36]

The emigrators worked at showing that they could not only spot potential villains when others might miss them, but also that they had a superior knowledge of the white slave trade and the methods of its traders, and that they understood how to thwart the traders' aims. The authors of the safe-passage narratives were careful to communicate these messages without stooping to the level of pulp journalism. Although their narratives were designed to shock and disturb their readers, actual discussions of sexual violence were almost completely absent. These texts relied on the readers' imaginations and on their familiarity with more explicit stories in the press. Although the emigrators took upon themselves the task of educating their readers about the white slave trade, they were careful to emphasize that knowledge that could be imparted through published texts alone would not necessarily save young women from entrapment. Young women were encouraged to gain an understanding of the dangers they faced while in transit, but they were also urged to get in touch with the TAS, GFS, YWCA, or one of the emigration societies for on-the-spot protection. According to the producers of the safe-passage narratives, only purpose-built organizations could do the sort of painstaking research required to ensure that all potential traps would be avoided.

As the spectre of the white slave trade lost some of its power towards the end of the nineteenth century, discourses about the international traffic in women were given new life in the emigrators' work by allusions to the Mormon threat. The TAS, BWEA, and affiliated societies eagerly absorbed the image of the villainous Mormon male, desirous of a harem of wives, into their narratives about unsafe passage. Their narratives joined with texts such as Arthur Conan Doyle's popular novel *Study in Scarlet* (1887), and a smattering of newspaper scandals around the turn of the century, to alert the British public to the dangers that Mormons' polygamous practices presented to young female travellers. The *Imperial Colonist* editor's commentary on a newspaper article reprinted from the *Commentator* provides a good example of the role that Mormons came to play in the emigrators' narratives. 'One hundred Mormon "converts," including eighty women, all bound for Utah, landed in Montreal from one ship the other day. Through Montreal alone 250 Mormon "converts" have passed on their way to Utah from Great Britain this season,' wrote the editor. She suggested that, 'in addition to being citizens lost to the Empire (which needs every one of her women), the deluded English women of these parties may well be lost in another sense.' The Mormons' indoctrination of young women with blasphemous ideas threatened their victims' souls, while their efforts to lure desperately needed single women away from their colonial destinations made them enemies of the British Empire: the fact that these women were directed away from imperial destinations meant that 'sturdy, honest, prosperous British settlers in Canada, Australia, and Africa must remain single perforce because of the scarcity of marriageable women.'[37]

The Mormon threat, like the white-slave-trade scare, justified the emigrators' claims that their safe-passage services were needed. Simultaneously, their discussion of the success of Mormons' efforts to redirect single women to Utah revealed that the men who should have been these women's natural protectors were failing to perform this important social duty owing to misplaced priorities and incompetence. The inability of the men who ran the British government to effectively deal with the problem of Mormon activity was noted in these texts with barely veiled frustration and anger. Dramatic tales of women's entrapment by and rescue from Mormons were paired with the emigrators' complaints about the government's comparative lack of interest in the problem. For example, in a 1912 journal, a letter from Canada outlining the efforts of two female emigrants (who had been warned of the Mormons through the YWCA) to rescue two fellow female travellers from the Mormons on their ship was placed ahead of an article about the lack of legal restrictions on Mormon recruitment. 'Expelled from nearly every European country, the Mormons have recently made Switzerland ... their working centre on the Continent, and continue to exploit Swiss girls without fear of legal interference,' wrote the *Imperial Colonist*'s editor. 'A hundred Swiss girls and a thousand European girls of all nationalities, under golden promises, are sent across the Atlantic – passage paid – to Utah city every year,' she continued. 'It is time that this traffic stopped. England and Switzerland are the only European countries in which Mormons are tolerated.'[38]

Records of emigrators' disapproval of the ways that male representatives of government bodies treated the safety of female travellers may be found at any point between the 1840s and 1930. But, as relations between the women's organizations and the British state improved,[39] and as these women increasingly attempted to promote more professional images of themselves, published indictments of British state policies and practices became more muted. In an article published in 1860 in support of emigrant ship matrons, Maria Rye presented an angry critique of the way that the migration of women and the employment of ship matrons had been handled by male authorities. In this article Rye made it clear that she had little faith in the intelligence or generosity of the men who managed migration to the colonies.[40] She noted that both the British Emigration Commissioners and the colonial immigration authorities fully understood the importance of good ship matrons to the behaviour of the emigrants.[41] Yet these authorities – who, as Rye pointed out, were themselves employed at large salaries – wanted high-quality matrons for less than the cost of hiring 'the lowest cabin-boy on deck.'[42] According to Rye, 'excessive selfishness characterise[d] the whole proceedings.'[43]

Maria Rye was exceptionally blunt in how she chose to deal with issues in need of reform. But it was not just a case of different personalities that determined that this sort of public condemnation of government administrators would not be published by the women who desired to manage the emigration of single women during and after the 1880s. When women like Ellen Joyce contributed to the safe-passage discourse in the late nineteenth and early twentieth centuries, they did so as representatives of large women's organizations. Within these organizations women created checks and balances to decrease the chance that aggressive literature would alienate those men who might otherwise become their supporters and allies.[44] The implicit support of state authorities for the women's protective work became an important element of the safe-passage discourse. Thus, when they felt that criticisms of the state were in order after the 1860s, the emigrators turned to more subtle methods of displaying them, leaving their more vitriolic outbursts for private correspondence.[45]

If government agents were not quite up to the task of protecting female migrants, then the men who ran the agencies that organized employment and migration for profit were presented as positively suspect. As Leonora L. Yorke Smith, head of the GFS Registry Department and Secretary of the Associated Guild of Registries, noted, corrupt employment agencies came in two classes: 'those which are dangerous to the pockets of those who come their way' and those which 'are responsible for much more serious evils.'[46] According to the women who sought to protect female migrants, employment agencies were often fronts for white-slave-trade organizations. Profit-motivated emigration agencies were not charged with this particular crime. But readers were informed that there were 'many agencies at work offering assisted passages to Canada which are dangerous and fraudulent.' As a result, 'some young women have been left without money, shelter or employment on arrival.'[47] The emigrators made it clear that such a predicament put many young women on the path to prostitution.

Just as government bodies and employment and emigration agencies could not be trusted to make women's safety a priority, those men for whom a female's safety should have been a primary concern could not be counted on to provide women with adequate protection. In the safe-passage narratives, fathers, brothers, and lovers tended to be absent or ineffective. The TAS *Annual Report* for 1902 provides a particularly detailed example of male incompetence. In this narrative an Irish brother and sister travelling to join friends in Australia arrived in London a day ahead of schedule (an early sign of questionable competence). Upon first sighting, it was obvious to the TAS workers that 'certainly the lad was no protection to his young sister. She had to manage for them both, though he was the elder and she scarcely more than a child.' The TAS took the girl into their hostel for the night, 'and her brother was given the address of a lodging for men near by, the address being written on a piece of the Society's paper that he might know where to come for his sister the next day.' The TAS workers were astonished when, 'in 20 mins he came back again, having confused the two addresses and not being at all aware that he had come a second time to the same house.' The TAS workers, now fully cognizant of the young man's inability to look after even himself, took extra precautions against losing him, and the next day brother and sister were seen safely onto their ship.[48]

Cases like this were designed to make the point that travelling with a male family member did not necessarily ensure women's safety. It is likely that the incompetence of the brother in this narrative was assumed to be due, in part, to his Irishness. In safe-passage narratives that featured young Irish women, the women were presented as being overwhelmed by train travel, crowds of people, and big cities.[49] The use of Irish characters allowed the creators of these narratives to provide their readers with a bit of extra humour. Yet, in the emigrators' writing, English girls were also regularly let down by their men folk who, owing to 'misunderstandings,' failed to meet them according to schedule at their travel destinations.[50]

Women's organizations like the TAS, the BWEA, and the GFS worked hard to convince the readers of their publications that, unlike men, they *could* ensure young women's safe passage. Moreover, they showed that the advantages that supposedly accrued to young women who chose to use the services of these emigration societies were significant. For these women, migration would be safe, comparatively inexpensive, and hassle-free. In an article entitled 'A Journey Under the Care of the SACS,' the differences between old-style (un-managed) migration and migration managed by women's emigration societies were highlighted:

> There is an idea that the departure of Colonists from the Old Country is generally attended with a vast amount of confusion, a multitude of unwieldy bundles and packages, a crowd of ill-assorted human beings jostling one another in hopeless discomfort, tears, and boisterous attempts at fictitious merriment ... [It] is certainly not a true picture of colonisation as conducted by any of the well-known societies now responsible for so much of the circulation of the arterial blood of the British Empire – its men, women and children. Perhaps this is especially noticeable in the work done by the Societies for the protected Emigration of women.[51]

Unlike the confused mass of miserable, 'ill-assorted human beings' that one might expect of a party of emigrants, the girls travelling under the care of the SACS were 'ushered into the special quarters reserved for them with such quiet method and order that few persons could have supposed that they were witnessing the departure of a large party on a journey of from six to seven thousand miles.' Moreover, 'There was no grumbling and no confusion – not even a solitary package had gone astray ... They seemed the happiest and brightest collection of passengers it was possible to imagine.'[52] Narratives about the experiences of

ANCHOR SIGN.
Used in the Emigration Department under which the Joyce Parties were recognised all over the world.

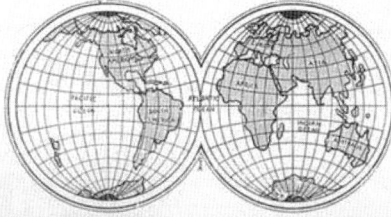

THE HON. MRS. JOYCE.
A Lady of Grace of the Order of St. John of Jerusalem and Commander of the British Empire.

1. A page from *Friendship's Highway: Being the History of the Girls' Friendly Society, 1875–1925*, in which Ellen Joyce, head of the Girls' Friendly Society's Emigration Department and a leading member of the British Women's Emigration Association for over forty years, is pictured with symbols of her work for the British Empire. (Mary Heath-Stubbs, *Friendship's Highway, Being the History of the Girls' Friendly Society, 1875–1925* (London: G.F.S. Central Office, 1926 [1925]), page facing 65.)

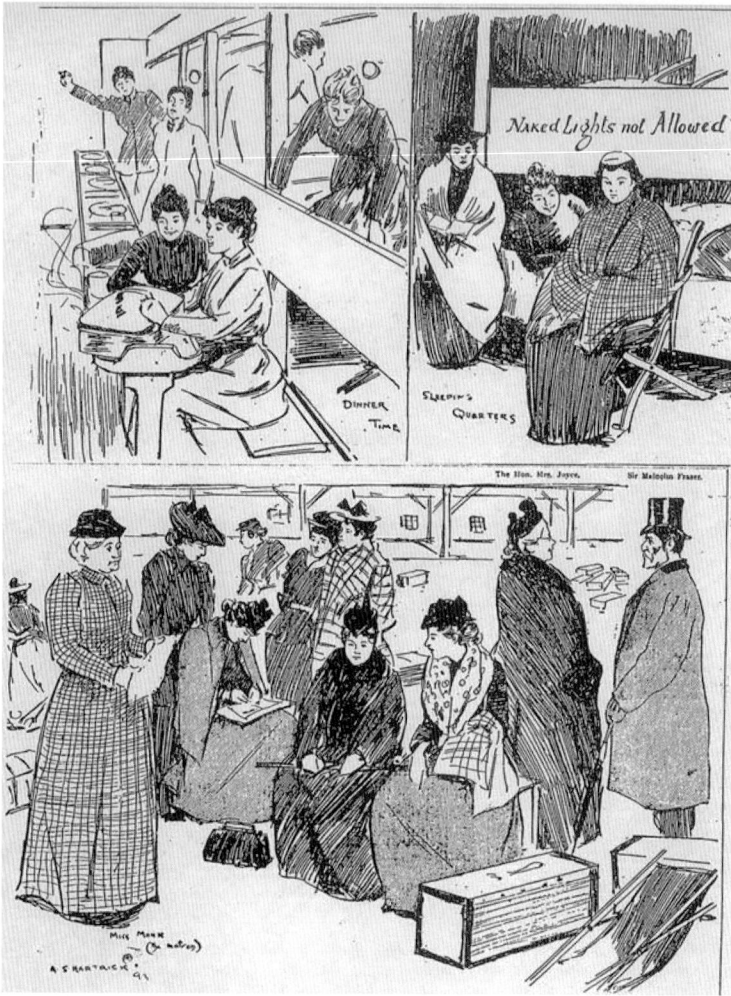

2. An illustrated newspaper report describes 'the departure of the first "protected party" of the year sent out by the United British Women's Association to Western Australia.' Forty-nine female emigrants set out on this journey, under the protection of the well-seasoned ship matron Miss Monk (pictured at bottom left). Also illustrated are Mrs Joyce and Sir Malcolm Fraser (bottom right), who joined the group to offer final words of wisdom and good wishes to the emigrants. (Miss Lefroy, Miss Bromfield, and Mrs Percival were also in attendance, but were not shown in the picture.) ('Women Emigrants to Western Australia,' clipping from unnamed newspaper source, 27 January 1893. Women's Library, London Metropolitan University.)

3. Three BWEA emigrants pose for a photograph on board ship, 1912. (*British Women's Emigration Association Annual Report, 1912*, p. 41.)

4. A group of immigrants gather together for a photograph outside the women's hostel at Calgary, 1912. (*British Women's Emigration Association Annual Report, 1912*, p. 29.)

5. Girls' Friendly Society Lodges, on the Prairies in Canada (top) and in Ballarat, Australia (bottom), served as places of accommodation, as employment agencies, and as social clubs. (Girls' Friendly Society Archives, uncatalogued.)

6. A group of GFS members break up a holiday camp in Australia. The back of the photograph reads: 'leaving camp – & feeling sad.' The suitcase labelled 'Wood' belonged to the local GFS club secretary

7. The Lady Bertha caravan, named for Lady Bertha Dawkins

FROM GREAT BRITAIN TO SOLVE OUR DOMESTIC PROBLEM

The Party of Girls who arrived in Sydney this morning by the White Star liner Medic, and will come through to Canberra.

8. The arrival of a group of specially selected domestic-servant immigrants is celebrated in the *Canberra Times*, 3 February 1927.

protected female travellers emphasized that this sort of travel was not only convenient and safe – it was also fun.[53]

The happiness of the chaperoned female travellers was easily explained in these narratives. Even well-heeled visitors who came to view the travel arrangements made for the emigrants were purportedly much impressed with the quality of the accommodation and provisions allowed for groups of protected female travellers.[54] Quoted opinions of the emigrants themselves were similarly positive. The editors of these organizations' journals were particularly fond of publishing letters from seasoned female travellers who attested to the superior travel arrangements of protected female parties.

The emigrators took care to inform their readers that the comfort, convenience, and safety women could anticipate when travelling under their care were the results of their own efforts, insights, and superior interpersonal skills. If shipping arrangements were found to be unsatisfactory, the members of the emigration societies went after the appropriate authorities until they had been assured 'that no exceptional overpressure by other passengers, or any other cause, shall again be allowed to interfere with the undertaking entered into by the steam-ship company.'[55] The emigrators emphasized that they only used the services of those shipping lines that understood that single female migrants had special needs. The quality of the accommodation at either end of the journey was likewise publicly reassessed and rated on a regular basis by the safe-passage providers, and only those that were deemed worthy were used by the organizations' chaperoned groups. Better safety and convenience of travel by train for single women were claimed to be the result of the efforts of the members of the TAS, who worked tirelessly to educate the managers and employees of railway companies about how they could improve travel for their vulnerable female passengers.[56] GFS associates went further than the members of most organizations involved in the safe-passage project in their attempt to protect girls from harm. They argued that girls who were members of their organisation were particularly blessed if they migrated under GFS care because this society offered protection exclusively to their own girls of certified purity.[57] Not only would GFS travellers be protected from violence, seduction, and inconvenience while in transit, but GFS girls would not be expected to travel with women less virtuous than themselves.[58]

The safe-passage narratives revealed that young women needed a small army of responsible, knowledgeable, and well-connected people to ensure that their movement would not end in disaster. Fool-proof travel plans needed to be carefully mapped out, the respectability of temporary and longer-term accommodations had to be ascertained, and someone had to scrutinize the credentials of new employers. In the larger discourse that the women constructed around these narratives, it was evident that the network of mutually supportive organizations of female emigrators was the appropriate place to look for this care.

A central aim of the various organizations that were involved in the safe-passage project was to transform 'unsafe' public spaces through which young women in transit had to pass, into domesticated, safe environments. The members of these organizations strategized about how to encourage – and enforce – appropriate codes of conduct in contexts that, previously, had been informed by a less 'refined' moral code. Central to their efforts was the imposition of a maternal gaze upon typically male-dominated, public spaces. When possible, they literally inserted female guardians into public venues. When this was not possible, they relied upon their voluminous correspondence with men in positions of authority, and their careful coaching of female travellers about what they ought to expect from male authority figures, to improve the conditions of public spaces. *Warning Signals*, a pamphlet written by Joyce on travel safety that was distributed to all young women who came in contact with members of the BWEA, SACS, GFS, and affiliated organizations, offers clear examples of the emigrators' methods.[59] In a section on 'Colonial Railway Travelling,' Joyce instructed emigrants to 'plan to have their sleeping berths together.' She noted that 'on no account should single women in the Colonist or Tourist Car in Canada make up their beds in a part where the men are.' She lamented that 'there is no part for women kept separate as there ought to be.' Still, 'The conductor of the train will help to arrange for women to be together at one end of the car if he is asked to do so.' 'We hope to get this system altered,' Joyce wrote; 'but [until that comes to pass] it is a very strong reason for going with a party protected by an experienced Matron.'[60]

The volunteer emigrators were joined in their safe-passage work by the societies' paid employees, who were chosen by the societies' members and employed to work under the members' direction. The women's organizations hired women to work as ship, train, and hostel matrons and servants, station visitors, and secretaries. As front-line representatives of these organizations, these employees played a vital role in the safe-passage program. The management of the matrons' and station visitors' images was thus of central importance to the identities of these organizations.

The women who ran the female emigration societies insisted that respectable female chaperones were an essential part of any attempt to emigrate young women safely. Because of the peculiar nature of ocean travel,[61] ship matrons held a special place in the emigrators' safe-passage discourse.[62] In the emigrators' literature, the ability of young women to make sensible decisions when out of their familial context was always in question. But the long shipboard journey to another continent posed more than the usual set of challenges for girls who desired to remain respectable.[63] As one article in the *Imperial Colonist* put it, 'the long idle, eventless days, the natural excitement of those on the verge of a new life, the feeling of freedom and irresponsibility engendered by a break with the past and the consequent shaking off of old restraints and conventions, [and] the natural feeling of home-sickness and tendency to emotionalism' all tended to undermine any reticence and good sense that a girl might usually possess.[64] The job of the ship matron was to 'guard against intimacies which are patently undesirable, or casual offers of help or employment from strangers, to check irresponsible rowdyism, whilst at the same time to encourage good fellowship and all forms of healthy recreation.'[65]

The emigrators differentiated their own treatment of the problem of single female migration from that of various government bodies,[66] run-for-profit emigration agencies, and shipping companies by pointing to their own commitment to using carefully chosen chaperones for all the female emigrants entrusted to their care.[67] By the beginning of the late 1880s, the emigrators' successful manipulation of the ship matron's image had turned the matron into a powerful symbol of well-organized female migration.[68] The transformation of this public image of the ship matron involved careful hiring practices, rigorous scrutiny of matrons' shipboard work, and energetic promotion of matrons in the organizations' publications.

In constructing the persona of the ship matron, the editors of the organizations' publications drew heavily upon the logs, letters, and anecdotes of the matrons themselves. Not only was it part of the matrons' job description to record, in detail, their work with the migrant passengers under their care, but it was also in their own best interests to help nurture the sort of image of themselves that their employers chose to promote.[69] Matrons presumably held positions of authority over their charges. The organizations that used their services tried hard to empower them as much as possible. They attempted to get governments to officially recognize matrons' work, they worked to have shipping lines solidify matrons' authority and status, and several of the organizations required that the women who travelled under their care sign forms committing themselves to obedience to the matron. But in reality the matrons' influence was largely restricted to the relationships that they could forge with the emigrants. They had little power to force good behaviour in their charges beyond the threat of unfavourable reports to prospective employers, and any actions they took against unruly passengers, or any changes they wished to make to their charges' travel arrangements, required the support of the vessels' captains and crews. Yet, according to the narratives, if a matron could persuade a majority of those around her that she legitimately represented respectability and good order, she would have little difficulty in finding support for her work.[70] The matrons, like the readers of the safe-passage narratives, were encouraged to believe that the most powerful weapons they could possess were convincing maternal personas. It was thus essential to their ability to do their work effectively that their charges learn about how they ought to relate to the ship matrons before embarking upon that portion of their journey.[71]

The images that the emigrators created for their other front-line workers had much in common with the images of ship matrons, even though these workers had significantly different relationships with migrant women. Hostels' matrons were stationary, and presumably had a fixed place within their greater communities. These women were expected to act as mother figures, at the head of a household of constantly changing daughters. Their job was to provide a safe and comfortable home away from home for young females dislocated from their real families, and to use their connections to secure respectable jobs for those in need. The emigrators promoted the idea that the hostels would become the young women's social centres, where the matron-mothers would preside over social events, encouraging positive attitudes and elevated thoughts. In her capacity as surrogate mother, the hostel matron was expected to be concerned about the welfare of the young women who passed through her home, keeping in touch with them after they had moved on, and arranging for assistance for them in times of need.[72]

Like the matrons, TAS train-station and port visitors were expected to carry themselves in a manner that denoted dignity, respectability, and competence. TAS workers had a less motherly image than those of the ship and hostel matrons. Although ship and hostel matrons had the capacity to become quite heavy-handed in their treatment of recalcitrant young women, they paled by comparison with the TAS port and station visitors. Unrequested interference in the activities of misbehaving young women was part of the TAS worker's job description. TAS annual reports regularly applauded instances where their visitors had forced the separation of previously unacquainted men and women who, in their opinion, were ill matched.[73] Although the TAS publications liberally recorded the gratitude of women saved from unwanted male attention, the visitors would certainly have infuriated some of the women they treated in this manner.

The TAS visitors were represented in these texts as urban guardian angels. Like the ship matrons, their very presence at major ports and stations was supposed to be enough to discourage rowdiness and incivility. Within a couple of years of these workers' existence, the TAS was confident that the station visitor had been promoted so effectively that her presence had come to signify safety. According to the TAS annual report for 1887, the Society had proof 'that our work is spoiling the trade of those who linger about the stations in the hope of entrapping innocent girls' in that 'more than once these persons have tried to personate our station-visitor.'[74] Emulation was seen as a clear indication that viewers were convinced by the station visitor's constructed identity.

The images of the paid helpers that entered the emigrators' publications were carefully crafted to suit the needs of the organizations they represented. In the case of ship matrons and station visitors, the organizations required characters who could be both domineering and indisputably feminine. They had to be capable of intimidating aggressive men into compliance with their wishes. Simultaneously, they were expected to earn the respect of the young women they sought to protect. They needed to be able to domesticate public spaces with their auras alone.

The production of the public personas of the paid helpers required tact and creativity, for, in reality, the relationships between the safe-passage promoters and their paid employees were not always harmonious, and few of these workers would have matched all of their employers' expectations. Some of the women hired to work as matrons became passionate about their jobs, and were clearly loved and respected by their employers and the women they chaperoned. Mary Monk (shown in figure 2) serves as a good example. She worked as a ship matron for twenty years, and chaperoned over two thousand female emigrants to the dominions.[75] These jobs were very demanding and did not pay well. Some of the women who took them on found that they were not well suited to the work, or that the small pay was not worth the dedication expected of them. The minutes of the organizations' committee meetings demonstrate that the personalities and actions of the paid employees could be a source of strife for the women who ran these organizations. Yet their publications reveal none of these problems. For example, the TAS had a series of difficulties with its London station visitor, Miss Rowe. TAS committee members spent a good deal of time determining the legitimacy of their paid secretary's accusations that Rowe was insubordinate and disrespectful, and that she lacked 'the tact or discretion necessary for the functions confided to her.' Although the members of the TAS decided that these accusations were probably overblown, they were horrified when they discovered that Rowe might be handing out tracts for unrelated causes at the railway stations where she worked. They demanded that she desist, 'even in her private capacity.'[76] However, none of the TAS publications for the period of Rowe's employment reflect any of her employer's concerns about her work performance.

The safe-passage narratives' matrons and visitors were not faceless, nameless women. In fact, some of the women who worked for these organizations became well-known entities to the regular readers of the societies' journals and other publications. Yet, their public personas were always uncomplicated and stereotypically maternal. Any tensions that might have existed between the paid workers and their employers were papered over, so that in the safe-passage narratives the matrons and visitors looked more like voluntary emigrators than employees. This blurring of the lines between the emigrators who worked for the cause on a voluntary basis and the paid matrons and station visitors was furthered by the fact that well-off emigrators sometimes chose to take on the role of chaperone or hostel matron for a spell themselves. In such cases, the decision to do so received extensive coverage in the organizations' literature.

The women who ran the female emigration and affiliated societies were also represented by carefully constructed characters in the organizations' publications. As the smart and savvy managers of other women's migration, they played a critical, if understated role in the safe-passage narratives. More than any other character in these narratives, the image of the emigrator was supported by evidence presented to the public outside of the literary narratives themselves. In their representations of themselves, the emigrators bore little resemblance to other contemporary images of female reformers. These were no manly feminists, prudish social reformers, or well-meaning but naive Lady Bountifuls. The women who were at the centre of the safe-passage discourse were not angry, arrogant, or isolated from the real world. Rather, they represented themselves as sympathetic individuals who were passionate about helping out less-fortunate women while promoting the best interests of empire. They had keen business and political senses, and they understood the ways of the world better than most men. In their celebrations of their own involvement with this field of work, and in the obituaries that they published to memorialize key players in their organizations, the dignity, respectability, and good sense of these women were highlighted. The photographs and illustrations of the organizations' leading 'ladies' that were reproduced in the organizations' publications were chosen to enhance their images as noble, intelligent, attractive women.[77]

The obituary of Louisa Mary, Baroness Knightley of Fawsley that appeared in the November 1913 issue of the *Imperial Colonist* serves as an excellent example of the emigrators' representations of themselves in their published writing.[78] Lady Knightley held several important positions in the GFS between 1878 and her death in 1913. She was also the first president of the SACS, serving in that position from 1901, and she was the *Imperial Colonist*'s editor from its inception in 1902. The author of her obituary was Ellen Joyce, who was arguably the safe-passage project's most able and dedicated promoter.

In her reflections upon the life and work of Lady Knightley, Ellen Joyce listed an impressive number of causes that had benefited from Knightley's involvement. Joyce noted that Knightley was not only a philanthropist involved in a range of projects related to women's issues, but also a well-respected (though unofficial) politician for the Conservative Party, and the president of the Conservative and Unionist Women's Suffrage Society. However, her involvement with many causes had not resulted in a half-hearted relationship with the safe-passage project. In fact, according to Joyce, 'Amongst all her activities and interests, the work of Protected and Imperial Emigration has, since the year 1900, when she joined the [BWEA], had her chief and centred attention.'[79]

Lady Knightley's obituary focused upon her reputation as one of Britain's most respected women of the social elite. Joyce noted that 'her active political life and her association with leading men of the day, gave her a somewhat unique experience of the views taken by politicians and reformers on questions of national and social importance, and in the methods and procedure of public business.'[80] Her friendship of fifty-two years with Princess Christian (who also supported the safe-passage project through her patronage of female emigration societies) and her close ties with other members of the royal family were cited at length in the obituary, so that her image was well rounded as a woman who had access to the ears of Britain's most influential authorities. Lady Knightley had status and insight, but she also had influence: 'Men, as well as women, accepted the good judgement and moderation of her opinions.'[81]

Joyce's depiction of Lady Knightley was designed to leave no doubt that this woman had been eminently qualified for the job of managing and directing the movement of young females. According to Joyce, Lady Knightley's personal credentials were indisputable:

> Her cultured thoughts were expressed in simple, strong, and courtly English. All who worked with her became impressed with the thoroughness, the integrity, and the sincerity of her purpose; the single-mindedness, the unselfishness, the righteousness of her daily life, made an atmosphere which fostered friendship and stimulated its reproduction. Her understanding sympathy with the difficulties connected with all associated effort, enabled her to adjust differences which might have obstructed excellent work.[82]

In this obituary Joyce demonstrated that young women ought to have felt truly grateful that Lady Knightley had 'concentrated the powers of her cultivated intelligence on [female migration's] problems.'[83] In a classic Ellen Joyce move, this obituary also gave its author an opportunity to suggest that those wishing to donate money to a good cause in Knightley's name could not do better than to provide funds for an institution that truly reflected Knightley's interests: the Joyce Hostel at Kelowna, British Columbia.[84]

Lady Knightley was only one of many emigrators involved in the provision of safe passage for women who were discussed in their organizations' publications. She was not the only emigrator reported to have friends in high places, and she was not the only woman described as being exceptionally insightful, dignified, talented, and charming. The vignettes of the female emigrators that appeared in the women's journals formed a part of a much-publicized system of mutual respect and admiration.

In their representations of themselves, the emigrators made it clear that they were a group of women who understood that their relatively privileged social status required that they work together in harmony to improve conditions for all women.[85] In an article on this subject, Ellen Joyce informed her middle- and upper-class readers that as prominent female philanthropists in their communities, GFS associates would be expected to give advice and assistance to members of the working class who wished to migrate. She told them that it was, 'therefore, of great consequence that Associates should be themselves possessed of correct information, and able to advise their Members as to the safest way to emigrate, and the proper steps to take.'[86] Their project was fundamentally political. According to its founder, the primary aim of GFS associates was 'the raising of the standard of womanhood.'[87] Similarly, the TAS advertised that 'the TA is essentially woman's work, and as such the Committee know it will appeal to those who, because they are women themselves, must strain every nerve to keep their sisters out of danger and thus do what they can to secure what is truly "Women's Rights," i.e., the raising of the whole standard of womanhood.'[88]

The safe-passage discourse openly questioned some of the most central of men's paternalist claims, asserting that women were more qualified than men to act the part of protector. Yet, although the emigrators aimed to replace the men who failed to provide adequate protection for young women in transit, few of them would have written these texts with the intention of seriously undermining the norms of gender relations. Their actions and accusations certainly annoyed a range of men in positions of authority, but generally these women were not perceived of as a threat to patriarchal power. For the most part, their ambitions concerning the management of younger women's migration were tolerated – and even encouraged – by the men who ran the British and colonial governments, and the transportation companies. Men in positions of governmental power and men who ran the larger shipping companies tolerated these ambitions because the female emigrators' involvement gave imperial migration a better image with minimal financial input from the state or business interests.

The safe-passage discourse evolved in opposition to contemporary paternalistic arguments – such as those presented in the Jack-the-Ripper narratives explored by Judith Walkowitz – about how women were in need of male protectors. Simultaneously, it was constructed against the discourse of the New Woman. As Walkowitz has shown in *City of Dreadful Delight*, narratives of sexual danger were particularly effective at gaining the attention of the late-Victorian public. Stories about abduction, seduction, and the plotted ruin of young virgins captivated while they scandalized Britons. The emigrators and their associates who worked at protecting young women from a host of social evils got great mileage out of the sexual-danger scares that took hold in English society in the

1880s. Themselves convinced of the dangers that young women in transit faced, and of the ineffectiveness of men as protection against these dangers, the emigrators formulated their own versions of sexual-danger narratives. In creating and publishing the safe-passage narratives, these women used their ability to produce and disseminate an alternative discourse in order to improve their own positions of power and authority, to alter the travel experiences and identities of the women they aimed to protect, and to reform the practices of the men they saw as threatening or indifferent.

The young single females in the narratives published by the women's emigration societies and affiliated organizations were shown to be vulnerable, naive, and ignorant – individuals in need of protection. In their attempts to assert their own rights and expand their own spheres of power, the emigrators endeavoured to undermine other women's claims to self-determination. Through regularly repeated, reworked, and augmented narratives about the certain relationship between young women's unsupervised travel and sexual transgression, female emigrators encouraged young wage-earning women to believe that to make a move on their own, be it to a new job, across the city, or to a different continent, was to court danger. The authors of the safe-passage narratives tried to enforce their own moral code in public places – a code that left no space for any interaction between previously unfamiliar men and women. They encouraged all female emigrants to travel with their protected emigration parties, and they attempted to direct all searches for employment through their own hands.

To what extent these narratives were convincing to the members of the general public, and to the specific groups targeted by them, is obviously a subject for debate. There is plenty of evidence that young women resisted the safe-passage narratives' messages and the self-identities they were supposed to take from them.[89] Clearly, many of the women who used these organizations' services would have done so without buying into the emigrators' visions of gender relations, class relations, and the dangers inherent in their own unsupervised movement. These narratives would have been used and reworked by young female travellers, just as the emigrators used and reworked more mainstream narratives of sexual danger.

Yet, in spite of the fact that they were sometimes resisted, reworked, or outright ignored, the emigrators' safe-passage narratives, combined with other elements of the safe-passage project, did achieve some of the results that their designers had intended. Their campaigns to alert women and their families to the dangers inherent in unchaperoned travel clearly heightened some people's fears of moral and physical danger. The sheer number of women that these women's organizations aided in one way or another is an indication that the public perceived a need for their services.[90] And even when read critically, the letters that these organizations received from grateful young women and their families reveal that the emigrators' efforts to protect female travellers were solicited and appreciated. Dorothy Harris, reflecting upon her own migration experiences in her youth, emphasized this point. She recalled that whenever she had needed a new job, her mother had asked GFS associates for their help in securing a suitable post. Even though Harris was eighteen years old in 1919, her mother would not allow her to travel across London by herself. 'A lady came to the station to meet me and took me safely across to the other station,' Harris recalled. '[We] were never allowed to travel alone in those days.'[91] By the early twentieth century these voluntary societies of women had become the recognized authorities on matters pertaining to safe travel for women. Articles featured in a wide range of British newspapers, including the *Morning Post*, the *Spectator*, and the *Daily Mail* promoted the women's safe-passage programs, and cited the opinions of these women as experts.[92] The safe-passage discourse had convinced key members of the public and of the British and dominions governments to see women's migration from the female emigrators' perspectives. Over the course of the second half of the nineteenth century, these women had carved out for themselves a larger and larger share of the management of safe passage. Their success in gaining power in this realm of work was the result of their manipulation of public feeling, their careful image building, and the consolidation of and cooperation between different groups of like-minded women.

chapter 3

'Grit and Grace': A New Class of Women for the Colonies

In 1906 Kathleen Saunders undertook a 'mission' to Canada on behalf of the British Women's Emigration Association (BWEA). 'The main object of my mission,' she wrote, 'has been to find openings for gentlewomen by birth and education with high principles, whose quiet influence will be felt wherever they are.' Saunders published a summary of her findings in the *Imperial Colonist*. Having discovered that Canada had few jobs to offer British gentlewomen, her summary began with the somewhat disingenuous statement: 'Home Help – what a novel but what a comprehensive name!'[1] By 1906, there was nothing 'novel' about the home help. Ladies' Helps, Mothers' Helps, Domestic Helps, Companion Helps, Helpmeets: the occupation had been renamed again and again, but the concept behind it remained remarkably similar to that which was promoted by female emigrators back in the 1860s. The home help was an educated woman who would perform general household duties, for an employer of a similar class background, under a social contract with her employer that would allow her to retain her privileged social status. In other words, like many female emigrators before and after her, Saunders had undertaken to find work opportunities overseas for educated British women. Like the others, she concluded her search with nothing much to offer beyond a glorified version of domestic service.

In Saunders's opinion, 1906–7 was an excellent moment at which to become a home help in western Canada. Owing to the availability of relatively well-paid domestic work in eastern Canada, competition from better-qualified domestic servants from the 'Old Country' was unlikely in the West. Asian men likewise offered limited competition: 'Now that the poll tax of $200 is exacted from all Chinese entering the country it has practically barred the way for any more to go in, and those already there, knowing how valuable their help is, can make their own terms, which are far beyond the reach of most people.'[2] A few months after Saunders's paper was published, Ellen Joyce presented a similar argument, but her commentary upon the need for home helps in Canada contained a slightly different emphasis: 'The heavy tax imposed on Chinamen makes the introduction of Englishwomen a matter of British importance,' she wrote. If Englishwomen did not take up the opportunity offered, Joyce warned, 'the field will be occupied by Swedes and Norwegians, Germans and Americans; it is worth a great effort to be on the spot soon.'[3]

On the surface, the various points that Saunders and Joyce brought together in their notices about the need for home helps in western Canada make little sense. Essentially, they were encouraging well-educated British gentlewomen to take up the most general type of domestic service work (a form of employment that working-class women increasingly shunned whenever possible), for less remuneration than Canada's much-abused Chinese immigrants would willingly accept! The logic behind the emigrators' proposal only becomes apparent when the particular socio-political context within which the emigrators were working is understood. The emigrators were ardent imperialists whose voluntary labour relating to British emigration had everything to do with improving the empire's racial and cultural integrity.[4] The emigrators felt that the influence of well-educated British women was critical to the appropriate evolution of colonial and dominion societies – societies that they saw increasingly drifting away from imperial ties. Yet educated British women's perceived cultural value was out of line with their paid labour value. Throughout the British Empire gentlewomen found themselves at a significant disadvantage on the labour market, both in relation to men of their own class and in relation to working-class women and men with more marketable skills. The disconnection between these 'values' meant that those who wished to increase the number of educated female British emigrants in Canada and Australia had to think creatively about how to respond to the limitations placed on their emigration work. Through an examination of the emigrators' promotion of educated British women as domestic workers to colonial employers, and of colonial home help work to educated British women, this chapter will extend the analysis of the emigrators' imperial project. It will show how the emigrators were concerned about more than the safety of the empire's migrant women; they also aimed to transform the white settler societies into communities that reflected a 'respectable,' feminized British ideology.

The emigrators' determination to oversee the migration of large numbers of British women to the empire's less thoroughly colonized regions during the late nineteenth and early twentieth centuries evolved both against and within a conspicuously masculine context.[5] In fiction and in documentary-style travel literature, colonial frontiers were represented as masculine homosocial spaces in which danger and adventure, mateship and rugged independence thrived. They were presented enthusiastically by British imperialists as environments in which men could shed the negative effects of an over-populated, over-civilized homeland. As Anne Windholz has noted, by the end of the nineteenth century, 'the literature of empire ... permeated fin-de-siècle popular culture, not least as an antidote to the degeneracy perceived as threatening British manhood and, by extension, nationhood.'[6] This 'literature of empire' taught boys and men that time spent on the margins of the empire would transform them into real men – men who, unhampered by feminine influences, would be free to rediscover their masculine identities.[7]

Anne McClintock's definition of the imperialist venture as a masculine enterprise – one in which male dominance was asserted over symbolically feminized peoples and territories – is compelling. She writes of the imperial order as a 'Family of Man' – 'a family that admits no mother.'[8] Over the past couple of decades, historians of women have worked hard to highlight the presence of women in the imperial context, exploring not only how women were the victims of imperialism, but also the ways in which women promoted and subverted British imperialism.[9] Their findings tend to support McClintock's assessment of the culture of imperialism in the late nineteenth and early twentieth centuries. Historians of women and imperialism agree that there was a general assumption that empire building was men's work: women were barred from holding formally recognized posts within the state-building institutions of the empire; female imperialists and adventurers had to fight against insinuations of impropriety, amateurism, and manliness in their efforts to get involved in the imperial venture; and women's informal relationships with colonized imperial subjects were regularly portrayed in the press and by the British and colonial governments as detrimental to the imperial project.[10]

Yet the assumption that imperialism should be a male monopoly was not shared by all subjects of the empire. Some contemporary observers argued that the mother should play a significant role in the imperial cause, even if that role was ultimately played out within the family of man. Adele Perry's study of colonial British Columbia explores the regulatory and reforming efforts of 'missionaries, politicians, journalists, and freelance do-gooders,' many of whom saw the presence of more white women as essential to the formation of a civilized society.[11] These critics saw white settler societies' frontier spaces as problematic for the very reasons that these spaces excited the imaginations of the phalo-centred authors of adventure narratives and their readers. In the masculine discourse of empire adventure, the absence of British women from the frontier was presented as a bonus; for those who wished to turn frontier spaces into civilized outposts of the British Empire, the absence of appropriately respected female settlers was a central aspect of the frontier problem.[12] Reformers regarded with scepticism the idea that the average 'unattached' British man was capable of acting as an effective civilizing agent. They argued that the young British men who went out to civilize these raw spaces and their peoples were more likely in the process to lose their own typically British masculine virtues of self-discipline and control than to enhance them. In this view, frontier environments nurtured the least savoury of male attributes; without the right sort of women, white male settlers could not maintain civilized identities. They noted that the absence of respectable British women in the relatively sparsely populated parts of the white settler societies ensured the emergence of lawless, immoral bush cultures, in which alcohol, gambling, violence, and cross-race and otherwise deviant sexual relations were prevalent.[13]

The women who were members of British female emigration societies in the late nineteenth and early twentieth centuries became key figures in a project to reform Britain's masculine empire – a project designed to correct the deficiencies evident in an all-male imperial enterprise. Like other reformers, they worried that the imperialist efforts of the 'superior' race could never be successful without the integration into colonial societies of sufficient numbers of those who embodied the civilizing attributes of that race. They also feared that white men on the frontier threatened the racial integrity of the imperial project by becoming overly influenced by their new, raw environment. Without the presence of marriageable women of British origin, male settlers could not be trusted to resist the lure of mixed-race or cross-cultural relationships. In the eyes of these female imperialists, the solution lay in racial regeneration through colonization by the right sort of women, who, if need be, would settle into their new communities as educated home helps until ready to marry. In all these perspectives there was much that the female emigrators shared with other reformers of colonial societies. Yet these women's vision of the empire differed from those of most male authors in important ways.[14] The female emigrators were committed female imperialists.[15] They conceived of the empire as a space in which the mother was a dominant force, and they presented themselves as the empire's grand matriarchs, working from the centre to ensure that suitable women would be in place to domesticate and appropriately populate the periphery. Central to this program was the construction of a discourse of imperialism fundamentally different from that which foregrounded men and their activities.

The female imperialists who ran the female emigration societies of the late nineteenth and early twentieth centuries did not all share the same politics about the place of women in British society. As Julia Bush has shown in her study of the upper-class members of these organizations, some were committed suffragists, while others were dedicated to a more conservative, anti-suffrage understanding of women's proper sphere.[16] Nevertheless, these women, along with their middle-class co-members, were able to find within a female imperialist agenda to feminize the empire a set of ideas that could appeal to all of them. The assertion by the British Columbian representative of the BWEA that 'there is no greater or better civilising power in the world than that which a truly good woman possesses' might well have been the BWEA's motto.[17] In the female emigrators' imperialist discourse, women were empowered to act as agents of the empire. The narratives published by the emigration societies showed women engaged in colonial adventures as heroes, civilizing uncivilized native peoples and white men and conquering harsh physical environments. The image of a British woman, empowered by her intellect and by her femininity, subduing and improving man and nature could work for female imperialists of all types. As part of a campaign to promote female emigration, it was also an image that could be made attractive to young prospective emigrants from a wide range of social backgrounds.

The female emigration promoters believed that the success of their program of empire feminization necessitated the formation of a new class of women for the colonies. They envisioned the emigration of well-educated women who, for the good of the British Empire and for their own self-fulfilment, would tackle work usually assigned to the least empowered members of the working class and, in so doing, would transform that work into a well-respected career. Conscious of the ways in which British class and gender conventions had ordered their own expe-

riences and identities, the women who promoted female emigration proposed a radical reordering of class and gender relations in the colonies.
They worked to reformulate domestic workers' identities. They argued
for a new meritocracy. Whereas the male version of the literature of
empire showed how, on the frontier, men would rediscover and reassert
masculine power, the literature produced by the female imperialists
claimed that those parts of the white settler societies that were in the process of being claimed and civilized were ideal locations for women to
demonstrate what it meant to be a true woman. On the frontier, the right
sort of women would be free to impose female imperialism.

Academics have noted the explosion of literature dealing with masculinity and empire at the end of the nineteenth century.[18] A parallel
increase in literature focusing upon women in the imperial context is
evident for the same period.[19] The writing of women involved with the
BWEA and associated societies constituted a significant contribution to
this body of literature. As with most other authors of imperial literature,
the female imperialists constructed their narratives with the intention of
doing more than just entertaining their readers. The women who ran
the female emigration societies wrote to educate Britons about the colonies, to encourage the emigration of a specific class of women, and to
promote their own philanthropic and imperialist activities.

The female imperialist agenda to domesticate the British Empire
required the movement of large numbers of single women from Britain
to the colonies. Promoters of female emigration argued that special
measures had to be taken to ensure the establishment of a healthy gender balance in British white settler societies.[20] Yet even more important
to the women who formed the female emigration societies than sheer
numbers was the quality of the female emigrants who would settle in the
colonies. From the 1860s, female emigration promoters were consistent
in their arguments that the emigration of the wrong sort of women
served only to impede the proper domestication of the empire. In their
annual reports and in their published essays and lectures, they claimed
that they discouraged as many, if not more, women than they encouraged to emigrate. The members of the BWEA and affiliated societies
took it as a point of pride that they facilitated only the movement of
respectable, capable young women.[21] They pointed out that if the emigrant women were to act the part of imperial missionaries, they had to
be fully capable of taking on that role.

The female emigration promoters' arguments about quality reflected
their concerns about the emigrants' class and race/ethnicity. As Ade-

laide Ross put it in an essay published in the early 1880s, 'English women are, in general, the most beautiful in the world, and yet our national emigration has often, by selecting the female emigrants from workhouses, sent forth the ugliest hussies in creation to be the mothers – the model mothers – of new empires!'[22] Within the published and unpublished documents created by the female emigration promoters may be seen a well-established system of rank by which the missionizing and civilizing potential of prospective female emigrants were assessed. Firm Christian (but preferably not Catholic) religious convictions were considered a definite asset. Emigrants from England and Scotland were ranked above those from Ireland,[23] and women who had been raised in major cities were considered more suspect than those from rural, less tainted social settings.[24]

The exact nature of the 'undesirable' female colonist (as understood by the female emigrators) changed over time. The mass emigration of the Irish during and after the potato famine of 1845–9 resulted in a dramatic increase in Irish populations overseas.[25] Moreover, the patterns of Irish migration differed significantly from those of other ethnic groups. Whereas other migrations in the nineteenth century were dominated by men, Irish migration in the second half of the century was dominated by single women.[26] Maria Rye, who promoted female emigration in the years closely following the potato famine, wrote that she considered 'an influx into the colonies of a body of women infinitely superior by birth, by education, and by taste, to the hordes of wild and uneducated creatures we hitherto have sent abroad' to be the best possible cure of vice and immorality in the colonies.[27] The women Rye referred to as 'half-savage' originated in the 'wilds of Ireland and Scotland.'[28] By the end of the nineteenth century, emigration from Britain's periphery was no longer of major concern to British female emigration promoters. The problematic Irish woman of the mid-nineteenth century had been replaced in the emigrators' literature by 'foreigners,' such as Afrikaner women in South Africa and women from eastern Europe in Canada.[29] While the undesirable female settler in the emigrators' imaginations changed over time, female agents of civilization and imperial loyalty remained, by definition, of English or, sometimes, Scottish descent.

Young British women of respectable working-class backgrounds could be seen as worthy candidates for emigration if they displayed evidence of attitudes and abilities appropriate to their class position and gender. The women who ran the emigration societies wrote positively about how, if carefully selected, such women would do a great service to the empire both as domestic servants and, later, as the wives and mothers of loyal colonial citizens. They encouraged working-class women to emigrate, and they worked hard to ensure their safe passage and happy and productive integration upon arrival at their destinations. However, as Bush notes in her discussion of upper-class female imperialists' emigration work, 'Working-class women, and especially domestic servants, were regarded as careless, self-interested and morally vulnerable, even if they had led hitherto blameless lives.'[30] Women of this class could not hope to compete with the civilizing and missionizing power of women of a 'higher' class.

The fact that women of middle-class backgrounds were usually ineligible for subsidized migration, and were actively discouraged from emigrating to the colonies, was cited as one of the main justifications for the formation of the Female Middle-Class Emigration Society (FMCES). In the paper that she presented in 1861 at the Social Science Congress in Dublin to gain support for her female middle-class emigration project, Maria Rye emphasized that working-class women were already supported in their efforts to emigrate, and that it was women of a higher class who most needed the help of philanthropists and reformers.[31] When the BWEA began its work in this field in 1884, its members made it clear that women of the servant class might travel with their protected parties of emigrants, but that they would not be provided with loans through the association.[32] In 1911 the Colonial Intelligence League (for Educated Women) (CIL) was established for the sole purpose of promoting and facilitating the imperial migration of women of a class above that of the normal domestic servant.[33]

Educated women held a special place in the female imperialists' agenda to domesticate the empire. But not all female imperialists defined educated women in the same way. In fact, determining what constituted an 'educated' women could be an activity that required careful negotiation between different female emigration promoters. Correspondence between Mrs Mary Agnes FitzGibbon, who established a hostel for gentlewomen in Vancouver, British Columbia, and women of the CIL in Scotland and England highlights this point. It appears that when she opened her hostel, FitzGibbon had a stricter definition of the educated woman in mind than did women in Britain, as responses to her letters display some consternation at her insistence that only women of gentle birth would be received. Mrs Ferguson wrote from Edinburgh: 'We in Scotland have rather a different type of individual from what is meant in England by the term "gentlewoman" ... but I expect that you would include in such a term women who had had a thoroughly good secondary education, and those who came from the teacher class, many of which class we have already placed in Canada as Home Helps.' Ferguson went on to argue that this class of women 'would probably be more valuable in Canada than those that in England are termed "gentle-women."' Ferguson suggested that maybe Mrs FitzGibbon was unaware of this, as 'it is difficult for anyone not acquainted with Scotch quite to appreciate these National distinctions.'[34]

The letter that FitzGibbon received from Caroline Grosvenor of the CIL in England indicated an even clearer disagreement with FitzGibbon's understanding of the educated British female emigrant. 'We are doing our very utmost in the C.I.L. to keep up the standard of efficiency, character, physical health, etc.,' wrote Grosvenor. 'If a woman of education comes up to our standard in all these ways, we cannot possibly refuse her because we do not consider her to be socially Class A.' Grosvenor made it clear that she believed Canadians would 'quite rightly value efficiency' over 'birth or breeding.' Drawing a hard line between women of good education and women of gentle breeding was impossible, she wrote, as '[the] daughters of men in business are often absolute ladies, while daughters of some professional men are nothing of the kind.'[35] Whatever her misgivings about the British emigration societies' standards, FitzGibbon did ultimately manage to come to an arrangement with the CIL.[36]

The female imperialists' visions of the ideal female emigrant were informed by their convictions about the relationships between class, race, gender, and personal identity. They worked from the assumption that only British women of a superior class and breeding – women who had been properly schooled in the virtues of being a British lady – were capable of fulfilling their mandate to domesticate not only settlers' homes, but the empire. In the literature published by the female emigration societies, educated women were presented as having a monopoly over the best of British virtues. As Ellen Joyce put it in one of her many essays on the topic, educated women 'are imbued with the traditions which are so all-important in forming character and moulding customs in a new country.'[37] The assumption that women of a higher class were best suited to female imperial roles determined that although most of the women whom the emigration societies chaperoned out to the colonies were of the working class, their publications were dominated by rhetoric that was designed to encourage educated women to emigrate.

Most single immigrant women went into domestic service work when they first arrived in the colonies in spite of the increasing tendency of young women in Britain and in the colonies to shun domestic service,[38] and in spite of the efforts of British female emigration societies to find alternative careers for single women heading overseas. Throughout this period the colonies had insatiable appetites for British women who were willing to undertake domestic service, but offered few alternative occupations to prospective female immigrants. Again and again the women involved in promoting and facilitating the emigration of women to the colonies tried to scout out unconventional occupations for the women who came to them with the intention of emigrating, but who did not relish the idea of domestic work. Their efforts met with limited success.[39] The types of occupations available to women were few and gendered female. Women who wished to work outside of domestic service might be employed as factory workers, shop assistants, teachers, nurses, or white-collar workers; but openings in these fields were inconsistent, comparatively few, and usually required specific training and experience. Working on the land was likewise a limited occupation for women, who were discouraged by popular opinion and by legislation from undertaking what was commonly considered men's work.[40]

The reality of women's work options did not fit well with the female imperialists' agenda to populate the colonies with educated women. The colonies did not want educated women for domestic servants; educated women did not find the idea of colonial domestic service appealing. This incongruity made for some difficulties for the emigration promoters. The female emigration societies thus had three aims when writing their promotional literature. Through their writing they aimed to convince the colonies that the immigration of educated home helps would be to their benefit; they tried to sell colonial emigration to women with appropriately 'gentle' class backgrounds; and they worked to transform women who technically did not match their definitions of refined and well-educated ladies into female emigrants who approximated genteel home helps in attitude, outlook, and behaviour.

Leading residents of the British colonies were not shy about publicizing their understanding of the best sorts of immigrants for their communities. Canadian and Australian governments were anxious to attract men with capital to invest, labourers skilled in identified trades, and undifferentiated physical labourers for specific building projects.[41] Families with agricultural experience were preferred for land settlement.[42] Single women destined to do domestic work were also eagerly sought; but established colonials made it clear that these immigrant servants ought to be respectable members of the working class, who had already been trained or were likely to be easily trained to play the part of a subservient female labourer.[43]

Well before the creation of the late-nineteenth-century female emigration societies, philanthropists and British government bodies had established a tradition of trying to pressure the colonies into receiving people who did not match colonials' definitions of preferred immigrants. Robin Haines's work on assisted emigration from Britain to Australia in the early decades of the nineteenth century has shown that government-assisted emigrants were not the depraved, physically inferior individuals that colonials claimed they were. After all, the Colonial Land and Emigration Committee had endeavoured to select for emigration only individuals and families that were likely to succeed overseas.[44] But the fact that the men, women, and children who were sent to the colonies by philanthropists and poor-law guardians were typically those who had been living in severe poverty, had been the inmates of poorhouses or orphanages, or were reformed criminals looking for a new start in life determined that colonials would object to their arrival. As Paula Hamilton has illustrated, colonials particularly objected to the arrival of the single women who emigrated under these sorts of schemes. As much as the philanthropists and British government officials might try to convince colonials that under the right circumstances these immigrants would become community assets, and despite the ease with which women from impoverished backgrounds were employed in Australia, community spokespersons and colonial officials continued to declare them 'most unsuitable to the requirements of the colony and distasteful to the majority of people.'[45] Colonials remained largely unimpressed and unconvinced by the rhetoric of philanthropically motivated female emigration.[46]

The Female Middle-Class Emigration Society was the first in a series of female emigration societies established to promote the emigration of women better educated and more refined than working-class women. But colonial authorities were as dubious about female immigrants of the middling sort as they had been about the under-class women before them. Whereas immigrant women of a lower class had been associated with moral contagion in the minds of established colonials, gentlewomen were considered economic liabilities. Projects to send gentlewomen to the colonies raised fears that without ready friends and family they would become burdens on the colonial public.[47] Colonials argued that there were many jobs for capable domestic servants, but few for well-educated but unskilled lady's helps. Critics of the projects to send educated women to the colonies noted that individuals who had been raised to be gentlewomen could not adapt to situations that required long and hard physical labour. Well-educated helps expected to do lighter work and have more privileges than their employers found desirable or even possible. Moreover, the educated British women's expectations that they would reform and civilize the communities into which they settled were not well received overseas, where the idea that British women's civilizing influences were required met with resentment. Colonial employers and authorities argued that if the emigration promoters really wanted to help the colonies, they would send only thoroughly trained, hard-working women of working-class backgrounds.[48]

The women who ran the female emigration societies were well aware that the opinions of prospective employers in the colonies were hugely influential in directing the flow of female migration. Not only did colonials determine what jobs were available and under what circumstances they would be offered, but they also constituted a significant interest group that could put pressure on governments to alter immigration policies. The emigrators were conscious that colonial women's organizations lobbied their governments to better promote emigration to British women of the servant class and to financially assist domestic servants' immigration,[49] and that because of the persistent and often forceful pressure put upon colonial administrations to increase the immigration of servants, this class of worker was constantly in the foreground of government studies, immigration policies, and parliamentary debates concerning immigration matters.

The emigration promoters attempted to win over colonial employers to their cause by showing them the logic behind educated home helps. S.R. Perkins offered a typical analysis of the colonial domestic servant shortage problem in an article published in the *Imperial Colonist*. She pointed out that from 'nowhere in the world, and certainly not from Great Britain, can an adequate supply of domestic servants be obtained' for the colonies. Well-trained servants of the working class could pick and choose their jobs in Britain; there was no real incentive for them to leave home. 'Only under the new conditions of treating those who help in the household on a footing of equality can a sufficient supply of helpers now be secured,' she wrote. It followed that 'in these circumstances the more refined the woman helper is the better for the family she enters.' Colonial employers of domestic help could decide the matter for themselves, she argued. 'If ... they remember the inevitable loneliness of the woman ... if they make her feel at home, see that she has society and reasonable recreation, her descriptions of her new life will lead others at home to follow her example. It is only thus that the tide of women's emigration will rise to what we and the Colonies alike would wish to see it.'[50]

The promoters of the educated home help argued that employing gentlewomen immigrants made good sense beyond the fact that the severely restricted domestic labour market meant that colonials could not afford to be picky. They explained in detail how educated women made better domestic helps for cultured employers than did bona-fide working-class servants in the colonies' less populated regions.[51] Educated women could provide lonely housewives of the servant-hiring class with valuable companionship to an extent that could never be true for employees of a lower class. In an article entitled 'Home Helps,' Kathleen Saunders outlined the sort of relationship that she expected would develop between the colonial mistress and her educated home help. She imagined a young woman who 'will make her employer's interests her own, and who will work for her as the good elder daughter would do who is always looking out and anxious to save her mother in every way she can think of.' In cases where the lady of the house was closer in age to her employee, Saunders saw the relationship as rather like that of two sisters. '[What] a happy life can be led by two young women working together with the baby as a common bond of interest!' she effused.

Educated women were supposed to make good domestics because they were of similar class backgrounds to the women for whom they worked, and could thus provide valuable social interaction. But there were also many other reasons why hiring an educated domestic helper made good sense. Because of her similar class background, the home help could also be employed in homes where there was no possible provision of a private room for the employee. As Lady Lyttelton put it in a paper presented at a conference held by the South African Colonisation Society (SACS), there were 'many families of refinement but limited means in the country districts, who cannot afford to keep ordinary white servants, and who would have no accommodation for them in their small houses, if they did – but to whom, the help of a gentlewoman, who would turn her hand to everything in a competent manner, and yet who could be made one of the family, would be of real service.'[52] Such were the benefits of employing someone who could ostensibly fit comfortably into the family circle! The home help was also a better bet than a working-class servant because she was a bargain. An examination of the wages offered to different classes of domestic workers, as they are listed in the *Imperial Colonist*, reveals that educated home helps could expect to receive significantly less remuneration for their services than domestic servants of the working class.[53] Moreover, according to the female emigration promoters, educated women made better domestic workers than women lacking formal education, as they could tackle their labour with their hands *and* their brains.[54] In return for low wages and some social generosity, a colonial employer could gain herself a competent and willing worker and a fine companion.

The emigrators were aware that the promotion of the educated domestic help would not be enough to undermine the colonials' reservations; they also had to address the negative stereotype of the educated female immigrant. Conscious of colonials' sensitivity to attitudes of English superiority, the emigration promoters encouraged their gentlewomen emigrants to practise inconspicuous colonization. For example, in the March 1909 issue of the *Imperial Colonist*, prospective emigrants were told that Australian employers would be more willing to consider using educated home helps if they did not have such 'airs and graces,' and that Canadians would be merciless about female immigrants' attitudes of martyrdom.[55] The editors of the *Imperial Colonist* emphasized this point by publishing the opinions of interested colonials. 'Do bear in mind and send out quiet, sensible, level-headed English girls to uphold the character of their race,' wrote a patron of the BWEA from Toronto. 'The Scotch and North Irish get on much better and are both loved and respected.' Some English girls are so 'ignorant,' she continued, 'that they imagine they only have to teach the inhabitants, and you can imagine that this is not a popular attitude, or a true one either.'[56] Female emigrants were warned that colonials would know best how work ought to be done in colonial conditions, and that any attempt to enforce English practices would not go over well.[57] The emigration promoters encouraged female emigrants to understand their colonizing mission in terms of inculcating the colonials with the spirit, tone, and ideals of respectable Britishness rather than of informing colonials' technical knowledge about the performance of daily tasks.

In their published literature, the female emigration promoters emphasized that the women they sent out were young, adaptable, healthy, and exceptionally competent. They argued that because of, rather than in spite of, their superior breeding and education, the women whom they desired to see settled in the colonies were capable of grappling with physical hardship and limited means in rural settings with good grace and fortitude. An educated woman had the capacity to be a 'philosopher' about her circumstances.[58] Educated women made ideal home helps in the less populated régions of the white settler societies, their promoters claimed, because they were much more than just working-class servants. Although this perspective was adopted by some colonial employers – the educated home help became quite a popular commodity in some colonial contexts[59] – this was a battle that was fought by the promoters of female emigration again and again in the decades between 1860 and 1930. It was hard to convince colonials that educated women would perform satisfactorily as domestic servants, and the occasional bad press that educated domestics did receive tended to confirm colonials' doubts.[60]

If settled colonials were dubious about well-educated women from Britain transforming into contented domestic servants in the less-populated regions of the empire, so too were the young women who were targeted as the ideal type of emigrant. In their promotion of imperial migration to educated women, the women who ran the female emigration societies focused upon three interconnected themes: they explored how single gentlewomen's precarious economic and social status could be salvaged by emigration; they published narratives of female emigrants' lives filled with adventure and romance; and they encouraged young women to believe that by emigrating they would be doing something worthwhile, even heroic, with their otherwise wasted lives.[61] They would not be domestic servants, they were told. Rather, they would work as 'companion helps,' which would entail no loss of social status. Young women were told that by choosing to go to a colony they would find financial security, an improved social identity, and a chance at self-fulfilment and lasting happiness. Last, but certainly not least, they were encouraged to believe that they would be doing a great service for the empire.

In the 1840s and 1850s few reformers and philanthropists interested in the condition of women in Britain promoted philanthropically sponsored emigration as a viable solution to the problem of impoverished gentlewomen.[62] But after the publication of the 1851 and 1861 censuses, in which the growing 'surplus' of women in Britain was highlighted, reformers with varied gender politics began to turn to emigration as a relatively easy, practical solution to single educated women's precarious financial circumstances. In 1861 Maria Rye began to promote a feminist account of the benefits that would accrue to single women who were willing to start anew in the colonies.[63] In 1862 William Rathbone Greg published a fundamentally anti-feminist argument in support of the same solution to the surplus woman problem.[64] The public debates that ensued stimulated a good deal of public interest in female migration.[65] Once the association between the use of the discourse of female redundancy and increased interest in female emigration had been made for the British context, female emigration promoters made regular use of redundant-women rhetoric in their lectures and writing. The issue of surplus women in England during this period has been raised in almost every study of female emigration.[66] But only recently have historians adequately emphasized the extent to which the concept of female redundancy was manipulated as a rhetorical strategy by emigrators.[67] The emigrators tried to make sure that single women were conscious that their social and economic difficulties were endemic to their status as *single* women, that their situation was shared by the huge majority of single women in Britain, and that their situation was likely only to get worse as they aged. They attempted to manipulate women's understandings of their own economic and social situations so that they would be read in ways compatible with the emigrators' visions of imperial migration.

Although the discourse surrounding the gender imbalances in Britain and the colonies was useful for the promotion of imperial migration to single British women, the emigration promoters were soon made aware that this demographic 'problem' was understood quite differently overseas. As Adele Perry has noted for British Columbia, the FMCES failed to establish committees of local ladies who were willing to offer assistance to gentlewomen immigrants on their arrival in the colony.[68] The FMCES experienced similar difficulties with lukewarm support in the Australian colonies.[69] In part, this disinterest in aiding the FMCES was a result of colonials' sense that the shortage of women would not be solved by the importation of this class of immigrant. In the colonies, single gentlewomen were 'surplus' regardless of what a census might indicate. This lack of colonial support for their efforts was a serious impediment to the FMCES's work with educated women.

It was only in the 1880s, with the formation of the BWEA and the establishment of an international network of like-minded female imperialists, that an aggressive, long-lasting promotional campaign to entice single women above the working class to emigrate was begun. However, although the members of the BWEA did make use of surplus-women arguments for emigration, other arguments were used more powerfully and consistently. The excess of women over men continued to feature in British censuses right through the early decades of the twentieth century.[70] But as Michele Langfield points out, Australian officials were particularly blunt when communicating their reservations about encouraging the immigration of women to correct perceived gendered imbalances between Britain and the colonies. Representatives of the Australian government argued that 'women now outnumbered men in Australia and [they] did not propose to increase the "surplus."'[71] As late as the 1920s the statistical imbalance of the sexes in Britain was still being used to stimulate the movement of single women – but by this point it was British government agencies other than the women-run Society for the Oversea Settlement of British Women (SOSBW) that were using surplus-women rhetoric.[72] The women who ran the female emigration societies had learned from experience that colonials, and indeed the emigrants themselves, were more likely to be moved by other ways of understanding educated women's migration.

The late Victorian period was an appropriate moment for the enthusiastic construction and promotion of the female imperialists' discourse about the educated home help. With the building of extensive railway systems, frontier spaces were no longer as inaccessible as they had been at the middle of the century, and, as we have seen, travel had been made significantly more respectable by this point, so that middle-class women were no longer as concerned about risking their reputations by migrating. This was a period in which class and gender definitions and identities were in flux. Images of the New Woman circulated widely in British society, stimulating discussions about women's roles, abilities, and limitations.[73] Likewise, in Britain and in the colonies movements were afoot to fundamentally alter the nature of domestic work. Through scientific management and new technologies, reformers were working to transform household work into a less labour-intensive, 'cleaner' occupation. These efforts to transform the physical labour involved in the maintenance of the domestic sphere were allied with attempts to 'elevate Housecraft to the dignity of a Fine Art.'[74] The timeliness of the message to start life anew as a useful home help in one of the colonies was not lost on the emigration promoters. Even Ellen Joyce, who was one of the more conservative emigration promoters in terms of her ideas about women's sphere, made use of the current rhetoric about 'new' understandings of women's place in society to promote her cause. As she noted in a paper entitled 'Openings for Educated Women in Canada' (a paper that was largely a promotion of careers in domestic work), not only were young women coming around to the understanding that economic independence and self-fulfilment through work were preferable to a parasitic existence, but so too was the 'new father,' who had come to know that 'his girls will lead happier lives if they are filled with work than empty with idleness.'[75]

In their construction of the model educated female emigrant, the emigration promoters were able to draw upon already established literary models. According to Elizabeth Thompson, mid-nineteenth-century authors such as Susanna Moodie, Catharine Parr Traill, and Anna Jameson became the originators of a tradition of backwoods heroines when they published their fictional and non-fictional accounts of women emigrants' experiences. Themselves gentlewomen experiencing and critically observing white settler life, these authors created 'a new feminine ideal – the Canadian pioneer woman.'[76] The image of the pioneer woman that emerged from these women's texts was of a 'self-assured, confident woman' who was capable, positive, and energetic.[77] These books were designed to entertain and enlighten British audiences, and to serve as guides for emigrants headed for the colonies. Their illustrations of life on the frontier were often romantic, but they were not intended to be promotional texts. In some cases, the publications explicitly aimed to caution gentlewomen against leaving their homeland.[78] Yet the representations of educated female settlers that were embodied in these works served as a template for later depictions of gentlewomen at work in the colonies. The pioneering gentlewoman became a familiar, identifiable character type.

Thompson argues that Catharine Parr Traill was the most significant of these female writers because 'she defined most clearly and succinctly the role of the pioneer woman,' and because she specifically intended that her writing would be of use to prospective emigrants and newly settled women.[79] In the colonial society of British North America, Traill imagined that she was witnessing the dissolution of the traditional British class structure. She anticipated (hopefully) that its replacement would be a new 'meritocracy based on education and manners.'[80] According to Thompson, Traill's novel *The Young Emigrants* (1826) 'sets the stage' for the elaboration of the new pioneer gentlewoman character type. 'The central dilemma of the book,' writes Thompson, 'the question of most concern to the young female emigrants ... is the issue of one's social status in Canada. Can a woman remain a lady in Canada, living as a Canadian pioneer, and performing what are essentially "unladylike" tasks?'[81] In this novel, and in her later work on the female pioneer, Traill's answer to this question was an unequivocal 'yes.' Traill argued that the daily tasks of a pioneer woman were not incompatible with gentility, because gentility is derived from personality, decorum, and attitude – not from the avoidance of essential daily labour. In her opinion, with the appropriate socialization and education to guide them and give them confidence, women living on the edge of civilization could define their own social identities. 'One thing is certain,' wrote Traill, 'that a lady will be a lady, even in her plainest dress; a vulgar minded woman will never be a lady, in the most costly of garments.'[82]

Traill's interpretation of the gentlewoman's status as a colonial settler is significantly more positive than that of Moodie, whose *Roughing It in the Bush* (1852) details at great length Moodie's own trials and tribulations as a settler, and her wistfulness about the loss of her genteel status. Traill's contention that gentility and 'roughing it' are compatible was not shared by Moodie. The tensions between these two perspectives are telling (Thompson defines them as those of idealism versus realism) and may be seen echoed over the next three quarters of a century in the narratives created by the female emigration promoters and the responses that those narratives received.

The female emigration promoters recognized that the rough, physical image of domestic service did not appeal to educated women. The stated missions of the female emigration societies clearly indicate that finding employment other than domestic service for single women was a central aim of their work, and the minutes of their meetings reveal their frustration about their inability to find sufficient alternative occupations for educated women.[83] Caroline Grosvenor, the chair of the CIL and the author of its first annual report, conceded that in their efforts to direct educated women towards the colonies, the members of the CIL faced 'very special difficulties.'[84] Prospective emigrants were informed that other employment options were severely limited, so that only the most qualified women could hope to successfully find such work. By contrast, opportunities for paid employment within the domestic sphere were abundant. Because of the lack of alternative work options for single women in the colonies, the society had 'first to bring home to the lady who desires to try her fortune in the Colonies the absolute necessity of complete and efficient training in the [household] arts.'[85] 'Under certain circumstances,' Grosvenor wrote, 'this work is absolutely suitable to the educated woman.'[86] The 'certain circumstances' to which Grosvenor referred were those that could decrease or eliminate the educated woman's sense of loss of caste upon taking up domestic labour.

In her biography of Maria Rye, Marion Diamond explores the challenges faced by the emigrators who wished to convince educated women and colonial employees that a middle-class status and domestic service were compatible. As Diamond notes, although a woman's occupation could be of critical importance to her social status, class identity was also determined by a woman's 'relationships with men, as daughter, sister and wife, and by many subtle indications relating to education, accent and manner.'[87] In England, crossing the divide between respectable and working-class employment was impossible for educated women who desired to maintain their relationships with people of their own class. However, in emigrating to the colonies the possibilities for combining paid domestic work with a gentlewoman's status were presumably greatly enhanced. In this gendered 'class ambiguity,' Rye and those who would follow her in this work saw a vast field of opportunities for adaptable, well-educated women.

In order for the educated home help to feel that she had not irredeemably lost her genteel social status, her employment had to take place in a particular social environment. According to the female emigration promoters, only in rural areas could such environments be found. As Grosvenor noted in a CIL annual report, 'in the large towns (in Eastern Canada, for instance), where class distinctions have already taken root and flourish vigorously, we do not recommend this particular kind of work for educated women.'[88] The ideal situation for a home help was one in which no other domestic help was employed, and where the woman would be treated as one of the family. Young women would be attracted to working as home helps in such contexts, wrote the editor of the *Imperial Colonist*, as they would not have to worry about 'losing caste by having to associate with those who are less educated than themselves.'[89] Grosvenor concurred: 'The real lady feels no degradation' in performing household work. Rather, 'what she does dislike and rightly, is to find that by reason of her work she is considered to have sunk in the social scale and is no longer treated as an equal by those of her own class.'[90] In order to assure educated home helps that they would be employed in the right sort of household – one in which the employers were of the appropriate class themselves, and where the help would be treated like a lady – the intervention of the emigration societies and their colonial representatives was essential. At least in theory, the employment destinations of educated home helps were carefully vetted by the female emigration societies before the young women contracted to work there.

The promoters of educated women's emigration made extensive use of testimonies from emigrant women and from colonial employers to prove their point that gentility and working as a home help were not incompatible. A letter from ES, a home help working in Cariboo, British Columbia, is typical of those that were published in the societies' journals and annual reports. 'I have now been here almost two months,' ES wrote, 'and feel I can safely say that I am settled. I am doing the work for, and looking after an elderly lady and gentleman, and am treated just as a daughter ... I have felt quite at home from the first day.'[91] Ostensibly private letters from prospective employers to the emigration promoters were published in the *Imperial Colonist* to make the same point. 'I may tell you I want a young lady more for companionship than help, for I am devoted to the work, but I am right away in the country – a widow – living alone, and I should much appreciate a companion,' reads one such letter. The author, a recent English emigrant herself, declared that she was looking for a surrogate daughter as hers had all married and moved away.[92] In a long article entitled 'Are Educated Women Wanted in Canada,' Georgina Binnie-Clarke, who had had first-hand Canadian experience and was considered by the emigrators to be an authority on the position of women in Canada, cited an example of one English lady-help with whom she had become acquainted to press home the point that in Canada 'no woman of refinement need hesitate to take up domestic service.' Despite a hard day of work, the young lady in question 'always contrived to appear at table as neatly and becomingly attired as a woman of leisure. She was always included in any invitations that came to my host and hostess, and was a very welcome guest among the neghbours [sic]. She took part in all the amusements and recreations that came to cheer one on one's way, and she also enjoyed the privilege of keeping her own pony, and rode whenever a successful navigation through the daily round permitted.'[93]

In their publications, the emigration promoters emphasized that educated women with the right sort of personalities would not lose status by performing the work of a domestic helper, because they would be doing the same sort of work that was done on a daily basis by their employers. In the colonies' rural districts, all women performed such work, as they had no option, readers were told. 'Many delicately nurtured gentlewomen, not being able to procure the help upon which they have always depended, have trained themselves to do every kind of work,' declared Mrs Skinner. These women, like the paid, educated home helps, 'have found ... that the refinements of education, which they at first thought so useless in the colony, were really a help in the end. The broader intel-

ligence linked with willing hands soon brought forth splendid results.'[94]
In the country districts of the colonies, expert housewives had transformed housekeeping into a highly respectable career. In an article on
'Farm Homes in Canada,' Mrs Alfred Watt explained why educated
women were better suited to the work of running a farm home than
were women of a lower class:

> She is away from big libraries and must be herself a 'reference' for the chil-
> dren ... Her emergency chest must have the home remedies which she
> must know how to make. Her knowledge of agricultural operations must
> be sufficient to make her an intelligent help-meet in what is an arduous
> and complicated method of earning a living. Her knowledge of home nurs-
> ing and home sanitation and sanitary appliances must be practical. And
> she must know food values and the common symptoms of diseases ... This
> is only part, and only the house and practical part, for the farm woman is
> nearly always in charge of the vegetable and fruit garden and poultry ...
> [Greater] still, she has the responsibility of the mental and moral wellbeing
> of the family.[95]

In a presentation of pioneering household work that is reminiscent of
those published by Catharine Parr Traill and others over half a century
earlier, Watt depicted educated women as having skills and knowledge
that could transform pioneers' household work into a career eminently
suitable (even best suited) to women of their class.

The promoters of female emigration encouraged educated women to
believe that emigration to the colonies to work as home helps would
prove an effective way to gain economic independence while maintaining their genteel social status. They argued that under the special circumstances that could be found in rural parts of the colonies, paid
domestic work would be appropriate for the educated woman's class
position and social identity. They claimed that as a home help in the colonies, an educated female could determine her own value; women with
energy, ability, and intelligence would 'find their own level,' and would
become well-respected and beloved members of their new communities.
Prospective female emigrants were assured that an intelligent woman
could make a wonderful, rewarding career out of domestic service.

Although home help employment was enthusiastically promoted by
the women who ran the emigration societies, a home help career was
seldom presented as an end in itself.[96] The emigration societies never
lost their interest in finding alternative occupations for educated

women. 'Not that we could on any account belittle the profession of Home-help,' the editor of the *Imperial Colonist* hastened to assure her readers; 'some women find the position so agreeable that they do not wish to exchange it for any other.'[97] But the reality was that most women could not envision themselves working as home helps for life. The position was thus frequently promoted as a stepping stone – 'a jumping off place for other kinds of work.'[98]

Home help employment was recommended for women with a wide range of aspirations. 'Artists, musicians, teachers, typists, trained nurses, the women with some strong bias, will find openings in Canada for their own particular gifts if they have but self-restraint to "bide a wee" and take up life in its simpler aspects becoming what the Germans term "the housewife's prop,"' advised M. Montgomery-Campbell in an article written for the *Imperial Colonist*. 'Real talent is certain to find its outlet in the end,' but in the meantime the home help will be 'saved by the shelter of home-life from many sharp experiences in a new country.'[99] A position as a home help was presented as an ideal way to acclimatize oneself to a new physical and social environment while living in a context that provided financial security and possibly a degree of emotional support. It was also endorsed as an ideal context in which to gain valuable skills and knowledge for setting up a home of one's own, or for starting a farm or other business.

Although the topic of heterosexual love and marriage was purposely avoided by many of the women who wrote promotional literature for the female emigration societies, it was clearly in the back of most emigration promoters' minds as a powerful incentive for single women to emigrate. As Bush has shown, there was often a discrepancy between what the emigration promoters said in their private correspondence and what they put in print.[100] Negative public reactions to the mid-century work of Caroline Chisholm and Maria Rye, which had arisen due to press representations of female emigration work as husband-finding missions,[101] had taught the female emigration promoters of the late nineteenth century that references to marriage ought to be dealt with carefully in their writing. Too much enthusiasm about marriage in their promotional literature could once again open up a can of worms. However, the assumption that most young women desired to become wives and mothers, and the understanding that marriage was more likely to be attainable in the colonies' less-populated regions, lay behind much of the literature produced by the female emigration societies from the 1840s to the end of the 1920s.[102] As one contributor to the *Imperial Colo-*

nist somewhat defensively put it in 1909, 'Many girls in this country know that in the West there are prospects of marriage to farmers. This is indeed an attraction. Why should it not be? Few girls are worth their salt ... if they hope not one day to be queen of a home.'[103] As an announcement in the *Imperial Colonist* of an emigrant home help's impending marriage made clear, emigrants who married well after spending time as domestic helps were admirably fitted for their future work as the mistresses of their own homes. 'One of our capable girls who went to an isolated part of the country as mother's help, is to be married shortly to an English gentleman owning a large ranch and many cattle,' the announcement read. 'Possessing both education and a complete knowledge of the management of a home, she has every chance of a happy life before her.'[104] Taking up a job as a home help in the colonies ostensibly made educated women more, rather than less, desirable matches for wealthy men.

Marriage predominates in published lists of the emigration societies' enumerated 'successes,'[105] but it was not the only logical result of working for a time as a home help in a colony. Life as a paid helper working outside of colonial urban centres was also presented as an invaluable education for women who wanted to take on business or farming ventures of their own; and, in fact, these career choices received more space on the pages of the emigration societies' publications than did marriage, which, it seemed, required no explanation. Businesses more easily gendered female were especially promoted in the *Imperial Colonist* and in other literature written by the emigration promoters as likely avenues of success for capable and energetic educated women. Farms specializing in poultry, fruit production, and bee-keeping received regular attention in these publications, as did boarding houses, bakeries, and businesses related to needlework. But women's involvement in farming activities that were more usually considered the preserve of men also received enthusiastic support in the emigrators' writing.

In spite of the fact that care was taken to emphasize the pioneering women's femininity, many of these narratives had explicitly feminist implications.[106] Women who struck out on their own and succeeded as colonial farmers in the face of social and physical impediments were celebrated throughout the quarter-century of the *Imperial Colonist*'s publication.[107] Women such as the daughter of Admiral M. of Norfolk, 'a well-known London lady journalist,' and four ex–army nurses who 'were suffering from "the returned soldiers' disease"' after the end of the First World War were applauded in this journal for their successful farming endeavours. These women were depicted as smart, gutsy, and overflowing with vitality. Two English sisters who made a 'brilliant success' of farming in Manitoba, operated '1,120 acres of mixed-farm' completely by themselves. 'Even to-day when they are rich and prosperous and there is no longer any reason why they should not hire male help extensively, they prefer to perform themselves all the tasks of the large establishment,' wrote the author of 'Some Canadian Women Pioneers.'[108] The cautions that often accompanied such success stories would have served, if anything, to increase the hero status of these vigorous women.

Educated women were encouraged to see emigration to the colonies and employment in someone else's home as a logical path to financial stability, self-fulfilment, and sanctified heterosexual love. But not all of the promotion was so serious. Life as a colonial home help was also presented as jolly good fun. Emigration was held out as an adventure or, as the letters of young female emigrants described it, 'a picnic.'[109] Gentlewomen in the colonies had the freedom to be unconventional (within strict parameters), unbound by archaic social conventions and the whims of respectable society. The life of the home help was especially indicated for the 'girl who declared that most hardships would be compensated for by freedom from veils and gloves.'[110] The female emigrants' letters revealed that rural life did not mean isolation. Horse riding (a much commented-upon activity) allowed for a never-ending round of outings to dances and other social events. The beauty of the new settler's physical environment was the focus of a great amount of attention, as was the argument that the climate and physical activities tended to improve the health and attractiveness of the young women who moved out to the colonies' rural spaces. Whether a woman's destination was Australia, South Africa, New Zealand, or Canada, she was informed that the environment would suit her better than that of her homeland. A rural home-help existence would turn young women into more vibrant, healthy, and interesting versions of their former selves.

The literature created by female emigration promoters emphasized the suitability of educated women for home help work in the colonies. It was promoted as an excellent temporary career choice for intelligent women with drive, great inner strength, and more than a usual share of energy. In this literature these qualities were presented as those most likely found in educated women. The emigration promoters nurtured images of women who had been well schooled in middle-class values and manners, yet who shunned the idle ways of gentlewomen. Their published open letters were directed at the woman who 'is not inclined to fritter her life away ... in an attempt at that hateful status called "gentility" on a straightened income.'[111] Refined and accomplished, yet pragmatic and unpretentious, these women were portrayed as embodying all that was best of British femininity, with none of their own class's vices.

Not only did the female imperialists seek to increase the number of well-educated British women in the colonies, they also worked at transforming women into their image of the ideal female emigrant. Their literature was both promotional and prescriptive. The emigration promoters were clear about what constituted the ideal prospective emigrant. As Joyce put it, the most suitable candidates for emigration were young women who

> live mostly in the country, they belong principally to the middle classes or they are the daughters of professional men and men of both the Services, they do a great deal for themselves in their own household, they become handy with children in the nurseries of their younger brothers and sisters, they do their own dressmaking, and many of them keep poultry, sometimes to a profit, most of them get bonnie complexions by gardening. They have been high-school girls, and get used to competition in study, and to being good-tempered in games in the hockey field. Their education is very thorough and well grounded as far as they have gone on with it.[112]

However, few such women were forthcoming, and even the young women who came from the social backgrounds portrayed as ideal for making a success of a home help career required some special coaching about how to approach their new social roles. The images that were evoked in this literature were thus designed both to entice prospective emigrants and to inspire those who had already made the decision to settle in the colonies to become, by example, key components in an imperialist project. The *Imperial Colonist* and other related publications taught British women how to be both genteel and successful in the colonies while undertaking the noble mission of improving colonial society.

The emigration promoters presented their readers with images of colonial societies in which women found their level within a new meritocratic system. These images allowed room for generous definitions of respectability and gentility. In essays clearly intended for a readership of working-class girls, the emigration promoters wrote of emigration in terms that encouraged their readers to identify themselves with women of a higher class. In an essay that was widely circulated to young women just prior to, or during, their emigration, Lady Knightley of Fawsley admonished: 'Seek in all things to uphold the standard of purity, to be gentle and refined, real ladies in the truest sense of the word.'[113] Being a 'real lady' in this context did not necessarily require solid middle-class or genteel parentage.

The emigrators worked hard to make a success of their program to settle a new class of women in the colonies. They wheedled and bullied colonials into giving their carefully selected home helps a try, and they established extensive systems of support for these women overseas. The emigration promoters actively discouraged educated women from choosing destinations that they considered to be unsuitable, and they were untiring in their promotion of those colonial communities and women's organizations that were particularly hospitable to home helps.[114] They carefully instructed their chosen emigrants about how educated home helps ought to behave and what sorts of attitudes they should hold. In their lectures to, and publications for, emigrating women the emigration promoters made it clear that all reasonable steps had been taken to ensure the emigrant's success. The rest, the departing women were told, was up to them.[115]

The failure of individual women to settle comfortably into the colonial home-help identity was usually explained in terms of personal character flaws. 'The qualifications for success in Canada,' Joyce wrote to her female emigrants, 'are adaptability, capability, courtesy ... "grit and grace."'[116] If a woman was not a success, she obviously lacked one or more of these traits. Evident attitudes of superiority were especially highlighted for criticism, as nothing else was as likely to anger employers. Central to the literature promoting the career of the colonial home help was the assumption that British women of gentle birth were superior to the colonials they were going out to serve. After all, theirs was a colonizing and civilizing mission. Yet, to demonstrate such an attitude was presented in the emigration promoters' literature as evidence of a lack of good breeding – a sign that the woman was wanting in courtesy and refinement.[117]

Educated women who chose to give the occupation of home help a try in the colonies were expected to take their decision very seriously. The women who encouraged and facilitated their settlement in the colonies told them in no uncertain terms that their failure to make a good go of their new careers would not only affect themselves, but would also have a negative affect upon the organizations' future efforts to help out financially troubled gentlewomen. As one Canadian correspondent put it, 'So much depends on the girls themselves. If they are capable, sweet-tempered and adaptable, they not only succeed themselves, but make the way so much easier for others who shall follow.'[118] Every generation of educated female emigrants who left Britain's shores to work as home helps in the colonies was lectured about how the demand in the colonies for educated home helps 'will depend upon the attitude adopted by the educated women who first go to the Dominion to undertake this type of work ... It is in their power to make or mar the future of the scheme.'[119] The identities that emigrant home helps formed as workers and as citizens would determine both the extent of colonial employers' demands for their labour and the likelihood that educated home helps would receive government-subsidized transportation to the colonies.[120] Upon the female emigrants lay the ultimate failure or success of the home help project as a whole, and, by extension, the female imperialist agenda to domesticate the empire.

Until recently, historians examining the work of the female emigration promoters of the late nineteenth and early twentieth centuries have understood this work as fundamentally conservative with respect to women's socio-economic roles and gender relations. James Hammerton's study *Emigrant Gentlewomen: Genteel Poverty and Female Emigration, 1830–1914* set the tone for discussions of this subject in 1979. Hammerton found in the work of the FMCES of the 1860s a clear example of feminist effort, after which imperial female migration work reverted back to a disappointingly un-feminist project, informed by a commitment to a gendered separate-spheres ideology.[121] This reading of the female emigration promoters' work as conservative has been brought into question by Bush's recent work on Edwardian female imperialists. Her careful analysis of the relationships between female imperialists, Edwardian society, and the women's movement provides an excellent context for a review of the discourse that emerged in and around the *Imperial Colonist* in the early twentieth century. Although Bush emphasizes that most of these women were not feminists, and that their associations were not fuelled by feminist agendas,[122] she does argue that the female imperialist associations were 'powerfully linked to a broader British women's movement, fed by the mingled currents of feminist equal rights activism and gender-conscious social reform.'[123] She shows how women with divergent views on such critical questions as women's suffrage could amicably work together to promote female imperialist agendas. Female imperialism could be embraced by women with varied political perspectives.

In her introduction to *Imperial Objects: Essays on Victorian Women's Emi-*

gration and the Unauthorized Imperial Experience, Rita Kranidis argues that middle-class female emigrants from Britain were 'commodified' in the debates between Britons and colonials about their migration. According to Kranidis, these 'undesirable, "superfluous" English women' had no '*practical* assignment of imperial duty in the colonies – they were being exported as surplus commodities.'[124] Although this was certainly true of the literature produced by some of the other parties involved in the management of imperial migration, it cannot be said of the female imperialists who ran the female emigration societies of the late nineteenth and twentieth centuries. Central to the female emigrators' work was the identification of educated women's practical imperial duties. In the emigrators' literature, educated female emigrants were represented as imperial agents on a civilizing mission of critical importance. Far from dehumanizing the female emigrants, the female imperialists highlighted their strength of character, their civilizing talents, and their extensive practical capabilities.

The dominant image of educated female emigrants that the emigrators created for public consumption was one that celebrated feminine power. Female imperialists nurtured visions of a new class of women for the colonies – women who had not been allowed to come of age in their own British society owing to a rigid class structure and male privilege. The emigration promoters depicted the colonies as environments in which such women could thrive, to the benefit of themselves and the communities in which they settled. The creators of this vision were not blind to the limitations of colonial contexts. They directed single women of the appropriate backgrounds and education to specific contexts within the colonies, and they chafed at the social and legal impediments in the colonies to women's adoption of male-dominated occupations. Nevertheless, these women saw in the colonies possibilities unavailable in Britain. They targeted frontier spaces that they imagined to be more open to the influence of women with character, ability, and determination. These were traits that they portrayed as fundamental to the make-up of educated British women.

The female emigration societies had to overcome a number of obstacles in order to implement their imperial domestication program. The high costs of transportation and settlement were a constant source of difficulty for the emigration promoters, who usually dealt with women who had limited financial resources. Likewise, the class of women they were most interested in seeing settled in the colonies were not easily convinced to leave their British homes. The attractiveness of emigration to the colonies was particularly undermined by the fact that domestic service consistently dominated the colonial employment scene for women. The emigration promoters worked hard to find funding from colonial governments, colonial employers, and philanthropically minded colonial and British citizens to support female emigration. They also worked to open up alternative career options for women emigrating to the colonies, and to improve the image of colonial domestic service. The promoters of female emigration had to pacify their project's critics, win converts to their vision of the empire, and convince single women that emigration would prove rewarding and fulfilling.

The result was a body of promotional literature that contained a multilayered argument in favour of educated women's emigration. It reflected the emigrators' efforts to respond, at least rhetorically, to the demands of a number of other interested parties. Colonial governments and prospective colonial employers, British supporters of philanthropic efforts, the popular press, and the women whom the emigration societies hoped to move all demanded different things of the emigration societies and provided them with different kinds of problems. The female emigration societies' work was circumscribed by the costs of travel and settlement, by the employment opportunities available to single women, and by the desires of potential female emigrants. Their promotional literature was designed to convince sceptical and hostile members of the British servant-hiring classes that the emigration of young single working women would not deprive them of scarce servants because the emigrating women would never have condescended to working in domestic service in their homeland. It sought to convince dubious colonials that the women they desired to help emigrate would be good for the colonies. And, most important, it aimed to entice young single women to start life anew in the colonies. With their writing, the women involved in this work attempted to justify their requests for financial aid, to negotiate amicable relations with potentially hostile parties, and to reorient the public mindset about the gendered nature of the imperial project.

Domestic service was not necessarily the preferred focus of the female emigration societies' promotional efforts. Rather, their endorsement of household work was the result of unavoidable constraints imposed by the gendered nature of the labour economy. Domestic service was primarily a means to an end – the end being the proper feminization of the empire. The female imperialists had unbounded faith in the abilities of suitably educated women to be successful in whatever venture they might undertake. They assumed that if educated women were forced by financial difficulties and a limited range of employment options into taking up domestic work, they would be able to turn the situation to their advantage. Their promotional literature was not just about establishing good homes in the colonies. Nor was it just about planting an adequate number of future mothers of the race throughout the empire. It was also the product of these women's efforts to promote a female imperialist ideology. Through their literature, and through their practical work with government administrators and women in the dominions, these emigrators endeavoured to empower 'superior' British women who would work as agents of the empire. Given space to grow, to move, and to prove their worth, educated women would use the inherent personal advantages born of their race, class, and education within the mother country to carve out meaningful roles and identities for themselves, and to reshape the mutable male environment of the colonial frontier.

chapter four

Letters 'Home': Female Emigrants and the Imperial Family of Women

The November 1910 issue of the *Imperial Colonist* features a series of four letters written by A. Glanville, who had immigrated to Canada under the auspices of the British Women's Emigration Association (BWEA) earlier that year.[1] Glanville's letters touch upon various aspects of her life between her departure from London in March and the writing of the fourth letter in October, 1910. They tell of her work as a nurse in a Columbia Coast Mission Loggers' Hospital 140 miles up the coast from Vancouver, then at a hospital in Revelstoke, British Columbia. They also hint at Glanville's changing state of mind. The first couple of letters exude enthusiasm, in spite of her obviously heavy workload and trying work conditions. They show that she revelled in her position of authority at the mission hospital, and that she had fallen in love with her physical surroundings. 'It is all so wonderfully new to me and the whole coast is truly beautiful. I feel so well. God has been good to me!' she gushed.[2] The last two letters have a completely different tone. On 3 September the hospital in which Glanville was working burned down. At the time Glanville was working alone. She managed to evacuate all of her fourteen patients, but she lost the building, equipment, supplies, and most of her personal belongings, including all of her books and papers. Within a few days her superiors had assigned her to a new post at another hospital in the province. But Glanville now questioned whether she was in a suitable condition to take on the heavy workload and responsibility again required of her. Her enthusiasm seriously shaken by the shock of the fire, she indicated that she might have to give up her current position for something less taxing while trying to regain her physical and psychological strength.

Like other emigrant letters published in the *Imperial Colonist*, Glanville's were selected by the journal's editor for their promotional and educational value, and because they illustrated points that the emigrators were trying to make in their own writing and lectures. The letters communicated their author's gratitude for the trouble the emigrators had taken on her behalf. They emphasized the physical beauty of Glanville's new environment and her sense of joy at her new circumstances. They highlighted the adventure involved in imperial migration, as well as the potential for romance. Glanville reflected at length upon her surprising discovery that the loggers were 'a very interesting lot of men to nurse.' She wrote that 'a number of them are Old Country men, gentlemen, and one wonders at finding them logging in the back woods of Canada.'[3] The correspondence also shows that Glanville was both touched and flattered by the attention she had received from the men in the logging camps she had visited. Finally, these letters add weight to the emigrators' arguments that emigrating to the empire's frontier spaces required exceptionally strong, adaptable, resilient women, and that for women of this sort there was a world of good work to be done.

The emigrant letters published in the female emigration societies' annual reports, promotional literature, and journals during the late nineteenth and early twentieth centuries have been used by historians interested in a range of subjects relating to the activities of British female emigrants and the workings of female emigration societies. But because these letters were solicited, selected, and edited by the emigrators – who did so in the interests of their own and their societies' agendas – historians have become wary of using them as if they can provide insights into the inner workings of migrant women (the authors of earlier, in-house histories of British female migration showed no such reluctance[4]). Obviously, these published letters need to be read with due sensitivity to the circumstances in which they were created and reproduced. But assuming that the letters were in fact written by the emigrants (and the evidence certainly indicates that they were), to read them only for what they can tell us about the women who produced the organizations' publications is to deny their potential value as sources of information concerning the emigrants themselves. The fact that these emigrants were writing the sorts of letters that the emigrators liked to read and reproduce should not completely undermine their value as emigrant-authored texts. Historians of women emigrants have noted again and again that we have access to remarkably few documents about the emigrant experience written by single women.[5] Only a small fraction of the emigrants' letters that do exist have anything to say about emigrants' relationships with the women who oversaw their migration.[6] As this chapter will show, published emigrant letters, like those by Glanville, are a potentially rich source of information for a range of topics that are difficult to access through other means.[7]

Like historians of other philanthropic and social-reform endeavours, historians of managed female migration have shown that middle-class women's self-empowerment came at the cost of poorer women's right to self-direction. As Jan Gothard writes, the members of female emigration societies 'sought, without malice and with the best intentions, to take away the agency of emigrating women.'[8] The logical correlative of emigrators' success was thus the emigrants' disempowerment. In their analyses of emigrator–emigrant relations, historians have highlighted the fact that being managed could be oppressive, and that emigrants' responses to being managed ranged from self-destructive shows of resistance, through tolerance, to the welcoming of the protection and other services provided by the emigrators, as long as they were short lived. Studies of British female emigrants tend to make three key points about the relationships between emigrators and emigrants: that the twinned themes of 'protection and control' were omnipresent; that emigrants' agency was usually demonstrated through various forms of (passive and active) resistance; and that where emigrants embraced the emigrators' schemes, their embrace was a practical, short-term strategy to ensure safety and convenience while in transit.[9]

In these analyses of the emigrator–emigrant relationship, historians have tended to explore with greater care the meanings of this relationship for the emigrators than meanings for the emigrants. This focus on the emigrators is understandable given the fact that it was the emigrators who created the masses of sources that historians have found so useful in their studies of managed British female migration. Yet the published letters of Glanville and other women who emigrated under the auspices of the BWEA and other female emigration societies suggest a more complicated, and sometimes more positive, relationship between emigrant women and the female emigrators than is to be found when assuming that agency necessarily equalled resistance or short-term strategic tolerance. These letters illustrate that some emigrant women found maintaining their relationships with the network of female emigration supporters useful on a number of levels, and that their interest in using the services provided by this network changed according to their circumstances.

What I want to explore here is the fact that a significant number of single female emigrants sought to maintain, and in some cases strengthen, their ties with the emigrators after their arrival in Canada or Australia. In this chapter I will look at some of the reasons behind emigrants' continued engagement with the British emigrators. In so doing, I am not seeking to dispute the arguments that have been made by Gothard and others about the emigrators' intentions, or about the meaning that the emigrators' supervision had for most of the emigrants who travelled under their care. The relationships that existed among these women were founded on significant inequalities of access to material resources and systems of power and authority. This power differential lay under the surface of all emigrator–emigrant correspondence in the late nineteenth and early twentieth centuries.

Nevertheless, a close examination of the emigrants' letters that were reproduced in the emigrators' publications reveals a set of relations that was more complex and of longer duration than has been acknowledged in most histories of this subject. Emigrants responded to the oppressive aspects of the female emigration societies' programs, as well as to the opportunities offered by these organizations, according to their own sensibilities and agendas. For some emigrants, the benefits that could be realized from extended involvement with an international, imperial network of women who shared opinions on a wide range of matters made it worth trying to deal positively with the rest of the emigrators' program. Moreover, by embracing the concept that emigrators and emigrants were all one big happy family of imperial women, the emigrants were able to help shape the structure and identity of that family. In so doing, they also contributed to the evolution of managed female migration.

The emigrants' letters that I draw upon in this book were written by a minority of those who went out under the supervision of female emigrators. Not only did these particular emigrants choose to write back to the emigrators (clearly, many of those who were not obliged to do so would have opted not to write), but their letters were also considered of sufficient inherent interest to be published as substantial entries in the emigrators' monthly journal. Obviously, the emigrators chose to avoid publishing solidly negative commentary on the emigration experience. Their own agendas – to promote emigration and their own management of that migration – always determined which letters would be given space and which would not. As a result, the extent to which the opinions and attitudes expressed in these letters are representative of a larger base of emigrant perspective is difficult to assess. But there is plenty of evidence to suggest that the individuals who wrote these letters were not unique.

I have noted in earlier chapters that there were three different groups of women who together made up the international network of women who supported single British women's imperial migration; there were the British emigrators belonging to the British female emigration socie-ties; there were the women who worked at reception in Canada, Aus- tralia, Southern Africa, and New Zealand, often on a voluntary basis; and there were those who worked (usually for pay) as matrons on ships, on trains, and in the hostels at either end of the emigrants' jour-neys. Because of the opportunity for long-term personal interactions, emigrant women were most likely to forge lasting relationships with people involved in reception work. The women who ran women's hos-tels tried to make these institutions a home away from home. At least in theory, their jobs dictated that they encourage return visits. Should an emigrant so desire, the hostel could become the centre of her new social world. On the other hand, it was unlikely that a settled immigrant would again meet the British-based emigrators or matrons who had overseen the earlier stages of her migration. Yet the nature of emigra-tion societies determined that the emigrants' correspondence with Brit-ish-based emigrators would be relatively well preserved. It was the British emigrators who collected and published emigrants' letters in the *Imperial Colonist.*

Like most of the letters from emigrants that were reproduced in the emigration societies' publications, A. Glanville's correspondence had originally been sent to individual British female emigrators with whom she had become acquainted in the early stages of her migration. In this case, the letters were sent to Ellen Joyce and Grace Lefroy, the two emi-grators most likely to receive female emigrants' letters during the 1890s and early years of the twentieth century.[10] Like so many of the women who emigrated with the BWEA, Glanville lacked financial means of her own, and had required a loan from the association in order to pay her way to Canada. As the BWEA's secretary, Lefroy would have had exten-sive correspondence and possibly some meetings with Glanville during her preparation for departure. It was also Lefroy who would oversee Glanville's repayment of the loan.

As with most of the emigrants who were featured in the *Imperial Colo-nist,* a serious search would have to be undertaken before more could be learned about Glanville than is offered in her published letters. But in spite of their brevity, these letters can be surprisingly revealing. For example, Glanville's correspondence indicates that before deciding to emigrate, she had received formal training as a nurse, and had done four years of 'Queen's Work' in London. She had no specific destination in mind when she set off for Canada, leaving it to a superintendent with the Victorian Order of Nurses at Ottawa to select a post for her in British Columbia. It appears that she had no close friends or family in Canada. The contents of her letters suggest that she conformed to the stereotype of the sort of woman most likely to continue a relationship with the emigrators after settlement: she was fairly well educated, and probably from a lower-middle-class family.

Glanville sailed from England on 16 March 1910 in the SS *Lake Champlain*, along with seventy-one other BWEA emigrants. Before the group's departure, the emigrants had gathered at the Wortley Hostel in London. While there, they met with Ellen Joyce, who had come from Winchester specifically to meet with them. They were also introduced to Mrs Forster of Toronto, who had connections with the Toronto Girls' Friendly Society, and Miss Townsend, 'who had lately made a tour in Canada and who knew nearly every place to which the travellers were going' – both of whom, like Joyce, had plenty of advice to give the departing emigrants.[11] Miss Black, a veteran matron, was in charge of the group while they were in transit. It is unclear whether Glanville travelled as a second- or third-class passenger – the group consisted of both.[12] The ship's destination was Saint John, but Black would have accompanied Glanville and her fellow westward travellers by train at least as far as Montreal.

It is clear that many of the emigrant letters that were published in the *Imperial Colonist* were constructed with the understanding that they might end up, in part or completely, in print. Emigrants who read the *Imperial Colonist* or other publications put out by the female emigration societies would have read excerpts from other emigrants' letters, and the fact that the emigrators urged them to send back letters containing news of how they were getting on would have made some emigrants think about the relationship between the writing of these letters and the emigrators' published texts. But some of the letters that the emigrators published were likely intended for their recipients' eyes only. Glanville's letters fit into the latter category. In spite of the fact that Glanville was mindful of the role that the emigrators played in the dissemination of colonists' news, her letters to Joyce and Lefroy do not appear to have been written with the possibility of their later publication in mind. They read as if they were penned in haste – private communications rather than carefully arranged statements of fact and impression for a potentially larger audience.

A careful examination of Glanville's letters and those of other emigrants reveals a complicated set of factors that influenced the letters' construction. At a basic level, a sense of obligation motivated Glanville to communicate with Joyce and Lelroy. She was obliged to write because of her outstanding monetary debt to the organization. Like other emigrants who wrote back, Glanville also felt the need to express her gratitude for the efforts these women had made on her behalf before, during, and after her migration. Most of the published letters reveal that part of the debt that emigrants felt they owed to the emigrators was one or more letters after they had settled into their new environments. These letters thus regularly began with some form of apology for the fact that the promised letter had taken so long to come to fruition. Ellen Joyce – and other emigrators who took their leads from her – explicitly requested letters from departing emigrants, often noting the subjects on which she wished individual emigrants to communicate once they were in a position to supply informed opinions. Joyce instructed nurses to report upon nursing conditions; she asked women going out to settle on the land to write back about their farming experiences; she suggested that home helps might think about how those who would follow could best prepare for this field of work; and she asked all female emigrants to keep an eye out for new career openings for capable women. The emigrators understood that settled emigrants were excellent sources of up-to-date information about matters relevant to emigration work, and they made it clear to departing women that their communications would be of great value to the emigrants who would follow them.[13] A large number of emigrants seem to have taken these requests to heart, and the result was a stream of letters back overseas that outlined colonial conditions in a way that prospective emigrants might find useful.

Glanville wrote back because she felt obliged to do so. But, like other emigrants, she also wrote back for more personal reasons. Settled emigrants used the fact that the emigrators worked as disseminators of their news to further their own agendas. For example, the emigrators regularly received settled emigrants' requests for assistance in advertising investment opportunities and properties for sale. The Topham sisters were typical in several respects. To Miss Vernon (another key member of the BWEA), I.M. Topham wrote: 'I hope you will not think we are troubling you too much, but possibly among the numerous girls who ask the B.W.E.A. at home for information there might be some with a knowledge of dressmaking who would like to start for themselves. We opened this shop a year last May and have really done very well, but the indoor life does not suit me. I was ill and in hospital for a long time last winter, which I cannot afford, and my sister would not keep it on alone ... If you could do anything to help us in the matter we should be greatly obliged.'[14] Mrs Eugenie Reeves, who wrote to the editor of the *Imperial Colonist* in 1921, had similar hopes that a mention in the journal might solve her business worries. More than a decade and a half after her relationship with the BWEA might have ended, Reeves found it expedient to again use the services provided by this imperial network of emigrators. Her letter indicates that she thought the editor might 'introduce a buyer' for her farm in Saskatchewan. At nearly seventy years old, Reeves was looking to sell the property she had homesteaded with her son after emigrating to Canada as a BWEA emigrant sixteen years earlier.[15]

Women who wished to advertise their training facilities were also periodically featured in the emigrators' literature. Mrs Horsfall's promotion of her Canadian Home and School for Gentlewomen in Cape Breton, which was featured in journals throughout 1902, and the 1915 advertisements for the Haliburton College in Victoria, BC, were probably paid-for advertisements.[16] But it is evident that similar businesses outlined in letters sent back to the emigrators were inserted as news items in the body of the *Imperial Colonist* because they were considered part of the general information about colonial conditions and opportunities that emigrators and emigrants alike ought to know about. For example, the November 1918 issue of the journal noted the establishment of a new training facility in Australia. In an article entitled 'Helping Daughters of the Professional Classes on the Land in N.S.W.' Mrs Maurice J. Barlow noted that 'two ladies, Miss Brace and Miss Alcock, who have been trained by Miss Turner [at the training school at Arlesley near Hitchen, England], have taken up 30 acres of land on the Northern Rivers in New South Wales.' Barlow explained that this school took on women who had already received some 'colonial' training at British institutions who wished to be further initiated 'into the particulars of that State.'[17] She also outlined the conditions upon which Brace and Alcock were willing to take on students, thus limiting the number of requests for training that these women would receive from unsuitable applicants. Undoubtedly, women like Miss Brace and Miss Alcock wrote back to members of the British emigration societies about their business ventures because they perceived that they would benefit from the informal promotion.

In Glanville's case, the emigrators were not asked to advertise a business venture. It was charitable donations that Glanville was after. '[Now] I am writing to you[,] may I beg for my hospital?' she asked Lefroy. 'Of course it's a crude little place and many, many things are wanted, should you know of anyone wanting to do some good work.' She suggested hopefully that 'there are many little comforts missing, both in wearing apparel and household things.'[18] To Joyce, a month later, Glanville wrote: 'Of course everything is crude here, and we want many, many things yet, little aids to comfort, one misses things at every turn ... I enclose a leaflet about our work.'[19] Like other emigrants writing back in times of more pressing hardship, it is possible that Glanville's subsequent description of the devastation wrought by the burning of her hospital was aimed at soliciting a more substantial sort of aid.[20] But even, if she did not imagine that some wealthy philanthropist in Britain might take up her devastated hospital as a pet project, it is evident that Glanville assumed that her letters would result in expressions of sympathy and understanding about the fact that she could not pay back her loan as quickly as had been anticipated.

Readers of the emigrators' publications would have known that pleas for aid in times of extreme need did not fall upon deaf ears. Throughout the *Imperial Colonist* are scattered references to 'gifts' made by British benefactors to worthy overseas cases.[21] In the event of a newsworthy personal or local disaster, the editor of the *Imperial Colonist* was quick to solicit help. For example, an emotional plea for assistance was registered in the October 1908 issue of the journal, under the title 'A Pathetic Appeal,' from a correspondent living in Cranbrook, BC. 'Terrible fires have been raging all around us, and every moment we were afraid we should all be burnt out,' wrote Mrs Hyde Baker. Saved by a sudden change in the direction of the wind, the residents of Cranbrook found themselves in the position of playing host to over two thousand refugees from Fernie, a neighbouring town that had not experienced the same good fortune. Fernie was gutted by the fire in the space of only two hours. Those who managed to escape were forced to flee without their belongings. '[Most] of them arrived almost clotheless in their hurry to escape. They had to throw any superfluous clothes away getting through the burning woods down to the river or the railway track.' 'All the money the men are earning now will have to go to buying lumber to rebuild their homes,' wrote Baker. Many of the residents were recent immigrants (some of whom had travelled with the BWEA). Hardly any were insured. The struggle ahead – for the comparatively lucky Cranbrook hosts and for the Fernie refugees – was daunting. 'The winter will soon be on us; in Fernie the thermometer goes down to 20°, 30° and 40° below zero,' Baker noted. I wonder if I might beg some *warm* clothing, especially women's coats, cloaks and shawls?'[22] The response from the network of emigrators and their friends was immediate. The next month's journal recorded that two parcels of clothing had already been dispatched. The clothing would be delivered by 'one of the young women of the October 29th party, who happen[ed] to be going there.'[23] The maintenance of connections with emigrators post-migration could produce concrete benefits.

While emotional accounts of hard-luck experiences such as those related in Glanville's and Baker's letters were periodically featured in the emigrators' publications (they made for very interesting reading, and they certainly added variety to the contents), it is logical to assume that the emigrators received more letters of this kind than they were willing to publish. After all, their literature was designed to promote emigration. Emigrants' accounts of their never-ending struggles to find decent employment, recover from major setbacks, adapt to extreme weather conditions, and overcome homesickness and feelings of social isolation were unlikely to entice uncertain prospective emigrants.

We cannot tell from the available sources whether Glanville received material assistance, via the emigrators, for her mission hospital. But it is evident that she was regularly sent gifts of reading materials by Lefroy. Glanville registered her gratitude for these packages in passing – at the time she was distracted by more pressing concerns. The letters penned by other women who had settled in remote areas of the empire were more explicit about the fact that these parcels had important roles to play in the relationships that developed between emigrators and emigrants. References to the joy and comfort derived from these parcels of British newspapers, magazines, and journals featured prominently in some women's letters. 'Thank you for sending me the "Daily Mirror,"' wrote LC from Saskatchewan. '[We] get very little news here, as we are so far up country. This is a lonely homestead ... there is no school or railway closer than Crooked River, so I teach my children what I can, and we are very glad of anything to read and pass it on to other settlers.'[24] LHW wrote back to her British correspondent: 'I'm only out from the Old Country seven years and still think so much of home there. I have received a paper twice, which was very welcome. Any illustrated papers and magazines from the Old Land are such treats. We can get them in Canada, but way up here everything is so costly and very often unobtainable.'[25] Echoing these sentiments, EMR wrote back from Manitoba that the parcel of magazines that she had received helped to keep her connected to the social world she had left behind her: 'We are, as I told you before, very isolated up here. Besides my husband, two trappers, and two Indians, who put into the river to camp for one night, I have seen no one since August 16th of last year, until a week ago, when I went with my husband to Shoal River.' 'I thought perhaps I might see some other woman as a little change from masculine society,' she reflected. She was to be disappointed: 'I saw an Indian woman or girl in the distance, but that was all, and the only white man in the place was one left in charge of the trading store and post office.'[26]

The women in Britain and in the dominions' urban centres who worked with the female settlers understood that as culturally resilient as a woman like EMR might be, periodic reminders of her more civilized past and of her colonizing mission were important bulwarks against a loss of 'proper' perspective. Women whose daily social interactions with adults were with white men and people of aboriginal or mixed-race heritage needed assurances that they were different from, and in many ways more cultured than, their companions. One of the projects undertaken by the female emigrators to shore up settler women's abilities to withstand the loneliness of the Australian outback was the establishment of a visiting 'caravan.' The caravan, which was run by two female volunteers well trained in religious and social counselling, consisted of a ford vehicle filled with educational and medical supplies. The volunteers, working under the auspices of the Girls' Friendly Society, toured the loneliest areas of the countryside seeking out isolated households and communities. Their caravan, named the 'Lady Bertha' after Lady Bertha Dawkins, who had been instrumental in founding the program, was received by women in the bush with great enthusiasm (see figure 7). As one recipient of the caravan's services wrote to Lady Dawkins, 'I can't tell you how grateful the women are to have the caravan to visit them – some poor women don't see a fresh face for months on end – what they suffer can't be described … [Only] people who have been in the Bush and had the hard knocks of loneliness and misfortune can understand the help the GFS Caravan can give; one time I was over two months and never saw another woman, it was just terrible.'[27]

The emigrators were well attuned to the effect that their correspondence and gifts of reading materials, etc., could have upon homesick emigrants. A letter sent to the SOSBW's head office from the Settlers' Welcome Committee of the Victoria League, South Australia, emphasized this point: 'Poor things, [the immigrant girls] are generally very home-sick, and lonely and a friendly greeting and interest taken in them seem to brighten them up considerably. They are always given a letter of welcome ... and later on when I know where they are situated I write them a personal letter as Secretary (of my Committee). This small act seems to please them very much.'[28] The enclosure of a sprig of English heather in a letter; a surprise birthday present for a young woman unused to receiving gifts, because where she came from 'there was no money to spare' – these were gestures of friendship and support by individual emigrators that would help to confirm established links.[29] In the conclusion to a piece on the work of the Australian Victoria League, the *Imperial Colonist*'s editor was explicit about her sense of the significance of these acts of kindness. 'There seems no doubt,' she wrote, 'that such friendship, offered to girl immigrants when feeling lonely in a new land, has often more far-reaching results than even the givers can foresee.'[30] The emigrants' letters that were reproduced in this journal appear to support the editor's assessment.

A multilayered sense of obligation and a desire to tap into resources available through the imperial network of female emigrators combined to determine that emigrants like Glanville would write to the British emigrators shortly after arriving at their colonial destinations. But the emotional content that may be found in emigrants' letters requires further examination. For example, how are we to interpret the statements of affection in Glanville's correspondence? The fact that Glanville's warm introductions ('My Dear Miss Lefroy') and parting statements ('Kind regards, yours very sincerely') were not merely formulaic niceties is indicated by her use of cooler lines ('Dear Miss Lefroy,' and 'Yours sincerely') after Lefroy had offended her by raising the subject of her outstanding debt. These slight variations – terms of salutation that go beyond what were strictly necessary formalities – are suggestive of both Glanville's feelings for the woman who would receive her letters and her state of mind at the time of writing. Likewise, Glanville's effusions – to Joyce, 'I have thought of you so often and wished you could see my little hospital,' and to Lefroy, 'Oh I wish you could see this little place! It is wonderfully beautiful!' – could be read as more than an astute woman's efforts to play to the egos of two philanthropically minded supporters.

Miss Black, the matron who had chaperoned Glanville's party to Canada, also gained a position of emotional importance in Glanville's post-emigration world. Black evidently did the rounds of ex-emigrant visiting that were expected of all regular travelling matrons.[31] For some emigrants, periodic post-settlement contact with the matrons, who had played supportive roles in the life-altering experience of migration, proved to be comforting. Glanville certainly seems to have been one such emigrant. Her reference to a chance meeting she had had with Black is the only positive note in the otherwise thoroughly dejected letter she sent to Lefroy three weeks after the disastrous hospital fire.[32]

It is not surprising that Glanville would feel attached to Black. The emigrators tried hard to select matrons who would gain the respect and affection of their charges. As has been previously noted, the success of their project demanded that they do so, as the matrons had little other than their force of personalities with which to encourage emigrant compliance with their conduct rules and guidelines. The matrons were often resented for their heavy-handed treatment of emigrant women, but it is also clear that the efforts of matrons could sometimes be greatly appreciated.[33] In the same month that Glanville wrote back to Lefroy of a fortuitous meeting she had had with Black, another letter – this one sent to a matron by a group of female emigrants – was published in the *Imperial Colonist*. This letter, which was obviously written with the intention that it serve as a letter of reference or support, follows a tiresomely familiar formula, but I think it would be wrong to dismiss it as insincere. It reads:

> We, your party of second class girls, wish to express our appreciation of the thought and care and labour you have given that every arrangement should be made for our comfort. We want to say how much we value the protection and pleasant company which being members of your party has secured for us, and to thank you for your kind words and counsel, and for the high ideals you placed before us. We know your words of advice will help to carry us through the difficulties we may have to face, and thus prove that the seed has not fallen upon barren ground.[34]

In less formal ways, large numbers of emigrants made similar points about their matrons in their letters back overseas. As one of the BWEA's 'regulars,' Black took her role as a motherly friend to emigrants seriously. As another Canadian immigrant (this one writing a full eight years earlier than Glanville) explained, 'It is quite impossible to say all Miss Black was to us [during our journey]. The hardest thing we had to do after leaving England was to say good-bye to her. She took all our difficulties and fought all our battles, and in spite of her responsibilities was always bright and happy. We all owe the Society much, but the greatest of all our debts is for Miss Black.'[35]

Glanville's indications of fondness for Joyce, Lefroy, and Black were not unusual in the letters published in the *Imperial Colonist*.[36] In fact, some emigrants were significantly less reserved than Glanville in their statements of affection. EJP's letter serves as a good example. With the aid of the BWEA, EJP left Tilbury, Ireland, for Sydney in December 1889. Upon arriving in New South Wales, she settled into regular work as a governess. Her financial stability in Australia allowed her to help finance the immigration of her sister and her niece, both of whom also settled comfortably into colonial life. Through strict economy, EJP banked most of her pay and thus saved an impressive retirement fund upon which she could live from the age of 55 years. In her letters, EJP made it clear that she owed an enormous debt of gratitude to the British emigrators who had made her comfort in retirement possible. 'If I had remained at home I might have been working for ever and then have nothing. This is what your Society has done for me,' she wrote. EJP remembered that 'it was all through reading a letter from the Hon. Mrs. Joyce, written to the "Irish Times," that gave me the idea of coming to this country. Does she still continue this glorious work of doing good for the poor half-paid people of England?' she asked.[37] After twenty-one years in Australia, EJP continued to write to the women who had facilitated her emigration from Ireland. During that period, she had continued to benefit from the emigrators' benevolence in the form of gifts of clothing. Yet her letter indicates that although she was immensely grateful for the material assistance she had received from various BWEA members over the years, it was the emotional bond that provided the most compelling reason for her continued correspondence. While conscious of the inequality of the relationship, EJP made it clear that she regarded the recipient of her letter as her 'dear friend.'[38]

The migration process completely stripped some women of their previous systems of emotional and financial support. For others, the systems of support that they might have had in Britain had been dismantled even before they set off for new lives overseas. As Jan Gothard has shown in her study of single emigrant women in nineteenth-century Australia, a high proportion of single female immigrants had already experienced the loosening of family ties through their migration within Britain and or the death of family members.[39] The social dislocation that came with emigration was an important factor in some emigrant women's interactions with members of the imperial emigration network. Writing back to England from South Africa, emigrant JB put in words what many other emigrants merely hinted at when she told her emigrator correspondent, 'Your reply·[to my letter] has been quite a treasure to me' ... 'My few friends at home have almost forgotten me, although I write to them from time to time,' she wrote. 'My parents are both dead and my sisters and brothers married, so perhaps that accounts for it, but I still long to visit the dear old home, and mean to do so as soon as possible.'[40] JB was by no means an unsuccessful emigrant. Her letter made it clear that she had fared well in her employment as a governess, and that she was happily engaged to be married to a fellow Scottish emigrant in four months. Yet her desire for strong ties with people 'back home' was clearly evident. In the early twentieth century, emigration for many single women meant limited contact by mail with people who previously had been central to their lives. Actually reuniting with people from their pre-migration past was, in most cases, unlikely. In these circumstances, continued contact by post and in person with the comparatively mobile emigrators, who formed a psychological link between emigrants' past and present lives, took on a heavily loaded significance. This contact helped to ground emigrants who were looking for ways to make sense of unfamiliar situations. JB's letter was unusual in the extent to which its author was explicit about the relationship between her appreciation for the emigrator's interest in her and her sorrow about the absence of a satisfactory set of relationships with overseas family and friends. But the sense of wistfulness – of a need for the gap to be filled – and the corresponding idea that women working within the female emigration network might go part way to filling that gap, may be found in a great number of the letters published in the *Imperial Colonist.*

Regardless of whether the emigrants settled in Australia or Canada, these were women who had travelled far from home. Most of them would experience homesickness, periods of self-doubt, and radical reorientations of their self- and public identities. Some sort of social support was necessary for the successful integration of emigrants into their new communities. It was especially useful in cases where emigrants were not joining family or friends already overseas, because they were more likely than others to feel isolated. Within this context, the women who constituted the imperial network of emigrators were well positioned to gain the confidence and affection of single female emigrants. Furthermore, they were motivated by their imperialism to press their advantage in this respect. They were sensitive to the fact that the sort of colonizing work in frontier spaces that they wanted British women to do could not be done by women in isolation. Understanding that a system of support was essential, they worked hard to maintain ties with emigrants after migration had taken place.

Emigrants drew upon their sense of being a part of an international network of imperial, colonizing women when constructing new identities for themselves in unfamiliar social contexts. Membership within an empire-wide community of women emigrators and emigrants, who were linked by their ties to Britain and by their shared assumptions concerning the benefits bestowed upon colonial societies by the immigration of virtuous British women, provided emigrants with a framework within which to situate their own experiences and attitudes towards migration and settlement. For some women, this sense of community was immensely useful. It provided them with a clear sense of identity and purpose – not as outcasts from their homeland, nor as foreigners to their new locales, but as participants in a mass movement of like-circumstanced British female emigrants. This family of women helped to ground emigrants who might otherwise have felt unmoored in new surroundings in which they lacked familiar frames of reference. Their correspondence with British emigrators also provided them with an outlet for their frustrations with colonial society. Within these letters they could note their disapproval of Australian and Canadian habits and attitudes, comfortable in the knowledge that their thoughts would reach a relatively sympathetic audience. Finally, as newcomers to Australia and Canada, these immigrants were often painfully aware of their own knowledge gaps – their lack of expertise – relating to colonial social practices and the challenges posed by their new physical environments. But when writing back to the emigrators overseas, these same women were able to position themselves as experts. Their experiences as new immigrants gave them insights that prospective emigrants and emigration managers overseas desired to tap into.

Historians have tended to emphasize the social distance that existed between the imperially minded middle- and upper-class emigrators and the working- and lower-middle-class women who emigrated to Canada and Australia as assisted immigrants.[41] Clearly, this distance could be significant. However, for some emigrants the lines between emigrators and emigrants were easily blurred, because the relationships that they formed with members of the emigration societies were determined more by their sense of being part of a women-centred civilizing mission than by their sense of class difference. One way of demonstrating their affinity for the emigrators' project was to take up reception work (and thus, like the emigrators, to adopt the role of surrogate mother to new immigrants) themselves.

The importance of integrating recent emigrants into the emigration women's network became evident to emigrators and emigrants alike early on in the history of female emigration societies. An examination of the letters that were sent back to the Female Middle-Class Emigration Society (FMCES) in the 1860s and 1870s reveals that those emigrants who were going out to join friends or family overseas faired much better than did those who had no one to receive them.[42] The creation and maintenance of an extensive network of women who were willing to provide information about local conditions to the British emigrants, and who would serve as friends to emigrants who settled in their communities, became a crucial part of an effective support system for migrating single women. The list of women who would serve the imperial project in the colonies was in constant need of replenishment as new areas of settlement were added to the number of locations that the emigrators wished to cover, and as old colonial helpers lost interest in the program or moved away. In the early years of the female emigration societies – between the middle of the nineteenth century and the turn of the twentieth century – the emigrators relied almost completely upon the voluntary services of well-placed middle- and upper-class residents of the colonies for reception work.

But comfortably settled women of elite or solidly middle-class status tended to be committed to furthering the work of other social reform and philanthropic organizations, and the important work of interacting with new immigrants on a regular basis fell outside of the sphere of activities that most women of this sort were willing to perform.[43] Right through to the Great Depression, the patronage and support of leading ladies in colonial communities continued to be critical to the survival of the imperial female network, because these women were well positioned to raise needed funds and gain the ears of men with power. But increasingly, as individual, previously assisted female immigrants proved themselves to be committed to supporting the immigration programs that the emigrators had designed, the emigrators turned to using them as front-line receivers. Whereas the class bias of the emigrators had determined that they would naturally look to their social equivalents for aid in managing the reception of female migrants, previously assisted emigrants' persistent assertions that they were willing to provide welcomes for new chums ultimately resulted in the program's reorganization to accommodate this source of voluntary assistance.

Over the past couple of decades historians have explored the relationships between maternal discourses and women's bids for power in the public sphere.[44] They have debated the extent to which female philanthropists and social reformers were actually inspired to work for a new world order informed by a maternalist politics, as opposed to merely using maternalist arguments and rhetoric to further their own efforts to direct social and political change.[45] But the fact that a maternal discourse was used by middle-class women in their efforts to gain control over the lives of other women, of children, and of the poor in general, is now a standard theme in histories of women's philanthropic and social-reform work in the late nineteenth and early twentieth centuries. I have argued in previous chapters that in the case of managed female migration, it is clear that the strategic use of maternalism was critical to the success of women-run female emigration societies. By carefully manipulating and recreating discourses of gender difference, female emigrators positioned themselves as the logical managers of migrating women. Central to their efforts in this respect was their creation of a large number of written texts in which emigrator–emigrant relations were represented in terms of a surrogate family of women. In the emigrators' published literature and correspondence, single female travellers were portrayed as vulnerable innocents who required, and generally desired, guidance and protection; the female managers of emigrant women were represented as maternal figures – nurturing, supportive, and fierce on issues of protection. Familial rhetoric and metaphors in these texts performed useful functions. The patronizing tone of much of their advice literature helped to clarify the power differential that was at the heart of their relations with the emigrant women, who were often reliant upon the emigration societies for financial and administrative assistance during their emigration. At the same time, identifying themselves and their paid helpers as 'motherly' rhetorically transformed the emigrators' authoritarianism and intrusiveness into a more benevolent, kindly involvement in the lives of the women who travelled under their care.

How did the emigrants respond to the emigrators' actual and symbolic efforts to 'mother' them? There was a range of responses. Some women rebelled against the uninvited 'mothering,' others seem to have ignored it, while still others were willing to put up with the mother-daughter game for as long as they were in transit. As the letters discussed in this chapter demonstrate, there were also a significant number of women who, on some level, embraced the emigrators' maternal discourse. Even a superficial review of published emigrants' letters reveals that emigrants, like the emigrators, regularly made use of familial rhetoric in their correspondence. For example, emigrants often referred to ship and hostel matrons as 'second mothers,' and letters sent

back to emigrators in Britain were referred to as going 'home.' LG's letter back to Miss Evans in England is typical in its use of familial references: 'I cannot tell you how lovely a person Mrs. B. (the representative
of the S.O.S.B.W.) is – she is a second mother to us girls and nothing is
too much trouble for her to make us happy. Her home is open to us all
and we know there is a hearty welcome whatever time we call.'[46] Of
course, familial rhetoric was used in this way widely outside the network
of female emigrators and emigrants in the late nineteenth and early
twentieth centuries. References to the British Isles by emigrants and
their offspring as 'home' were common. Likewise, the term 'second
mother' seems to have circulated easily among young women during
this period. But in light of the concerted efforts by emigrators to establish the image of the happy emigrator-emigrant family of women, the
use of this language by the emigrants to describe their own relationships
with the emigrators carries added significance.

Historians of single women in the late nineteenth and early twentieth
centuries have noted the prevalence of independent spirits in their subjects. It is reasonable to assume that single women who emigrated from
Britain without kin would have shared outlooks and attitudes with the
working-class, wage-earning 'good time girls' of the city or the middle-
class, liberated 'New Woman.' It is evident that, in different ways and to
different extents, female emigrants did enjoy their independence and
liberty from conventional social constraints. Jan Gothard has shown that
the myth of the female emigrant as a husband hunter is largely groundless. Women emigrated to find paid work and financial independence.[47]
Yet, as Angela Woollacott has argued, it is useful to push beyond an
understanding of women's travelling as 'an assertion of independence,
a bid for self-discovery, and an escape from domestic gender constraints' to one that allows for more complex self-identities, and more
nuanced meanings of travel.[48] Woollacott suggests that we need to
understand how the particular socio-political imperial contexts in which
women moved, and the various combinations of ambitions and anxieties
that they carried with them, shaped the ways in which their experiences
were understood and then repackaged for consumption by others. In
the case of assisted female emigrants, this way of thinking about their
correspondence is extremely useful. The fact that single female emigrants embraced the roles of dutiful daughters to maternal philanthropists and social reformers does not mean that they looked to replace
one form of family dependency for another. Rather, emigrant women
were able to manipulate and use this discourse to forge useful relation-

ships with other women in a context where their usual networks of support were lacking. The role of surrogate daughter could, in fact, provide a context and identity that was empowering.

As the examples cited in this chapter illustrate, emigrants used the idea that they were a part of a family to solidify the system of support that was in place for their use, and to squeeze more out of their relationships with the emigrators than might otherwise have been on offer. Their embrace of the familial discourse served to promote the continuation of the emigration societies' services considered most worthwhile by the emigrants themselves. They used the emigrators' publications and informal communications system to advertise their business ventures and charitable endeavours, they encouraged the further distribution of British newspapers and magazines, and they tapped into a wide range of reception programs that the emigrators supported.

At the same time, the way in which the emigrants engaged with the emigrators' familial discourse contained an element of resistance to the emigrators' efforts to dominate them. By actively engaging with the emigrators and their work, the emigrants denied the emigrators the right to represent female emigrants and their relations with the emigrators just as they wished. They took the images related in the emigrators' writing and reinterpreted them to more closely fit their own senses of reality. The hierarchical nature of the emigrator–emigrant relationship was typically de-emphasized in emigrant letters, while emigrants' claims to adult status were validated through illustration. Not children, but intelligent adult members of this family of women, the emigrants writing back to the emigrators indicated that they were clearly capable of speaking for themselves. The letters affirmed that their relationship involved ·mutual dependency and support. As the emigrators themselves noted, the emigration societies' successes were determined by the actions and attitudes of female emigrants. The emigrants' letters played on this theme. In their writing to the emigrators, the emigrants suggested that they understood the emigrators' need for positive feedback from themselves. Post-migration, they noted their own continued affection for the surrogate mothers who had cared for them during the migration process, and they demonstrated their willingness to maintain ties – but on a more equal footing.

The letters that emigrant women sent back to the emigrators who had assisted them in their migration played an important role in the much larger process whereby individual emigrants affected, through their writing and through their actions, how they and others would be understood and treated. The correspondence reviewed here illustrates that emigrants were not simply either the passive or the resistant objects of emigrators' attention; their relationship with the emigrators was not solely about being managed or controlled. The emigrants took much from the system established by the emigrators. For many, it meant more than just loans and protection. Emigrants also gave back to the system advice and support to the next generation of immigrants, and praise and validation of the emigrators' work. The relationship between the emigrants and emigrators – or, perhaps more appropriately, the emigrants and the emigrators' imperial female migration system – was dynamic and multifaceted.

To look at the relationships that were forged between these women is useful when trying to understand emigrant women and their strategies for coping with the stresses involved in migration and colonization. Emigrants resisted the efforts of emigrators to control their movements and actions, and they used the services of the emigration societies in ways that the emigrators had not intended. But as Glanville's and other published emigrant letters suggest, some emigrants also embraced the emigration societies and what they had on offer along lines that *had* been intended by the emigrators. There is no evidence in the *Imperial Colonist* that Glanville's relationship with the emigrators and their emigration system would outlast her financial debt to the BWEA. Yet it is clear that in the months following her arrival in Canada, Glanville considered Joyce, Lefroy, and Black to be more than just the administrators and chaperone who had overseen her movement from one location to another. The emigrators gained their positions of importance in Glanville's life because they worked hard to that end, but they would not have been able to do so if Glanville's personal situation had not allowed it. Women such as Glanville retained contact with the emigrators in the months and years after their migration for their own reasons, and, as far as possible, they did so on their own terms. Emigrants' relationships with specific emigrators changed over time, according to the emigrants' financial and emotional needs. They continued to foster these relationships for as long as they served a purpose for themselves, and they quietly stopped writing when there was no longer an incentive to do so.

chapter five

Welcoming Women: Reception Work in Canada and Australia

For a great many Canadian and Australian men and women, the reputations of the spaces in which they lived (whether defined locally, regionally, or nationally) were a matter of extreme importance during the late nineteenth and early twentieth centuries. As historians with a wide range of interests have shown, the citizens of these young nations actively engaged in the process of national, regional, and community image building.[1] Australians and Canadians were both self-conscious about their international identities and anxious about the likely ramifications of negative stereotypes on immigration. The uproar that surrounded the publication of a particularly negative article in 1910 in *John Bull*, a popular British newspaper well known for its sensationalism, provides an instructive example. Louis Wain's 'Canada's Deathtrap: Further Warnings to Canadian Emigrants' was one in a series of similarly anti-emigration *John Bull* articles. Most of the article was about the plight of young men who had been enticed by false advertising to emigrate from Britain to the Canadian prairies. Upon arrival these men had discovered that there was no work, only bitterly cold weather and hunger awaiting them. Wain's representation of the Prairies as an unsuitable destination for respectable men annoyed Canadians, but they were infuriated by the section of the article that advised that the Prairies were 'No Place for Decent Women.' *John Bull*'s readers were informed that 'the woman population is composed largely of half-castes, ... redeemed women who have been sent out by rescue societies to fall back into a worse state than they were drawn from, and the lowest class of domestic servant who, if she is at all good-looking, soon falls away into wild life, for the girls are of too low a class for most of the men to marry.' Wain explained that the small number of women of a 'better class' who settled down into married life in the Canadian West suffered badly 'from hardships which only the brawny, strong animal type of countrywoman can stand.' He acknowledged that prairie towns did contain some good women, 'but they live in the midst of temptation,' he wrote, 'and are plagued by a class of men vulgarly nicknamed "remittance men" and their hangers on ... They crawl about with sunken heads, aged and care-worn, more often than not just out of their teens; their lairs are covered up brothels, and officialdom winks.'[2]

Had an article of this nature been published in Canada, it would have been received differently. In Canada, as in Australia, reform-minded citizens had long made careers of ferreting out and publicizing the moral shortcomings of their own societies. Damning articles by colonials were more likely to stir up regulatory and reform efforts than whole-hearted defences of the people and spaces thus attacked. But the fact that this article was published in England for a British audience meant that Canadians leapt to defend the Prairies' honour. The 'slanderous' depictions of the West in 'Canada's Deathtrap' became the focus of discussion in the House of Commons,[3] and Canadian authorities considered taking legal action against *John Bull* for its dissemination of such images.[4] The Canadian public fought back by publishing denunciations of the article and alternative representations of the communities and people of the Prairies. A flood of angry letters were sent to newspapers' editors, in which the treatment of women in the *John Bull* article was singled out for rebuke. As an article in the *Ottawa Free Press* put it, it was bad enough that men had been portrayed as little more than serfs, but worse still was the fact that 'it cast aspersions upon the character of the women who are doing their share to build up a greater Canada on the plains.'[5]

The controversy surrounding the publication of 'Canada's Deathtrap' brings to light a number of themes and issues that are central to an understanding of British female immigration to the dominions in the decades preceding the Great Depression. It highlights the explicit racism behind colonial settlement agendas. On the one hand, the 'casting of aspersions' upon prairie women included reminders that the West continued to be peopled by First Nations and mixed-race individuals. On the other hand, assertions that in fact prairie communities were made up of hardworking, respectable people involved the purposeful erasure of non-white inhabitants from the scene – a practice that was clearly evident in the publications of female emigration societies, where aboriginal and mixed-race people seldom received a mention. The controversy shows how efforts to attract settlers to the Prairies engaged recruiters in a myth-making campaign to convince an international public of the wholesomeness of prairie life, in the face of the less appealing, well-publicized image of a West fraught with desperation, lawlessness, and vice. It also shows how vulnerable even British immigrants could be to critical review.

Canadians, Australians, and Britons all understood immigration and settlement in gendered terms, and in this respect too 'Canada's Deathtrap' and the discussions it elicited reflect a larger set of concerns about women and migration. Problems with female immigration regularly came under the media spotlight during the late nineteenth and early twentieth centuries. As historians of single women in the city have shown, young independent women were seen by vocal observers as unstable signifiers, more likely to represent moral laxity than respectable femininity.[6] In the context of international migration, where single women were unloosed from their usual daily routines as well as from familial control, they were seen to be that much more susceptible to moral contagion. A wide range of issues relating to single female immigrants generated acerbic public commentary. The complaints of recent immigrants about false promises by immigration agents, or abuse at the hands of colonials, regularly found their way into the press, as did the complaints of Canadian and Australian employers about the shortage of prospective immigrant employees, or about their new servants' lack of training and inappropriate demeanour. Most captivating for the press in Australia were outraged travellers' protests about the morally suspect shipboard behaviour of the odd group of young immigrant women.[7] The immigrant female's ill treatment at the hands of government agents, employers, or host community or, conversely, the misuse of the public's benevolence by unworthy female immigrants and their promoters could easily blow up into a newsworthy public scandal.

Whereas the ability of a man to make a success of immigration was gauged by his capacity to achieve a (preferably independent) comfortable lifestyle, the measure of a woman's successful migration was her maintenance or improvement of her identity as a respectable woman. Concerns about the plight of the male immigrant revolved largely around the issue of misleading advertising and the raising of false hopes. The plight of the female immigrant was rather more complex. Not only did it matter what type of work a woman performed and for whom she performed it, but her identity was also affected by the society in which she found herself, and how she was perceived and treated there. As the 'Canada's Deathtrap' article suggests, there was an evident relationship between the female emigrant, her reception into a new space, and shifting perceptions of national character.

Mariana Valverde's discussion of reception work in *The Age of Light, Soap, and Water: Moral Reform in English Canada, 1885–1925* offers an evaluation of the politics and ideologies behind female reception work, and an assessment of how the agendas of social reformers affected women's experiences as immigrants. Hers is an analysis that is shared by many of the historians interested in this topic. Valverde points to the intersections of nation-building ambitions, eugenic and imperialist ideas, and class and gender prejudices that occurred in immigrant reception work. According to Valverde, the reception programs put in place by Canadian reformers were meant to enforce strict codes of behaviour. '[There] was no clear distinction between the work of providing help for those in need ... and the work of controlling, regulating, and even deporting those deemed undesirable because of their sexual irregularities or because of their "race,"' she writes. '[Coercion] and protection were but two sides of the same coin.'[8]

Valverde's point that reception work always had 'two sides' – one designed to uplift and support, the other to regulate and punish – is supported throughout this study. However, the emphasis here differs from that of Valverde by placing primary attention upon the efforts of Canadian, Australian, and British women to make immigration a less stressful, more successful venture for British female immigrants. Through their intervention in the immigration process, they attempted to ensure that both the immigrants and the host communities were satisfied with immigration arrangements. By offering new immigrants a warm welcome and a 'home away from home,' they tried to soften the women's feelings of loneliness and dislocation. By helping immigrant women to find respectable jobs that would suit their qualifications and temperaments, these women sought to ensure the immigrants' contented settlement into their new communities. Through their surveillance, guidance, and protection of the young women who came under their care, they reduced the possibility that their charges might stray from the path of virtuousness and thus gain the ire of the public. Their friendly overtures, combined with their efforts to lessen the likelihood that careless or disreputable colonials would harm or offend the immigrant women, were designed to ensure that the new settlers sent back overseas a positive image of their new homes.[9] Finally, by establishing close relations with the new arrivals, they were able to remind both the immigrants and the public of the immigrants' roles as models of civilized virtue. This chapter will show that the women who took up female reception work as a cause saw contented British female immigrants as critical to the formation of the 'right' sort of societies and to the development of positive national identities. Although they were certainly willing to punish miscreant emigrants, female reception workers put much more emphasis on effecting their reform and imperial agendas through the creation of the ideal emigrant reception environments in Canada and Australia.

Over the past couple of decades, historians interested in gender and social power dynamics have contributed greatly to our understanding of the potency of sexually charged discourses about space and place. Marilyn Lake, Judith Walkowitz, Carolyn Strange, Christine Stansell, Karen Dubinsky, and Adele Perry (to name only a few) have each revealed the ways in which specific geographic locations and social spaces were defined as sexually dangerous or disreputable.[10] In the work of all these historians, the role of the social reformer and philanthropist in defining these spaces as dangerous is highlighted. So too is the fact that these reformers and philanthropists felt that they understood best how to reclaim these spaces for respectable society. The women who dedicated their time, energy, and money to providing a welcome and aftercare for single female immigrants were likewise implicated in the creation and dissemination of stigmatizing discourses about public spaces such as railway stations and ports, and regions such as the Australian outback and the Canadian West. Simultaneously, they endeavoured to insert their own presence in these locations, and by so doing make them more clearly white, middle-class, and domesticated – in other words, more self-evidently safe and respectable.

Through a series of Canadian and Australian case studies, this chapter assesses the changing relationships among the various groups of people (Canadian, Australian, and British; representatives of the state and of voluntary organizations) who managed the immigration and reception of single British women to Canada and Australia between the middle of the nineteenth century and the Great Depression. On a day-to-day basis, these groups usually collaborated well. They each had their own agendas, yet they saw the benefit in supporting each other's work. However, an examination of the periodic conflicts that arose between these parties reveals a set of tensions that lay just under the surface of the migration managers' relations most of the time. Because of their relationships with the British emigrators, the women working at reception in Canada and Australia knew that the way that British immigrant

women were treated upon their arrival, and how they interpreted their
new social situations, reflected upon their host societies in important
ways. But they also understood that the immigrants were not the only
group of women whose status within Canada and Australia mattered.
The ability of middle- and upper-class women (be they British, Canadian, or Australian) to carve out for themselves well-respected, authori-
tative roles as the protectors of other women and children also reflected
upon the nature of these societies.[11] The experiences of women who
encountered concerted opposition from men in their search for positions of power in these fields of work were taken by women in Britain
and in the dominions as an indication that gender relations were in
need of reform.[12] This chapter argues that the interactions between
these different interest groups may be best understood as power struggles over how immigrant women should be received and by whom this
work ought to be managed.

The socio-political climate in which the reception of single female
immigrants was organized was charged with imperialist and nationalist
sentiments. The desire to increase immigration was an important motivation behind the federation of the Canadian colonies in 1867 and the
Australian colonies in 1901. Once federation occurred, immigration
gained the status of a national priority in each country. As historians
have made clear for both nations' histories of immigration, eugenic
beliefs played a major role in the formulation of popular attitudes about
immigration and in the creation of official immigration policies.[13]
Although Canadian and Australian observers periodically registered
grave concerns about the quality of British immigrants being received,
and although there were differences in opinion about the labour needs
of the new countries,[14] there was little public disagreement about the
fact that Britons were the most desirable immigrants.[15] The British
Immigration League of Australia was at one end of the spectrum regarding its members' willingness to dedicate time and money to the British
immigration cause. However, the League's stated mission outlined a
perspective that was probably shared by most colonials of British extrac-
tion. Its members desired to build up 'a new Britain in Australia, as dis-
tinct from an Australia composed of people from all the nations of the
earth.' They believed that this could only be achieved if large numbers
of 'suitable immigrants of British race' were encouraged to settle in Australia.[16] Single females were given specific attention within this call for
increased British immigration.

The Australian colonies' immigration policies of the late nineteenth century have been characterized as the result of 'personal and factional struggles for power.' As A. Martin points out, two broad camps were always at the heart of struggles over immigration policy: employers and workers. '[Employers] were well represented in the legislatures, and workers were always well to the fore in popular agitation – framing petitions, organising public meetings and forming protest bodies.'[17] In the case of female immigrants who were intended for domestic service, there were no such rival parties fighting over their value to the country. All parties tended to agree that more British domestic servants were desirable, so that as a group they were privileged in terms of government-subsidized transportation and other incentives over most other categories of immigrant. As a result, single female immigration was virtually synonymous with domestic service. The women who worked to promote and facilitate single female immigration encountered few opponents to the principle of importing British women to perform domestic labour. When voices were raised in protest about female immigration, the issues highlighted were usually those surrounding the problems of insufficient numbers of this class of immigrant, the 'quality' of the female immigrants, and the mismanagement of their recruitment, migration, and reception.[18]

Over the three-quarters of a century before the onset of the Great Depression of the 1930s, Britain's various white settler societies actively competed with each other for British immigrants. The scarcity of domestic servants for colonial homes resulted in fierce competition, which is reflected in the files that the Canadian and Australian governments kept on each other's immigration activities. Among other things, these files received government agents' complaints about the use of 'unfair' tactics in the search for more qualified female immigrants, and newspaper articles about the other country's immigration woes.[19] A particularly smug article published in the *Toronto World* in 1914 (saved in the Canadian authorities' 'Immigration to Australia' file) outlines Canadians' feelings about their overseas competition. Entitled 'Australia Hard After Emigrants. Canada's Chief Competitor Displaying Indiscriminate Zeal,' the article notes that Canadians and Australians shared a keen desire for well-trained English servants, but that Australian methods were not practised by Canadian officials. According to the article, an enthusiastic Australian emigration promoter devised an ingenious plan for securing experienced cooks for Australia. S/he constructed a letter outlining 'the advantages of life under the Southern Cross, and particulars of reduced fares, high wages,' and any other detail that 'a cook desiring to go to Australia would want to know,' and then sent copies of the letter to 'the cook' in homes throughout specially selected middle-class neighbourhoods in England. The cooks' employers were quick to register their disapproval of the scheme, and Canadian agents were equally quick to avow their higher moral ground.[20]

Competition within Australia and Canada was also sometimes heated, with different regions endeavouring to gain a greater portion of their countries' female immigrant populations. In Canada the promotion and management of immigration was centralized from Confederation on. Yet, as Marilyn Barber notes, 'Competition among the Canadian provinces for domestics was almost as great as competition between Canada and other countries.'[21] In Australia, the management of immigration was not centralized until after the First World War. Until that point, individual Australian states organized their own explicitly competitive immigration programs. As with Canada, the centralization of immigration work did not completely resolve this inter-state competition. Tasmanians regularly protested against the fact that female immigrants who were slated to go to their state were allowed, and even enticed, to stay in Melbourne; likewise, the Immigrant Agent for Queensland complained about the periodic loss of women requisitioned by his state to New South Wales.[22] Finally, not only was there competition between nations, and between states or provinces, there was also competition between different cities, and between urban centres and rural communities for this scarce labour commodity.[23]

The competitive climate of empire migration ensured that advertising the virtues of specific destinations became a thriving industry during this period. As with other types of immigrants, single women based their decisions about where to settle upon information they had received about the availability and conditions of work, and about the social and physical environments of the places to which they could afford to go.[24] Because of the peculiar cultural position of single female migrants, the facilities available for reception also played an important role in the promotion of specific destinations. A particularly well-run women's hostel or an enthusiastic and efficient committee of local women could make a significant difference to the experiences of young migrant women, and to how colonial cities and even regions would be depicted in their private correspondence and published letters. Young women's letters home likely played an important role in the decisions made by future female emigrants.[25] At the same time, the quality of reception that a young woman could expect to be offered was reflected in the British

female emigration societies' promotional literature. The British emigrators went out of their way to direct emigrant women towards destination's that they were confident would provide single women with an
appropriate reception.[26]

In the mid-nineteenth century, the reception and care of single
female immigrants were low priorities for colonial philanthropists. Most
of the impetus behind the establishment of reception committees and
women's hostels came from Britons. Historians of Scottish-born Caroline Chisholm have emphasized that she worked almost single-handedly
to improve the facilities for the reception of single female immigrants
in Australia. During the 1840s, hers was a largely unaided struggle to
change the attitudes of established colonial residents in regard to the
needs of immigrant women.[27] In 1850, members of the British Ladies
Female Emigration Society attempted to interest Torontonians in forming a reception committee to protect and welcome single women, but
the organization that resulted from this prodding took a long time to
come into existence, and within a few years it dissolved for lack of funds
and community interest.[28] When Maria Rye and Jane Lewin of the
Female Middle-Class Emigration Society (FMCES) started their work of
sending single women to the colonies in the early 1860s, they also found
it difficult to interest colonials in reception work.[29] The few women they
thought they had found to provide consistent, reliable care for their
emigrants proved to have only a limited interest in the cause. Some of
the early colonial contacts grew hostile to the demands of the female
immigrants, while others turned out to be mainly interested in the work
of reception as a business venture.[30]

Over the course of the second half of the nineteenth century, middle-
and upper-class women in Canada and Australia became more and
more interested in funding and managing hostels for immigrant
women. Yet, well into the twentieth century, the mark of British women
on these institutions remained conspicuous. British women (like their
male counterparts in other voluntary organizations)[31] felt that only by
being at the scene of reception themselves – for periodic assessments at
least – could they be sure that the welcome and protection provided
would be appropriate. Not only did representatives of the British emigration societies regularly do tours of the major urban centres in Canada and Australia to inspect and reform facilities for reception,[32] but
British women affiliated with these organizations also undertook to do
the work of receiving immigrant women themselves. Ishbel Aberdeen is
a good example of a British woman who became involved in managing

the reception of single women in Canada as part of her larger interest in stimulating and facilitating Scottish emigration. Aberdeen considered the quality of reception and aftercare in Canada to be critical to the success of emigration projects, and whenever possible she made her own supervision of the immigration process conspicuous.[33]

For about a decade the efforts of Octavia Fowler were held up in the emigrators' literature as a shining example of British female imperialist philanthropy. At some point in the early 1890s, Fowler, the daughter of the ex-mayor of London, decided to leave her home in England to do voluntary work in Canada for the sake of the empire.[34] She settled upon establishing a receiving home for immigrant women in Winnipeg, not because Winnipeg had any 'special claim' on her, but because she felt that Canadian cities 'ought to be provided with Girls' Homes in their order along the railway line.'[35] Montreal already had a hostel run by the Women's Protective Immigration Society (WPIS, renamed the Women's National Immigration Society [WNIS] in 1898), so Winnipeg should be next, she reasoned. To this hostel Fowler dedicated $500 per year for its first three years, along with her own labour as its superintendent. In 1900, when the home's committee decided to purchase a new house, Fowler donated a further $1000. Needless to say, reception committees in other Canadian cities eyed the good fortune of Winnipeg somewhat wistfully. '[We] commend to the notice of women of means, anxious to find interesting work, and an outlet for the truest benevolence,' reception work along the lines adopted by Fowler, wrote Helen McKinnon, the secretary of the WNIS. 'Miss Fowler's work in Winnipeg is an example of what can be done by one woman,' she enthused.[36] McKinnon was particularly concerned to point out that there were splendid opportunities available for setting up such a home in Vancouver.[37]

As an imperially minded British woman, Octavia Fowler was like many of the individuals who decided to run a women's immigration hostel during this period. In her history of the British societies that managed single female emigration, Una Monk mentions several such cases, including Miss Vernon, a woman who worked for many years on various female emigration societies' committees. Vernon chose to take charge of the Rosebank Hostel in Cape Town for the first year after the Anglo-Boer War as part of her contribution to the imperial migration cause.[38] Some of the women who became involved in running hostels and facilities to train newcomers had themselves travelled to the dominions as single emigrants under the protection of British female emigration societies. According to Monk, Miss Thomas, a graduate of Leaton College[39] who had gone out as a home help to Western Canada, 'was for seven years from 1909 the admirable matron of the women's hostel at Calgary, mentioned warmly and often in other settlers' letters.' Another emigrant 'stepped on first arrival into a post at the Immigrants' home in Montreal. Yet another became the first superintendent of a new Young Women's Christian Association (YWCA) hostel in a factory area of Toronto.'[40] Georgina Binnie-Clarke, an Englishwoman who took up farming in Canada in 1905 partly to prove that women such as herself could be successful independent farmers, arranged to take in single women from Britain for training on her farm.[41]

Well into the twentieth century, much of the impetus behind the formation and revitalization of reception committees and women's hostels continued to come from Britain. But by the end of the nineteenth century, interest in this work in colonial urban centres had grown considerably. With the boost in confidence that came with the emergence and solidification of women's organizations such as the National Councils of Women, and with the recognition and support that these women's organizations began to receive from governments, the women of Canada and Australia began to assert their own interpretations of how female immigration ought to be handled. Women in the dominions became more proactive about encouraging and facilitating single female immigration, and they became more involved in the regulation of landed immigrants.

This increased confidence and ambition did not mean that these women replaced British women in reception work. Rather, in the years around the turn of the century, Canadian and Australian women sought to collaborate with British organizations in reception programs. Not only did these women correspond with each other extensively, sharing opinions, ideas, and strategies, but they also met in person much more regularly than might seem likely. As has been noted above, representatives of the British emigration societies made regular trips to the dominions, where they networked with as many local women involved in reception work as possible. Leading Canadian and Australian women also made the trip to England, where they attended the meetings and conferences held by the female emigration societies, and socialized informally with the British emigration promoters. These meetings between Britons and women from the dominions were taken very seriously by both parties, and were duly recorded in the minutes of their societies' meetings, their annual reports, and their other promotional publications. As a British Women's Emigration Association (BWEA) annual report noted, imperial celebrations at which large numbers of women from the dominions were present were used to forge closer ties with colonial men and women who might provide useful overseas connections. The Jubilee Commemoration was seen by BWEA members as an opportunity to welcome 'distinguished Colonial visitors' and to explain to them 'that only women of character and capacity were sent out, and such as the needs of their own Colonies required.' In return for the BWEA's services in this respect, the 'influential co-operation' of the visitors was requested.[42]

The women who worked at promoting and facilitating the emigration of single women from Britain were keenly aware that the help of well-placed colonial women was essential to the success of their projects. In every annual report and issue of their journal, they emphasized that overseas women's efforts were invaluable, and they singled out for special notice those individuals and committees who had done especially good work. For example, in the 1896–7 *Annual Report* of the BWEA, the activities of women working in Perth were given special attention. The 'untiring and continuous' care of the GFS Associates in Perth for all of the BWEA's female emigrants – be they GFS 'girls' or not – was applauded. The BWEA indicated that it was particularly pleased with the efforts of Lady Gerard-Smith and 'a very influential Committee of the leading people in Perth' to establish a hostel for female immigrants.[43] In the March 1925 issue of the *Imperial Colonist*, Mrs Bond of Winnipeg was described as being a 'genius' at placing educated female emigrants. The success of the Colonial Intelligence League's work in Winnipeg was owed to Mrs Bond, wrote Caroline Grosvenor, formerly the chairman of the League: 'She never seemed to make a mistake, and the Committee of the C.I.L. had always a feeling of complete confidence in sending a girl to her.' Because of their faith in her abilities, the CIL sent sixty single women to Bond's care during the three years that she worked with them before the outbreak of the war – a number far in excess of what the area would have received had she not been there.[44]

The British women's consciousness of the services rendered to their projects by women working at reception overseas was mirrored by Canadian and Australian women's understanding that the British emigration societies could provide useful assistance and knowledge. An example of the enthusiastic adoption of British-originated ideas about the management of single female migration may be found in the work of Miss Calder. In 1890 Calder travelled from Melbourne to England with the intention of finding young women who would be willing to emigrate to her colony.

During her visit she 'acquainted herself fully with the [BWEA's] methods of selection, and she spoke on the openings in Victoria at several meetings.'[45] When she returned to Australia later that year, she carried with her 'credentials' from the BWEA, along with a circular letter outlining the BWEA's plans for a system whereby colonial employers and the BWEA would go half-and-half in loaning passage money to emigrant women, which would be paid back out of the emigrants' wages after they were settled. Shortly afterwards Calder moved to Tasmania, where she established a servants' fund along the lines suggested by the BWEA with the support of other leading local women. By the time the BWEA had published its *Annual Report* for 1892–3, the twenty servants that Calder had requested under the servant fund scheme had been selected, sent out, and settled in jobs for long enough that Lady Dobson, a member of Calder's Tasmanian committee, was able to report with some pride that '[all] the servants are still in the situations that they went to on arrival in Tasmania, and on the whole they have been a success.'[46]

Reception work was usually performed by committees of locally based women. But this work was never done in isolation. The management of single female immigration demanded cooperation with other related organizations. It is thus not surprising that most Canadian and Australian reception projects were allied in one way or another with international women's organizations. With the establishment and then expansion into the colonies of organizations such as the YWCA, the GFS, the Travellers' Aid Society, and National Councils of Women, the groundwork was laid for a well-integrated system of female migrant care. Even so, this system was not implemented with ease at the will of the women involved in these organizations. Government programs already in place had to be worked around, and reception committees had to deal with apathetic and sometimes antagonistic publics and resistant female immigrants. As the case of the GFS's reception work in Sydney indicates, the integration of women-directed reception work into the procedures already in place was not always smooth or successful. While some members of the colony had been won over to the idea that single women ought to be taken under the wing of benevolent ladies with British connections, large portions of the community viewed this sort of philanthropic work with scepticism and hostility.

The GFS was founded in England in 1875. The central organizing principle behind the establishment of this organization was that it was better to prevent a young woman's fall from virtue than to engage in rescue work after the fall. It was an organization devoted primarily to working-class women engaged in domestic service. The GFS accepted only those who had 'unblemished' records. Although girls of all faiths could join the society, it was explicit about its close association with the Church of England. The fundamental aims of the organization were to promote imperialist attitudes in young women and to nurture closer ties with the colonies; to instil strong Christian values; to school girls in obedience to parents and to employers; and to encourage pure and chaste femininity.[47] Central to the GFS's efforts to maintain their young members' respectability was its practice of commending them to GFS associates (middle-class GFS leaders) on arrival at their places of destination. When an emigration department of the GFS was formed in 1883, it was seen as imperative that an adequate system of reception be in place for GFS members who were emigrating. The GFS Central Secretaries for each colony were contacted by Ellen Joyce and asked to assign an Immigration Associate for each port and major city. The GFS branches in the colonies became responsible for meeting new immigrants, for ensuring that they were appropriately accommodated, for receiving their introductions and testimonials, which were then to be used when assigning the immigrants to employers, and for keeping in touch with the immigrants once settled.[48]

The New South Wales branch of the GFS was founded in 1880. When the Sydney associates received Joyce's request for their help in receiving and settling single women three years later, they responded with vigour. Their president, Annie Gordon, made contact with key immigration officials and secured promises that she would be allowed to take away from the immigration depot any GFS emigrants about whom she had been notified.[49] Determined to cover all of her bases, Gordon also wrote to the GFS in England requesting that Members emigrating to New South Wales be asked to sign a special contract before their departure. The contract specified that the emigrants would not 'hire with any employer on the public hiring day or any other time till she has seen the [GFS] Immigration Associate or received a letter from her telling her who the employer is, who has been found for her and with whom she will then hire agreeing to remain at least 3 months in the situation thus found for her at a fixed wage which will be current in the Colony.'[50] Although the circumstances outlined in Gordon's letter to justify her request were not commented upon in the minutes of the Colonial and Emigration Committee of the GFS, it is clear that she convinced the committee members that the situation in Sydney warranted this special set of precautions. Her suggestions along these lines were adopted.

For the five months before July of 1885, when the associates of the New South Wales GFS finally admitted defeat and announced their withdrawal from immigration work in the *Herald*, this society's work in the field of female immigration had been thoroughly scrutinized and critiqued by government officials, newspaper editors and journalists, and members of the public.[51] Supporters of the GFS, such as Sir Alexander Stuart, the colonial secretary, argued that in light of the fact that it was impossible to encourage an adequate number of respectable young women of the servant class to immigrate to New South Wales, any organization that could aid in this work should be seen as a boon to the colony.[52] 'A Redfern Housekeeper' pointed out that the guidance and protection afforded to virtuous young women by the GFS allowed women to emigrate from Britain who otherwise would never have done so. After all, she wrote, '[most] parents object to allow their daughters to come to a strange country unless assured of friendly help and care, and some guarantee that the situations obtained will be respectable.'[53] Promoters of the GFS cause claimed that the GFS's involvement in matters of immigration reception would improve the quality and quantity of the colony's servants.

The GFS's detractors held a fundamentally different view of the society's immigration work. Within the state administration, the GFS gained adversaries in Daley, the acting colonial secretary, and in George Wise, the New South Wales agent for immigration.[54] It appears likely that Wise provided evidence to the press for the anti-GFS campaign, and he provoked Annie Gordon into a state of fury by refusing to allow her to correspond privately or in her capacity as president of the GFS with immigrants at the depot on the grounds that she was meddling in affairs that were none of her business.[55] A number of authors of letters to the press agreed with the sentiments of 'A Sydneyite' who asserted that '[t]he sole desire of the ladies forming the committee of the GFS is to provide servants for themselves and their friends without the annoyance of attending the scramble of the hiring room.'[56] Outraged 'sufferers' recounted incidents in which it became evident that they could not hire a domestic servant at the immigration depot because the emigrants had previously been discouraged from hiring themselves out by members of the GFS, or in which their hard-won servants had been stolen from them by devious and intrusive GFS 'visitors' to their homes.[57] The most vociferous opponent of the GFS was the *Herald*'s editor, who claimed that 'a society for the protection of mistresses against faithless, lazy, and ill-tempered servants could easily justify its existence; but ... the elaborate protection of servants seems to imply a remarkable dearth of charitable objects.'[58]

As the unseemly struggle between the GFS and its detractors illustrates, the interest of middle- and upper class women's organizations in reception work relating to domestic servants was inextricably related to these women's own positions as members of the servant-hiring classes. They had a keen sense of the need for more domestic servants in their own communities and a comprehensive understanding of the various problems relating to domestic service in general. Having direct access to incoming British domestic servants held obvious advantages for middle-class Canadian and Australian women. As their critics were quick to point out, it meant that they could circumvent the tortuous and uncertain route to gaining new servants that most women of their class were obliged to take.[59] But these women's involvement with immigrant women was also related to their desire to be part of an imperial network of like-minded female philanthropists and reformers. These women saw themselves in a context that was much larger than Sydney, and they likely understood that their failure to establish an effective system of reception for single women would be perceived by British observers as an indication of their own inferior social status and organizational abilities.

Single women were the only class of adult immigrants whose hiring was fiercely controlled by the government of New South Wales.[60] As observers of the GFS fiasco pointed out, whereas government-sponsored married couples and single men were permitted to 'engage themselves when and where they liked,' single women were carefully contained and chaperoned, without the right to leave the depot before the official hiring day.[61] The women's special immigrant status was due to their dual identities as highly sought-after commodities in the labour market and as relatively young women set loose from family ties. British domestic servants with good references were scarce, jealously guarded 'prizes' who tended, to the great annoyance of emigrators and prospective employers alike, to act in ways that reflected their own understandings of their own best interests. At the same time, their gender ensured that they would be perceived as relatively vulnerable migrants, in need of careful protection.

As the case of the Sydney GFS illustrates, the fact that a reception committee was associated with a British sending society would not necessarily save it from the devastating effects of a determined onslaught by representatives of local or national governments and members of the public. The programs put in place by women working in the dominions had to be managed astutely. Great care had to be taken in negotiating with government officials, and a large local base of support had to be secured. On the other hand, as the following examination of the history of the Women's Protective Immigration Society[62] reveals, a more sustained show of support by the British emigration societies for a colonial organization could have a significant impact upon a local institution's fortunes.

In 1881 the Women's Protective Immigration Society (later renamed the Women's National Immigration Society) was established by a group of prominent Montreal women with connections to men in positions of power in Canadian and British governments and businesses.[63] From its foundation, this society was able to boast titled British supporters, including its patron, Princess Louise.[64] It was designed to be national in focus and imperial in its politics.[65] The principle upon which the society was established was that single female immigrants required special protection against moral and physical dangers – dangers that were predominantly associated with unscrupulous and predatory men. In 1882 the WPIS opened the first Canadian hostel for single female immigrants in Montreal. The WPIS home was non-denominational, and it was run by women for women only. In spite of chronic financial difficulties, the home gained a solid reputation in short order. By the early 1890s it was the linchpin in a well-oiled British female settlement program.

For the leaders of the Anglican Church, looking after the religious needs of immigrants to Canada was a task of significant importance.[66] In the context of Montreal, this meant that immigrants who were known to be Anglican were welcomed by a specially appointed minister, whose job it was to ensure that the immigrant was quickly incorporated into the local Anglican community. During the last decade of the century, the Anglican Church's Immigration Chaplain at Montreal was the Reverend J.F. Renaud, who took his job of protecting Church of England immigrants from the influences of other religious groups very seriously. His discovery in 1890 that the WPIS home's matron was Roman Catholic galvanized him into action. He infuriated the members of the WPIS with his abusive treatment of their matron during his visits to their home, so that ultimately they were obliged to refuse his entry to the home unless he was visiting on official duty. Undeterred, Renaud campaigned to have the offending matron fired. When it became evident that the WPIS would not relieve their Catholic matron of her duties, Renaud and his supporters in the Montreal Anglican Church community worked to stop the flow of single female migrants to the WPIS home. With the establishment in 1895 of the Andrews Home, an Anglican hostel for migrant men and women, these men's efforts to direct single Anglican women away from the WPIS home gained a new focus.[67] Renaud travelled to England to discourage the British emigration societies from sending women to the WPIS home, and he lobbied the Canadian government to hand over all or part of the WPIS's subsidy to the Anglican hostel.[68]

There were two other organizations central to the Montreal reception conflict: the BWEA and the Anglican Church's Society for Promoting Christian Knowledge (SPCK). Founded in 1698, the SPCK was primarily involved in the promotion of Anglican Christianity through the production and dissemination of religious literature at home and overseas. In the second half of the nineteenth century, the SPCK took on the task of selecting and paying for chaplains and matrons to minister to groups of emigrants while in transit.[69] By 1886 a firm relationship between the SPCK and the BWEA had been established. For the next eleven years, all single women who asked their clergymen for advice about emigration were put in touch with the BWEA so that they could be assured sound advice from a reputable source. All single women were directed by Anglican ministers to travel with the BWEA's organized parties, and for every group of emigrants that the BWEA put together, the SPCK provided a ship's matron. From its foundation, the BWEA had sent its parties of chaperoned female emigrants to the care of the WPIS in Montreal. It was thus to the SPCK and the BWEA that Renaud appealed in his efforts to redirect the flow of single female migrants from the WPIS home to the Anglican home under his control.

Renaud's campaign to convince the BWEA and the SPCK that the WPIS hostel was not an appropriate place of accommodation for Anglican women revolved around his assertion that the Roman Catholic matron posed a serious threat to the Anglican Church's influence over female immigrants. Initially, the BWEA seems to have paid little attention to Renaud's protests about its use of the WPIS home. Ellen Joyce, who had visited Canada in 1884 and in 1890, felt that she had a good sense of what was needed in the way of female immigrant reception. She was thoroughly satisfied with the services provided by the WPIS, and as an official spokesperson for the BWEA she took Renaud's attacks as an opportunity to make her support for the WPIS home public.[70] The SPCK also chose to avoid the issue of female reception in Montreal for as long as possible, preferring instead to leave the matter in the hands of the BWEA. But by 1895 Renaud's campaign was beginning to make things very uncomfortable for the clergymen who ran the SPCK. They received letters from churchmen with significantly more power than Renaud, desiring to know why an Anglican home should be passed over in favour of one that was run by a Roman Catholic matron. Ellen Joyce managed to satisfy the members of the SPCK only temporarily with her assertions that the WPIS had served the BWEA well in the past, and that she felt that the Andrews Home, which catered to both men and women (though in separate parts of the building), was less appropriate for young women than was the WPIS home. The fact that the members of the BWEA were 'unanimous' in their belief that reception arrangements should remain as they were could not outweigh the increasing pressure that the SPCK was facing from church authorities about this issue.[71] It was only a matter of time before the members of the SPCK's emigration committee would be forced to have a showdown over this issue with the women who ran the BWEA.

Between December 1895 and February 1898, correspondence concerning the reception of single women at Montreal dominated the meetings of the SPCK's emigration committee. Its members were barraged with letters from Renaud demanding to know why he was still receiving no single women at his home 'after all our work and the great expense the Diocese has been at in the establishment of the Home, after our expressed willingness to care for, provide and look after all women and girls belonging to the Church, [and] after the favourable reports made by your Chaplains of the Home.'[72] They also received letters from, among others, the Anglican bishops of Montreal and Quebec and the Archbishop of Canterbury questioning the use of the WPIS home over that run by Renaud.[73] In these letters, a strong case for the Andrews Home was made: Anglican women who emigrated under the care of matrons who had been paid by the Anglican Church ought to be directed by those matrons to Montreal's official Anglican home for immigrants.

In their response to the SPCK, the members of the BWEA were equally determined that only one future course of action was thinkable: the BWEA would continue to use the services of the WPIS because the Andrews Home was not an appropriate place for vulnerable young women. 'My profound conviction is that if I sent the girls to the Andrews Home I should simply be sending them into the very temptations which the whole system of protection under Matrons is built up to prevent,' wrote Joyce. The Andrews Home would provide young, unattached women with an opportunity of making friends 'with those very men who we are trying to save them from'[74] – wanderers, vagrants, and men with unknown pasts. But it was not just the fact that men and women were both housed at the Andrews Home that convinced the BWEA that this was not an adequately respectable destination for their charges. Joyce was convinced that Renaud was 'totally wanting in experience as to the management of Immigrants,'[75] and she likewise argued that Renaud's cousin was a poor choice for the home's matron.[76]

The BWEA would not consider using the Andrews Home. On the other hand, the WPIS home and system of protection had been well tried and found true. Joyce acknowledged that it was unfortunate that the WPIS home was non-denominational. But she refused to accept that there was anything wrong with the home's Roman Catholic matron, whom she claimed to know well, having even received her as a guest at her home in Winchester. There was no threat of losing young Anglican women to the Catholic Church through the work of this matron, she argued. On the other hand, Renaud's religion *was* a problem. Joyce knew that she would be reaching sympathetic listeners in the SPCK when she confided that 'the matter is unfortunately embarrassed by the element of Mr. Renaud and his party taking the position of extreme Protestantism.' Moreover, if Renaud had not annoyed the members of the WPIS with his 'overbearing conduct,' wrote Joyce, he would have continued to enjoy free access to this home.[77] According to Joyce, the difficulties that had arisen around the system of reception in Montreal were directly the result of Renaud's malicious interference.

Ellen Joyce and the women of the BWEA tried to convince the emigration committee of the SPCK of the logic of their decision to use the WPIS home rather than the Anglican one run by Renaud. But when it came down to it, they expected that the members of the SPCK's emigration committee would concede that the BWEA women were best placed to decide upon such matters. The core of their arguments for continued SPCK support revolved around their assertion of their superior understanding of the needs of young single women in transit.[78] In the BWEA's correspondence on the matter of female reception in Montreal, they contended that men were the central problem for female emigrants' safety and that men could not be counted on to make the right judgment calls concerning vulnerable women's protection. But as Joyce's discussion of the Andrews Home's matron shows, not all women were qualified to manage female migration either. Only women of proven ability and high moral standards were worthy of this important duty. To Joyce and the other women of the BWEA who debated the problems they were experiencing with the SPCK, the logic of these arguments was self-evident.[79] The difficulty lay in getting the members of the SPCK to cede this point. 'I hope your Committee will not press me to do what I know would be prejudicial to the morals and stability of my girls,' Joyce told the SPCK's emigration committee.[80] The barely veiled subtext to this request was Joyce's confidence that the men to whom she wrote would understand the moral consequences of a decision to ignore the seasoned advice of the BWEA for the sake of politics.

By the end of the nineteenth century, the members of the BWEA were able to point to a history of extensive experience and numerous successful emigration projects to their credit. More important, they could show that their intervention in female migration had made it respectable. The BWEA had gained for itself a reputation as an organization that could provide quality female immigrants. Joyce informed the SPCK that the BWEA had won the admiration of prominent Canadian statesmen, including Prime Minister Sir Charles Tupper.[81] She did not need to remind the members of the SPCK that the BWEA held the support of a wide range of British social, political, and religious leaders – of this they were fully aware.

Some of the members of the SPCK were clearly very uncomfortable about the situation in which they found themselves. For a variety of reasons, a showdown with the BWEA was not desirable. Not only did the BWEA manage female emigration efficiently, and thus provide a valuable service for the Anglican church, but the personal ties between these men of the church and the women of the BWEA were significant. For example, Reverend Bridger had worked closely with Ellen Joyce and Adelaide Ross for several years. He had likewise worked with Ellen Joyce's son, the Reverend A.G. Joyce, and with Adelaide Ross' husband, the Revered Alexander Ross. When the conflict between the SPCK and the BWEA reached its climax, Bridger attended a BWEA committee meeting in a vain attempt to bridge the gap between these organizations' positions and to explain that the SPCK, 'as a Church Society,' was 'compelled' to side with the leaders of the church rather than with the women who ran the BWEA.[82] It is unlikely that anyone else on the SPCK's emigration committee had as close a relationship with these women as did Bridger, but for political reasons other members of the committee were also wary of moving against the BWEA in haste. Ellen Joyce could not be attacked without the possibility of unwanted repercussions. She had friends in high places in the Anglican Church, and her emigration methods were well respected by influential people in Britain and overseas. As Mr Maitland pointed out in an SPCK meeting, they could not risk 'the appearance of persecuting Mrs. Joyce.'[83]

The minutes of Victorian committee meetings tend to be poor sources for discovering the emotions of the people who attended them. However, the feelings involved in the BWEA-SPCK conflict of 1896–7 were such that even this usually dry source is revealing. Mr Fanshawe of the SPCK was particularly outraged by Mrs Joyce's impertinence. At one meeting towards the end of 1896 he 'suggested that Mrs. Joyce should be asked whether she was the authorised agent of the Girls' Friendly Society and that if she answered in the affirmative she should be asked how she reconciled her position as the agent of a Church Society with sending Immigrant Women to such a Home' as that which was run by the WPIS. Understanding that this question would be rightly interpreted as aggressive by Joyce and the rest of the BWEA, the rest of the committee chose to ignore Fanshawe's suggestion. Undeterred, he repeated his request, only to be more forcefully shut down by the meeting's chair.[84] A couple of months later Fanshawe again urged the committee to formally put Joyce in her place. He requested that she be told that she must choose between working for the BWEA and for the Anglican Church. Assuming that she would choose the church, Fanshawe stated that 'Mrs. Joyce should be definitely required to undertake to work in perfect loyalty to the Church, and ... the female protective work ought to be put in other hands.'[85]

Although the other committee members would not support Fanshawe's suggestions, they did pass a couple of strongly worded resolutions that made it clear that the women who managed the work of the BWEA were to take their directions from the church authorities. In the future, they informed Joyce, male representatives of the church would have the authority to determine which girls would join the BWEA's emigrant parties; Mr Bridger would have veto power over the choice of matrons for the BWEA emigrants; and all emigrant women sailing out under the care of SPCK matrons would be placed in the Andrews Home upon their arrival in Montreal. Furthermore, 'Mrs. Joyce [was] asked to express her acceptance of, and concurrence in, this decision.'[86]

The women of the BWEA were outraged by the treatment they had received at the hands of the SPCK. Not only was the 'ultimatum' offensive, but the SPCK committee had made an obvious point by their lack of courtesy towards representatives of the BWEA who had been summoned to address their meeting. The Reverend A.G. Joyce, who had gone in his mother's place, described to the members of the BWEA how Mrs Chaloner Chute and he had been made to wait outside of the SPCK meeting for over an hour before he was called in. Chute was never asked in at all. Once inside, Joyce discovered that he had been asked to come to the meeting as a mere formality: 'Members were leaving the meeting and the question seemed to have been decided and they refused to hear any details.' Joyce's impressions of the SPCK members' meeting were corroborated by Chute. The BWEA women responded with their own, unanimously agreed upon, resolution that 'the Honourable Mrs. Joyce be empowered to convey to the Secretary of the Emigration Committee of the S.P.C.K. cordial thanks for the monetary help they have given in paying Matrons to take charge of single Women and that she should inform them that in the future the [BWEA] will themselves pay the Matrons they require for the Protection of the Women *entrusted to their care*.'[87]

When the Reverend J. Bridger was summoned by Grace Lefroy (the secretary of the BWEA) to receive formal notice of the association's decision, no amount of apologetic explanation about the difficulties faced by the SPCK in this matter could deter the women of the BWEA from their course of action. Instead, Bridger was told that although the women were pained by the fact that their resolution 'put them in apparent opposition to the Church,' they had no intention of transferring their allegiance to the Andrews Home, and that unless the SPCK relented, their formal relationship was over.[88]

The BWEA remained consistent in its support of the WPIS after the turn of the century. Like many other such institutions, the WPIS home in Montreal was forced to close owing to a lack of funds during the First World War. But the WPIS, the BWEA, and other women's organizations continued to work together, dominating the management of female migration until the British and Canadian governments absorbed these organisations and their affiliated hostels into state structures after the end of the war. The continued support of the BWEA for the WPIS in the face of pressure from the Anglican Church in Canada and Britain to cut ties for religious reasons is a testament to the firm relationship that had already been established between these women's organizations. Only one year before the attacks on the WPIS began (and after eight years of dealing with the Catholic matron), the BWEA recorded their complete satisfaction with the arrangements in Montreal. Not only did the women of the WPIS provide safe and comfortable accommodation, emotional support, and a respectable employment agency for the women who would remain in Montreal, but they also offered single female travellers an opportunity to refresh themselves, eat, and relax at their hostel 'whilst the train [was] being made up' for their journey further west.[89]

The women of the WPIS went out of their way to keep the women of the BWEA informed about the movements of their emigrants, and the WPIS was glowing in its praise of the British women's work. 'Your girls are thought a great deal of,' wrote the president of the WPIS home. '[We] depend of course upon the choice you make in England, and we are exceedingly grateful to you for the pains you take in your selection.'[90] The fact that these two organizations saw themselves as working together towards the same goal – the safe and happy settlement of respectable British women throughout Canada – was key to their representation of each other in their private and public communications.[91] Ultimately, the fact that the WPIS saw itself as an imperial and national women's organization meant that it kept the BWEA's confidence and support in the face of sectarian attacks from men with a completely different understanding of reception work.[92]

The Anglican men who opposed the British and dominion women's combined efforts to provide facilities for the reception and aftercare of female immigrants at Montreal were unusual in that they established their own reception program in competition with the one already managed by influential local women. Opposition more regularly came from the men who ran government immigration institutions or programs when they found themselves the targets of middle-class women's reform agendas. For example, women involved in promoting and managing female migration campaigned for many years for the reform of the government-run immigration depot at Kangaroo Point in Brisbane. The response that these women received from the implicated government agents was solidly hostile.

The most assertive complaints about the conditions of the depot and the treatment of women who were housed there came from the matrons who had travelled to Australia with the female migrants. A 1926 letter of protest about government policies, practices, and attitudes in Queensland, written by H.M. James, the Assistant Government Matron at Australia House in London, provides a good illustration of these women's grievances. This letter also does an excellent job of encapsulating James's (and other female emigrators') sense of the importance of this matter for Australia's national and international identities, and it highlights the attitude of female emigrators (paid and voluntary) about their own roles in the creation of the Australian nation.

James's letter outlines a number of problems with the reception of female immigrants at the Brisbane Depot, all of which reflected a lack of hospitality on the part of the government and an absence of respect for the dignity of the immigrants. In her opinion, no decent welcome to the new arrivals was offered. Rather, the women were immediately made to feel that they were inmates of a state institution. The beds that were made up were covered with grey blankets in the centre of which was 'the Government mark of the broad arrow ... conspicuous and suggestive,' writes James. The bathroom was a disaster, with only a filthy tub that would not empty and three basins that were lined up in front of a window that could not close and had no cover. Those women who desired to wash themselves had either to expose themselves 'to the gaze of curious eyes,' or give up and go without. Come time for sleep, the immigrants turned to their beds, only to find that sleep was not possible due to the bother of swarms of mosquitoes and huge black beetles. According to James, those responsible for the depot had not thought it necessary to put netting on the windows or provide mosquito nets to go over the beds.[93]

In her letter of complaint about the depot, James made it clear that her motivations for writing were not just related to the suffering of the women who had to endure a few days at the depot. She was deeply concerned about the sort of image that this reception would translate into through the immigrant women's reports home. '[The immigrant] looks at the great barnfull of beds and wishes she was back in London or Liverpool,' wrote James. 'Her little room may have been in the slums, but it was homelike and comfortable compared to this. If this is the way Australians live they seem to be scarcely civilised. They do not know how to make a decent cup of tea, nor how to furnish a room.' 'This is the first impression the British migrant gets of Australia, and Australians,' she mused, 'and first impressions stick.' The results are obvious, argued James: 'Is it any wonder that Australia and Australians are looked upon with suspicion on the other side, and that many prefer to settle in Africa, Canada and America or Europe[?]'[94]

James protested against conditions at the immigration depot as a concerned citizen of Australia and as a person whose work was to promote and oversee single female immigration to Australia. She was distressed by the knowledge that Australia would suffer as a result of this state of affairs, and she was indignant at the hostile reception that she got from Mr Abell, the Immigration Agent for Queensland and the person responsible for running the depot. Abell proved himself to be arrogant, condescending, and mysogynistic in his responses to James's concerns. When James asked him why there were no chairs for the immigrants' use, he told her, 'Oh! they would smash them.' James took it upon herself to remind Abell 'that these people were British subjects and not savages; that they were just as accustomed to the use of furniture as he was.' Abell informed James that he felt her complaints were all groundless, and that he was 'satisfied with the existing conditions.' Moreover, he told her that 'other matrons had complained, and that in future no matrons in charge of migrants would be allowed at the Hostel and he much regretted having given [her] the accommodation there on the previous night.' According to James, men like Abell were completely out of touch with the responsibilities of their work. Moreover, they were guilty of undermining the serious efforts of women like herself and the members of the New Settlers' League (who had provided the immigrant women with a 'really genuine welcome and pretty reception' on the day after their arrival) to promote Australia. Unlike Abell, the women of the League were 'truly interested in the development of their country and the unity of the Empire.'[95]

As Abell indicated, James was not the only woman to register her grievances about the facilities provided by the Queensland government for receiving immigrant women.[96] Between 1926 and 1929 this matter was raised a number of times with government officials, to no avail.[97] Only after the Women's Committee of the Queensland Division of the New Settlers' League (NSL, an organization funded and supported by the national and state governments of Australia) put together a forceful resolution about the need for reforms at the depot in 1929 did the Queensland government take the situation seriously. And even then, it seems likely that the matter was addressed only because of the strong endorsement of the Women's Committee's resolutions by Canon David Garland, the president of the League and a man with a history of amicable relations with Queensland government officials.

The manner in which female immigrants were received by colonials could have long-lasting repercussions for the reputation of a city or a region within the world of 'managed' female migration. The withdrawal of the New South Wales GFS from reception work during the 1890s would have been a source of significant annoyance to the British women who worked at promoting the emigration of GFS members. By humiliating the GFS Associates and disallowing their reception work, the government and citizens of New South Wales had contributed to the stigmatization of Sydney as a hostile environment for respectable single women. Clearly, James was highly sensitive to this sort of negative press; she would have been well aware of eastern Australia's unenviable history of conflict with female emigrators. After all, the British emigrators with whom James worked were not particularly reticent about sharing their opinions. For example, organizations working in collaboration with the BWEA came together in London in 1910 specifically to consider the question of inadequate reception in Australia.[98] An article published in the *Imperial Colonist* summarized the feelings of the attendees: 'The residents – the employers – in the Over-Seas Dominions demand "our best,"' wrote the journal's editor. '[But] what are they doing to take care of the newcomers on their arrival?' 'Is England right to trust her virtuous daughters to the temptations and dangers of any State or city which does not provide safe accommodation and guidance and protection for the newcomers?'[99] Clearly, a rhetorical question! The article concluded: 'It cannot but strike everyone how great is the contrast between the arrangements made by Canada, New Zealand, and South Africa, and those which prevail in Queensland and New South Wales. It is earnestly hoped that the Government of these two Colonies, who are so greatly stimulating emigration, will speedily take steps to remove what we do not hesitate to say, is, at present, a grave scandal.'[100] Seven years later the members of the Joint Council of Women's Emigration Societies became so exasperated with reception conditions in Australia that they sent a letter to the Australian High Commissioner asserting that 'no emigration society of repute would encourage women to go to Australia unless suitable conditions both for the journey and on arrival were provided.'[101]

As the sagas of the state-run immigration depots at Sydney and at Brisbane and the privately managed hostels at Montreal illustrate, it is possible to read the history of the relationships between female emigrators and the men involved in the male-dominated areas of immigration work in terms of a struggle for power. When women like James (or Annie Gordon of the New South Wales GFS) tried to reform or replace government-run facilities for female reception, they could expect to encounter resistance.[102] Through their struggles to gain control over the reception of female migrants, these women were engaging in a battle between reform-minded women and men in positions of governmental authority that was being fought on numerous other fronts during this period.

In the struggle for control over reception in the dominions, it was clear where the British women's emigration societies' allegiances would lie. From the perspective of the British women who promoted and facilitated the emigration of single women, hostels run by women, specifically for single women, had clear advantages over hostels like the Andrews Home or government-run immigration depots. They were overseen by well-connected women who would have shared views on many related issues, and they were managed by carefully chosen matrons. These homes offered more than just accommodation. They frequently offered immigrants an opportunity to receive some domestic service training in the colonial context, and they usually served as informal registry offices. At least in theory, the credentials of employers who sought domestic servants from these homes were scrutinized by the homes' managers in an attempt to safeguard the young women from questionable work environments. They also provided single women with a safe, racially and ethnically 'clean' place in which to stay while sick or between jobs, and with a positive, culturally reaffirming social environment in which to spend their leisure time.

The work of welcoming, accommodating, training, and providing aftercare for single female migrants required the mobilization of a large variety of human and financial resources. Some of these resources came from British individuals and organizations, some from the ranks of British emigrants, and some from women solidly situated within the dominions. Reception work also involved a significant amount of politicking and educating, aimed both inwards, towards other members of the imperial network of female emigrators, and outwards, towards relevant public bodies and government representatives. In previous chapters I have discussed the efforts of the British female imperialists to convince prospective female emigrants, governments, and publics to adopt their perspectives and agendas. The women who did reception work in the dominions also worked at promoting their own understandings of the needs of single female immigrants and of the communities into which they would settle. Although the relationships between women in the dominions and Britain (like those between women in the dominions and the dominion governments) were usually amicable, there were always implicit – if not explicit – negotiations about power sharing and about valuations of knowledge bases involved in these groups' interactions.

Lady Mary Orme Masson's Australian reception work illustrates how some women in the dominions were able to carve out for themselves positions of authority within the sphere of imperial migration. Through her involvement in this field of work, she helped to ensure that Australian women's insights and skills would play an important part in how immigration was managed. Masson was typical of women in the dominions who took up reception work, in that she was herself a British emigrant who continued to have strong ties with her homeland. She was born and raised in Edinburgh, which she left for Melbourne upon her marriage to David Orme Masson in 1886. She spent the rest of her life in Australia, although she appears to have gone back to Britain for visits on a number of occasions. When her children no longer absorbed as much of her time, she threw herself into philanthropic and reform work. Among the many causes that she embraced was work relating to the reception of British immigrants. She was a founding member of the Victoria League, the New Settlers' League, and the Country Women's Association of Victoria, three of the largest and most influential organizations in Australia dealing with matters pertaining to immigration.[103].

In the period following the First World War, Mary Masson became an important figure in the struggle for increased female influence over Australian immigration matters. In her interactions with the women of the Society for the Oversea Settlement of British Women (SOSBW) may be seen her attempts to build solidarity with the British women in the face of the Australian government's rejection of their claims to authority. At a meeting of the Australian subcommittee of the SOSBW in London in 1922, Masson confirmed the British women's suspicion that '[the] arrangements for receiving settlers were not ... satisfactory in Australia. No women officers are attached to the immigration Department and the placing is in charge of men officials.' She told the women who attended the meeting that 'the SOSBW was not recognised in Australia as being officially connected with the OSC [Oversea Settlement Committee]. She considered that no weight would be given to [the SOSBW's] recommendations until the Australian Federal and State Governments were officially informed that the Society was Acting as the Woman's Branch of the OSC under the Colonial Office.'[104]

Mary Masson's interaction with the members of the SOSBW reveals her determination that women should have positions of influence and power in the management of international migration. The work that she performed in the Australian context underlines her strong commitment to having Australian women take part in this management. Like a number of other women prominent in organizations such as the NSL, the Victoria League, and the National Council of Women of Australia, Masson worked hard to educate the public and the Australian government about the need for more' female activity and responsibility in this field. She became involved in efforts to ensure that Australian rather than British women would be responsible for selecting and protecting single female immigrants.[105] Masson also worked at stimulating reception work at the grassroots level. In an Australian radio broadcast in 1926, she explained the work of the NSL to her listeners, pointing out how there were a variety of ways in which women could get involved in reception work – from helping to provide welcome teas to immigrants just off the boat to organizing local committees of women who would take an interest in the settlement of newcomers to their communities. Masson encouraged more women to take up the management of NSL branches, noting that of the two hundred branches then in existence, 'among the most active are the seventeen managed by women.'[106]

In the decades preceding the depression of the 1930s, women in Canada and Australia grew increasingly assertive about their superior abilities to assess the needs of their own countries, and they became more and more confident about their understanding of the intricacies of imperial female migration. This new-found confidence was sometimes the cause of tensions between women in Britain and the dominions. As Julia Bush has illustrated, 'the British lady imperialists seldom wavered in their determination to build a world-wide web of daughter associations with the Mother Country's own societies in the leadership position for which social status and imperial destiny had qualified them.'[107] Some Canadian and Australian women came to resent these attitudes of superiority.[108] The assertion of will on the part of women in Canada and Australia was not always looked upon favourably by the women who ran the British emigration societies. In the early twentieth century, immigration societies in the dominions began to formulate projects and resolutions that were not always in line with the agendas of women working out of Britain. For example, the efforts of Canadians such as Mrs Ethel West (the head of the Presbyterian church's Department of the Stranger) to increase the ease with which women might be deported were the cause of much distress on the British scene.[109]

The urge for self-direction in the dominions did not mean the end of close ties between the British emigration societies and the women working in Canada and Australia. The British societies continued to influence work in the dominions to a surprising degree throughout the first three decades of the twentieth century, and women in the dominions continued to seek British support and guidance. Although Canadians and Australians had an appreciation of the fact that the British women who promoted imperial migration were often woefully ignorant of conditions in the dominions, this knowledge did not result in the abandonment of British schemes and methods. Rather, it led to concerted efforts by Canadian and Australian women to gain greater control over the imperial system of migration management that had been put in place by the women at the centre of the empire. Simultaneously, women in the dominions endeavoured to educate British women (and their own gov-

ernments and publics) about local conditions and their likely impact
upon the new settler. Canadian and Australian women were more and
more willing to take the initiative in organizing single female immigration, but the projects that they designed continued to rely upon the
insights and cooperation of the British emigration societies. Women in
the dominions continued to work closely with their British counterparts
right through the 1920s, taking from the British emigration societies
that which was of use to them, cooperating on schemes that were of
mutual value, and abandoning joint projects when they no longer suited
their needs.

Between the 1860s and 1930, the relationships between the women
who ran the female emigration societies in Britain, the women who
undertook reception work in the dominions, and the dominions' governments changed considerably. The influence of British women became
less conspicuous in the dominions as reception work became a less likely
vehicle for imperial ambitions. As the example of Mary Masson shows, the
personal and associational ties between women of the dominions and
women in Britain continued to be evident throughout the 1920s. But in
the post–First World War period, as the dominions' governments incorporated women's reception networks into their official plans for the management of immigration, Australian and Canadian women became more
active on the British scene.[110] With the increase in government control
over immigration reception in Canada and Australia, the dynamics
between the various parties involved in this work became more complicated. In some instances – such as that of the immigration depot at Kangaroo Point, Brisbane – women at the local, regional, national, and
imperial levels found that it was necessary to work together to reform
problematic reception facilities or dysfunctional aftercare programs. Yet
women working in the dominions increasingly found that they could
work effectively with government bodies, and thus had little need for
close ties with British organizations.[111]

Over the course of the late nineteenth and early twentieth centuries,
the nature of reception and aftercare work changed significantly. The
reception committees that were formed in the decades preceding the
First World War were the product of an era when single female immigrants were largely British. During this period reception work was intri-
cately tied to British imperialism. The women in Canada and Australia
who worked at improving the accommodation and aftercare of female
immigrants were rewarded for their cooperation with the British emigration societies in a number of ways: they received a greater proportion

of the female emigrants than did destinations that were thought to be less welcoming; they received the social rewards of friendships with women based in Britain (which were clearly of major significance to some of the women who worked in this field); and they received financial and moral support for their reception projects. But, as it became evident after the war that the flood of immigrants that had been anticipated from Britain would not materialize, and as a greater proportion of female immigrants were coming from non-British backgrounds, the priorities and agendas of the women who had worked at immigrant reception shifted elsewhere. In Canada, the cultural re-education and assimilation of immigrants became the new foci of reception work. In Australia, non-British immigrants were generally left to adjust to their new environments on their own. Women who had managed the reception of British female immigrants turned their attention to settlement follow-up work through the Country Women's Association and the New Settlers' League so as to ensure that British immigrants to rural areas remained upon the land.

Because of their unique status as valuable yet vulnerable cultural signifiers, single British women were subject to more care and protection than were any other class of adult immigrants during this period. The respectability of female immigrants reflected upon the organizations that facilitated their immigration and upon the social environment out of which they came. At the same time, the way that receiving communities treated these immigrants could be taken by the press and by British observers as an indication of those communities' levels of civilization. Some of the care provided by the networks of concerned British and dominion women was perceived by immigrant women as unwanted regulation and interference in their lives. For most of the unfortunate women who were the focus of deportation efforts, the work of the women who provided 'aftercare' was anything but supportive. Still, the extensive resources that were mobilized for the purpose of welcoming British women also meant that single immigrant women were supported through the migration period in ways that no other group of immigrants would experience. At least in theory, the imperial network of women who desired to see the settlement of large numbers of British women in Canada and Australia was dedicated to making their experience of migration and integration as comfortable and hassle-free as possible.

By looking at the links that were established between women in Britain and the women who ran the reception programs in Canada and Australia, it is possible to gain an understanding of the motivations and goals behind this work that is significantly different from that which emerges from studies that focus exclusively upon the efforts of British emigration promoters or upon the work of philanthropists and reformers in the receiving societies. In part, reception committees were formed and female immigrant hostels were established because of concerns about the need for positive images of colonial communities. What people in Britain thought about Canada and Australia mattered to the British emigration promoters because images of the various destinations were used to stimulate imperial migrations. Likewise, how Britons perceived Canada and Australia was a matter of concern for Canadians and Australians. It mattered not only because these countries were in the process of creating their own national identities – identities that were defined in relationship to Britain – but also because British immigration formed a critical part of Canadians' and Australians' nation-building strategies. Through their correspondence with British emigrators, Canadian and Australian women gained a heightened awareness of the fact that their communities were in competition with a plethora of other communities for British female emigrants. Their British correspondents made them sensitive to their locations' changeable statuses as destinations within the international flow of migrants. As the *John Bull* article 'Canada's Deathtrap' and the responses it received within Canada highlight, women played an important role within the discourses around immigrants and place. For imperially minded Britons, female emigrants carried within them (literally and symbolically) the future of the race and of the empire. For Canadian and Australian women whose own sympathies lay with British imperialism, the immigration of large numbers of British women was fundamental to their ideas of what their new nations should be. By inserting themselves into the contact zone between immigrant women and their new communities, the women who took up reception work were able to gain some control over both the discourse around the British female immigrant and the circumstances of her reception.

A comparative study of British female migration to Canada and Australia also reveals some basic differences between these two nations' attitudes towards the women who sought to manage migration. In Canada, relatively harmonious relationships were established between the state and female emigrators – both British and Canadian – over the course of the nineteenth and early twentieth centuries. In Australia, relations seem to have been more regularly fraught with tension. British emigrators criticized Australian systems of migration far more regularly than

they did those run by the Canadian government, and they found it difficult to convince Australian officials to take them seriously as British
government agents. Australian women likewise struggled to gain the
recognition of the Australian state for their work with immigrants.

Yet this study suggests that the similarities in how female migration
was managed in Australia and in Canada are more striking than are the
differences. Women in Canada and Australia established strong bonds
of support with women working out of Britain, bonds that were critical
to how they understood their place within the empire, to how they
chose to manage female migrants, and to how they elected to deal with
men who sought to undermine their immigration agendas. Canadian
and Australian women's increasing confidence over the period studied
here, combined with the evolution of the British Empire into the British
Commonwealth, altered the nature of these women's relationships with
each other. Yet Britons continued to play an important part in the management of Canadian and Australian female migration right through
the 1920s.

chapter six

Domesticating Canberra:
The Federal Capital Commission and
the Domestic-Servant Project

Three-quarters of a century after Caroline Chisholm implemented her program of protected female migration and reception in New South Wales, and sixty-five years after the formation of the Female Middle-Class Emigration Society, the Federal Capital Commission (the government body charged with overseeing the official opening of Australia's capital city) decided that Canberra desperately required more domestic servants than were locally available. Because of the capital city's symbolic importance, the commission decided that the provision of female labourers for Canberra's households should become a government priority. The plan that the Federal Capital Commission devised called for the importation of young female domestic servants from Britain, the establishment of a hostel for their accommodation, and an elaborate program of labour-relations management – all at the expense of the Australian Federal Government.

The 1926–7 Canberra domestic-servant project involved the creation of an unusually comprehensive set of documents concerning the immigration and settlement of single British women. Together, these documents outline the motivations and methods behind the project, as well as the response that the project elicited from people not directly associated with its implementation. Through a review of this project, this chapter will assess the impact of the female emigrators' work on how female migration was understood and managed in Australia in the 1920s. It will look at the relationships among female emigrants from Britain, dominion government officials, the press, British imperialism, and the making of Australian national identities after the First World War.

In the early decades of the twentieth century, Australians and foreign observers alike explicitly linked Canberra's emerging identity to that of the Australian nation. The city's symbolic importance was huge. As Lord Denman stated in a speech at the 1913 ceremonies to name the capital city, 'the traditions of this city will be the traditions of Australia.'[1] When the Australian parliament opened its first session at the new nation's capital on 9 May 1927, the story received 'worldwide interest.'[2] The grandeur of the event was marked by the attendance of the Duke and Duchess of York (later King George VI and Queen Elizabeth) as the guests of honour, and of Dame Nellie Melba, Australia's famous opera singer, who sang the national anthem. The individuals who managed Canberra's public face consciously aimed to turn this event into a symbol of Australia's coming of age, which, for them, was understood in terms of the country's position within the British Empire. Of critical importance to their sense of Australia's 'mature' identity was their anglo-centred, elite understanding of culture and civilization.

Australians' emotional investment in their capital city was such that even before the Australian colonies confederated in 1901, the subject of the capital city was the focus of fierce disagreement. Inhabitants of New South Wales argued that the federal capital ought to be Sydney; Victorians wanted Melbourne. A compromise location inland between these two cities was ultimately agreed upon, although most parties were not charmed by the thought of a 'bush capital.'[3] The fact that Canberra was to be carved out of 'untamed' countryside excited its designers; the clean slate presented by Canberra's location meant that creative imaginations could dictate how the city would work with limited resistance.[4] But the idea of going to live in a work-in-progress city disturbed those men and women who anticipated being transferred there. The location was not the only source of contention relating to the establishment of Canberra. Walter Burley Griffin, Canberra's principle architect, was unable to implement his plans for the city for more than three years because of obstructions put in place by hostile members of the government body assigned to Canberra's management at the time.[5] Conflicts about location and designs for the city, combined with a shortage of funds during the First World War, meant that it was a full two and a half decades after confederation before plans for moving the seat of government from its temporary home in Melbourne were finally implemented.

In the early 1920s the gap between the dreams of Canberra's creators and what actually existed was immense. The construction of the city was severely compromised by bureaucratic dissension, and by problems with funding and labour. Although many of these problems had been resolved by 1924, federal officials decided that Canberra required on-the-spot management by a well-informed, powerful administrative body to see the city through the next stage of its construction. The city was beginning to take shape in that the main roads and government build-ings were well on their way towards completion. Yet, there was no dis-guising the fact that Canberra was replacing scattered farms and bush. Homes and schools needed to be built, shopping areas and social ser-vices provided, and a wide range of other physical and social details dealt with. In order to see the construction site transformed into a model community, the federal government was willing to delegate control over Canberra's management to a few hand-picked men with impressive credentials.[6]

The Federal Capital Commission was an unusual governmental cre-ation designed to work through an unusual set of problems. The com-mission consisted of John Henry Butters, its chairman and only full-time member, two part-time assistants, John Harrison and Clarence Hardie Gorman, C.S. Daley, an employee of the Department of Works and Rail-ways who was the commission's secretary, and Colonel Owen, its chief engineer. The leading men in this commission were not 'typical' Austra-lians. They came from privileged backgrounds, and earned exception-ally high pay for their work. The significance of their duties is marked by the fact that Butters, as the head commissioner, received an annual income for his work that was significantly higher than that of Australia's prime minister.[7] Butters was made Knight of the British Empire for his work on the commission, and eight of his assistants were made officers or members of the British Empire at the capital city's opening ceremo-nies.[8] At its foundation, the commission became the sole authority 'responsible for the administration, design, and construction of Can-berra, as well as for the development of municipal activities and the control of private enterprise.'[9] In order to accomplish its goals, the com-mission was given complete control over all the land and other public assets of the Australian Capital Territory as well as a large working bud-get. As the city's leading figures of authority, the commissioners, along with their wives, formed the centre of Canberra's elite between 1925 and 1929 – an elite that had strong ties with England.[10]

Established in October 1924, the Federal Capital Commission held its first meeting in Melbourne early the following month. Although its mis-sion was to oversee the building of all parts of the new capital city, its pri-mary function was to facilitate, as quickly and as smoothly as possible, the transfer of Parliament and the public service from Melbourne to

Canberra. In January 1926 the commissioners were informed by Cabinet that they had little more than a year to prepare for the opening of Parliament and the transfer of all public-service departments other than the Defence Department. The transfer of public servants necessitated preparation for the reception of 664 officials and their families – 1637 individuals in all.[11] The related problems of transportation, accommodation, and infrastructure were enormous.

The commissioners' concerns about the domestic life of the nation's capital stemmed in part from their desire to assuage the growing scepticism that many public servants in Melbourne felt about Canberra as their future home. The federal government's public servants had been 'perturbed' by rumours of the impending move to Canberra for several years, and in 1925 became proactive by forming a Public Service (Canberra) Committee to determine the ramifications of such a move, and to protect the interests of those who would be forced to transfer. This committee created subcommittees to look into issues relating to housing and the relative cost of living in Canberra, 'and sought, as a first step, some assurance of the eventual repatriation to Melbourne of those forced to go to Canberra when retirement was near.'[12] Their findings confirmed the public servants' suspicions that the move to Canberra would mean a substantial increase in the cost of living for all concerned, and resulted in a demand that the government provide transferred workers with an income subsidy to make up the difference. Among other measures introduced by the government to help pacify the state's unhappy employees, Cabinet voted to pay 50 per cent of the cost of train tickets for public servants and their wives who wished to inspect the new capital city.[13] In the early months of 1926 the members of the Federal Capital Commission would have been well aware of the less-than-happy mood of the men and women they were supposed to see comfortably settled in Canberra in little over a year. It was in its capacity as overseer of the establishment of this new community that the commission came to see the provision of domestic servants for the population of Canberra as one of its more pressing tasks.

On 25 March 1926 Butters wrote to G.F. Pearce, minister for home and territories, outlining the domestic-servant problem that the commission had identified as a serious impediment to the establishment of a contented community in Canberra. By the time he wrote his letter, Butters and the other commissioners had come to believe that the situation was serious enough to warrant immediate government intervention. Butters noted that his personal experience with domestic servants and his work of overseeing the smooth functioning of Canberra's government-run hotels had 'kept very much in [his] mind the difficulty of securing domestic help.' He attempted to show Pearce that what might be understood as a purely domestic issue was, in reality, a potentially serious problem for the government:

> It will undoubtedly militate against a contented community if the higher paid Public Servant is unable to get domestic help for his household or has to pay such exorbitant rates to attract it from elsewhere as to seriously increase the cost of living. The lower paid class of Public Servant is affected also in that whereas in Melbourne the wife of such an officer is usually able to get a relative or friend to come in and help her out during the occasional difficult period, her chances of getting such assistance [here] would be greatly reduced.[14]

According to Butters, Canberra's domestic-labour scarcity problem was unlikely to find a satisfactory resolution without government intervention.

In his capacity as manager of the government's hotels, Butters had independently come to the conclusion that the lack of servants was a problem in Canberra. But his understanding of the nature of that problem and the solutions that he desired to see implemented were the result of discussions that he had had with Miss M.E. Chomley of the Society for the Oversea Settlement of British Women (SOSBW) in the early months of 1926.[15] Chomley, an Australian who had joined the SOSBW after working in London with the Red Cross during the First World War, was in Australia on official SOSBW business.[16] The plan that Butters proposed to the minister for home and territories clearly reveals her influence. Butters called for the recruitment of young single women who had domestic-service experience in Britain. Once enough women had been signed up to make a party, they would be carefully chaperoned from London to Canberra. More parties would be organized according to Canberra's needs. Butters' plan also included the establishment of a hostel for the servants' accommodation and the formation of a 'club' that would serve as both a social centre and an employment guild. The hostel and club were to be run by a matron employed by the state.[17]

In justifying his Canberra domestic-servant project to G.F. Pearce, John Butters drew upon arguments that had been made by British female emigration promoters for decades. Butters explained that the issue of domestic servants in Canberra was a multifaceted problem. He pointed out that there was no convenient pool of labour upon which prospective employers in Canberra could draw. He did not mention the possibility of drawing upon the labour of local Aboriginal communities. Evidently, any domestic service that might have been supplied by Aboriginal girls and women was not considered sufficient to meet the city's needs – either in quantity or in quality. In light of the policy of removing Aboriginal girls from their families for training in domestic service in other parts of Australia, this omission is noteworthy.[18] Because Canberra was a new white-settler society, there was no resident community of white Australians from which single daughters could be employed. Butters was confident that there was no point in trying to convince Australian women to move from other regions of Australia to work as domestic servants, because Australian women were no longer interested in working as servants in other people's homes.[19] Butters made it clear not only that servants would be difficult to recruit, but that those women who might have been willing to work as hired helps would be disinterested in remaining for long in a city like Canberra. In his letter to Pearce, Butters emphasized that it would be 'some years before the less intellectual class of employee, especially those who are unmarried, [would] find Canberra attractive.' Certainly, Canberra could not hope to compete with the 'many attractions available in a place like Sydney.'[20]

Finally, Butters was keenly aware that Canberra was unlike other 'instant' towns in that its instant population was to be made up primarily of white-collar workers, with an unusually high representation of middle-class and elite residents and visitors. Not only would a significant proportion of the population expect to use the services of female domestic helps, but the nation's capital's comparatively 'refined' population of politicians and civil servants would require that their servants be of a notably 'superior type.'[21] In Canberra in the mid-1920s, this class of workers was clearly absent. Butters pressed the point that as scarce commodities, even in large cities like Sydney and Melbourne, thoroughly trained, etiquette-conscious servants would have to be imported directly from Britain.

Since the mid-nineteenth century, British emigration promoters had argued that the only way to encourage young women into domestic service was to treat them with more respect. What was needed, they argued, was an elevation of the status of the domestic servant. The most common complaints of domestic servants were that service allowed far too little time off duty, and that other members of the working class looked down on the occupation. Eliminate these drawbacks to domestic service, the emigration promoters claimed, and service would lose its stigma.[22] The commissioners drew upon these ideas about improving domestic service as an occupation in the hope that their plan would prove to be more than a temporary solution to Canberra's domestic-servant problems. Their domestic-servant project aimed to make Canberra a model community in terms of employer–servant relations. As with many of the other problems that the Federal Capital Commission confronted, the solution that the members decided upon required an unprecedented degree of state involvement.[23]

The central aims of the commissioners' plan were to attract servants to Canberra and to keep those who arrived content in their new environment. In order to achieve these aims, the commission decided that the servant population ought to have a supportive home base, an assured minimum income and amount of off-duty time, and a respected position in the community. It proposed that funds be allocated for the building of a hostel for domestic servants that would be designed to accommodate forty-one residents and would require a significant kitchen staff. The commission estimated that the hostel could be established at a cost of £13,000, and that within a 'reasonable time' it would be self-supporting. In the meantime, Butters argued, 'any loss should be a community charge in view of the very definite public interest in meeting this want in the new city.'[24] The hostel was to serve both as a short-term place of accommodation for new arrivals to the city and servants between jobs and as a long-term home for those servants who might choose to provide their services 'by the day.'

Like hostels that had been established by women's organizations in all of Britain's white settler communities, the Canberra hostel was to be more than just a place of accommodation for domestic servants. It was designed to provide a safe social space where women could meet, relax, and enjoy entertainment during their time off work.[25] The 'Lady Matron' of the establishment would oversee the efficient working of a domestic servants' club, which was designed to promote pride in domestic service work and respect for servants within the larger community. All domestic servants in Canberra would be 'encouraged' to become club members. The club would require of its members – and of its members' employers – conformity to a long list of rules that were designed to enforce respectable behaviour and attractive appearance on the part of the servants, and appropriate wage rates and time off from the employers.[26]

Butters and the other members of the Federal Capital Commission imagined that the establishment of a hostel, a club, and some lifestyle options for domestic servants would help to ensure that they would enjoy living and working in Canberra. However, to the men who promoted this scheme, domestic service was not a career, but a respectable, dignified means of making money for working-class women. The domestic-servant project was designed to improve the image of domestic servants, but its creators had no interest in raising these women's status within Canberra's class structure. There was no sense that they should see the sale of their labour as a business enterprise. In fact, the project initiated a system whereby the labour of servants would be more tightly controlled. The government-sponsored servants' club dictated the terms of domestic employment so that servants could not be exploited, but the same terms were also designed to ensure that the chronic shortage of servants in Canberra could not be used to enrich individuals who had domestic labour to sell. Some of the control over domestic service was removed from the employers, but rather than awarding the workers more control over their labour, the commission invested its own representatives with this power.

Explicit in the commissioners' handling of the Canberra domestic-servant issue was a paternalist understanding of the relationships between themselves and the women they wished to settle. This understanding left no room for the kind of recasting of the identity of the single female immigrant that had been so essential to the work of female immigration promoters. Unlike the Home Help projects discussed in chapter 3, the Canberra domestic-servant project did not aim to provide single women with more power or autonomy. The commissioners' aim was to introduce an updated version of the traditional sexual divisions of labour and status in Australia's new capital city.

John Butters encountered no difficulty in having the whole of his plan approved by the federal government. However, G.F. Pearce did inform him that the recruitment of immigrants would have to be organized through established government channels.[27] It is not quite clear what this meant as the commission certainly managed to avoid the usual unwieldy and uncertain process of requisitioning domestics through the federal immigration department.[28] The Australian matron that Butters chose for the task of selecting and chaperoning the British emigrants was associated with Australia House, and she used their facilities while recruiting and interviewing prospective emigrants. Perhaps this was all that the immigration department required of the commission at that point.

The job of selecting domestic helpers of a 'superior type' for Australia's capital city was given to Miss Hawkins, a well-respected Australian woman familiar with Canberra's conditions who, conveniently, was in England at the time.[29] Her work in England and Scotland on behalf of the commission was initially hampered by problems of divided authority and communication among different sections of the Australian government. Particularly difficult was the initial refusal of the representatives of the Australian immigration department based in London to recognize Hawkins's full authority. Yet the lack of help from Australia House in London was more than made up for by the help she received from other women working within the extensive network of emigration promoters in Britain. Of particular significance was the fact that women within the SOSBW believed that the Canberra domestic-servant project was worthy of support. The SOSBW advertised the project in the *Imperial Colonist*, and acted as liaison between prospective emigrants and Hawkins.[30]

References to the Canberra domestic-servant project in the *Imperial Colonist* reveal that the SOSBW promoted Canberra in much the same way that other favoured destinations (usually outside of Australia) had been promoted previously. Delighted that, for a change, the Australian government was committed to establishing an appropriate reception program in Canberra, the emigrators emphasized this aspect in their promotion of the city. The *Imperial Colonist*'s readers were told of the area's physical beauty and of Canberra's beneficial climate. Prospective emigrants were informed that the scarcity of women at Canberra would result in a more privileged status for those women who chose to settle there. In their promotion of Canberra as a worthy colonial destination for single female emigrants, the editor of, and contributors to, the *Imperial Colonist* constructed predictable images of Australians and their new capital city. Canberra was presented in terms of its place within the British Empire. The journal's readers were encouraged to think of Canberra as both exotic and comfortably familiar. In a paper written by Lord Burnham, who had recently visited Australia, the *Imperial Colonist*'s audience was informed that among the advantages that an Australian destination had to offer English emigrants was the fact that Australians were, 'in manners and deportment – British to the core.' He wrote that the country's people are, 'to our everlasting pride ... an unbroken totality of British origin and British nationhood.'[31] In another article, the editor of the *Imperial Colonist* informed her readers that 'young women will be well advised to take advantage of this opportunity ... to join with those who are to lay the foundations of life in the future London of Australia.'[32] Australians' loyalties to their motherland were emphasized, and their efforts to construct a world-class national capital city were read as endearing attempts to emulate Britain's more mature society. The female imperialist agenda found voice in the *Imperial Colonist*'s promotion of female emigration to Canberra. Young women were urged to aid Australians in their quest for a higher level of culture by offering up themselves as agents of civilization. They were led to believe that as female natives of Britain, their emigration to Canberra could be of inestimable service to the formation of that city's identity.[33]

It is unclear whether prospective emigrants were attracted by these arguments or whether other inducements were involved for those who decided to make Canberra their destination. Whatever the case, the efforts of Dorothy Hawkins and her British associates to promote Canberra as an ideal destination for female emigrants were remarkably successful. At a time when British homeowners were complaining bitterly about the scarcity of trained domestic help, and when the Australian immigration authorities were incapable of encouraging more than half the desired number of female servants to come to Australia, Hawkins was able to select her quota of servants from a large number of applicants.[34] More impressive still, almost all the women Hawkins selected had actually worked as domestic servants in the past.[35] In November 1926 Hawkins informed the eagerly awaiting commissioners that she had only to receive passage money, medical certificates, and validations of references for each woman before she could provide them with a definite list of the names, credentials, and specific occupations of the chosen emigrants. She anticipated that such a list ought to be ready for the commission within a fortnight, and that the party would be ready to sail for Australia in mid-December.[36]

In Canberra, plans for the reception of the women were also falling into place. Since construction of the hostel would not be started until well into the following year, plans were made for the accommodation of the newcomers in a section of a government hotel that had been specially converted for the purpose. As news of the impending arrival of the domestic servants began to spread through the small circle of already established Canberra residents, the commissioners began to receive requests for servants. One eager prospective employer got into the reform-minded spirit of the affair, noting that what she really required was a 'sort of superior maid of all work,' but that she would be willing to refer to the maid as a 'working housekeeper' if the administrators felt this term would be preferred.[37] The commissioners informed individuals who had registered requests for the immigrant servants that it 'had not intended to allot the whole of these domestics in the first instance to the general public – the object was to obtain such help to be available for Civil Servants who might be transferred.'[38] However, most of these early requests were sent to the members of the commission by their own friends and acquaintances looking for favours. It appears that no such requests were ultimately rejected.[39]

On 7 February 1927 the long-awaited domestic servants arrived in Canberra, having departed England on the SS *Vedic* on 17 December 1926. Their passage had taken them to Melbourne, then on to Sydney, where they boarded a train for Canberra. Along the way they were treated to teas hosted by women involved in the Melbourne and Sydney branches of the New Settlers' League.[40] In all there were twenty-two women in the group, although one, a Miss McDade, was found to be missing on the morning of 11 February. To the disgust of the commissioners, she had been lured back to the 'glamour of Sydney.'[41] The women who arrived in Canberra as planned were quickly assigned to employers.

Officially, the commissioners were pleased with the early results of their project. The immediate domestic-servant crisis had been resolved, and upon questioning, the servants and employers alike had indicated that they were content with their situations.[42] However, in spite of the fact that the domestic servants and their employers quietly settled into their new routines and relationships, the arrival of these women quickly became the focus of a heated public debate. The immigrant domestics had been anticipated with great excitement by members of the Canberra community. In a long article on their arrival the editor of the *Canberra Times* spoke for many of the city's residents when he applauded the commission's intelligent response to the domestic-servant problem.[43] But the glowing review that the *Canberra Times* gave the domestic-servant project contrasted sharply with reviews that the project received from other quarters. Although there were other newspaper reports that presented the perspective of the commissioners,[44] the scheme as a whole received a significant amount of negative press from observers located elsewhere in Australia.

An analysis of this debate reveals some of the opposing views that Australians held concerning the ideal nature of the nation's capital. Negative commentary about the Canberra domestic-servant project did not focus on the more unusual aspects of the commission's plan. Nor did critics seem to have a problem with the fact that the government had involved itself in 'domestic' affairs. Rather, critics bitterly attacked the commission for its importation of foreigners to do jobs that might otherwise have been taken up by Australians. Although all parties agreed that Canberra should be a symbol of Australia's coming of age, they did not agree about what that might imply for the relationship between the capital and Australia's British heritage. Whereas Butters and the other commissioners assumed the superiority of British domestic servants to be self-evident, critics of the project insisted that these immigrants should be seen as foreigners, and thus as potentially inferior and certainly undesirable for Australia's capital city.

The 'nativist' attack upon the work of the commission came not only from several unhappy journalists, but also from politicians and from within other branches of the Australian federal government. In the most virulent denunciation of the commission's scheme, a journalist writing for the *Age* questioned the necessity of importing servants from elsewhere. He reported that the officials at the State Labour Bureau in Sydney felt that in the past they had adequately responded to requests for domestic workers in Canberra. He interviewed two members of parliament about their thoughts on the issue (both appear to have been ignorant of the scheme), and was delighted to record their responses. Mr Charlton, leader of the Federal Labour Party, indicated that if the servants had been imported to Canberra 'without it having been previously ascertained that no Australian girls were available, then an injustice had been done to the latter.' The second MP interviewed was much less careful in his response:

> Mr. Coleman ... said that he was not surprised at the girls being brought out, as it was in keeping with the policy adopted of using imported rubber flooring for Parliament House at Canberra, when Australian firms had tendered, and when many business houses had found Australian rubber flooring entirely suitable. Mr. Coleman went on to say that imported goods had been installed in the kitchen at Parliament House, and in the lifts.[45]

In the opinion of this MP and the journalist who recorded his views, the state-organized and funded installation of further 'imported goods' in the homes and hotels of the nation's capital was a serious offence indeed. The MP claimed to speak for many in his assertion that only Australian materials should be used in the creation of Australia's capital city.[46]

In her discussion of 'How Men Gave Birth to the Australian Nation,' Marilyn Lake writes that 'colonial men in white settler societies everywhere sought to assuage their resentment at imperial subordination by insisting on their status as "white men."[47] 'As colonizers and colonized both,' Australians of British heritage implemented policies that were designed to exclude or subjugate Asians and Aboriginals. Lake provides an example: 'Furniture manufacturers ... asked prospective consumers to choose the product made by "skilled white labour": "It is not a question of policy merely, but of a deep-rooted principle, one upon which the very foundation of our nationality rests."'[48] As the above example of reactions against the Canberra domestic-servant project indicates, similar arguments were being used against imported British labour by the late 1920s. Considering the cultural status assigned to British female emigrants by Britons and Australian anglophiles (like Butters), the opinions communicated in these attacks would have been considered antagonistic in the extreme.

The fuss that was raised around the arrival of the British women forced Canberra's top officials to marshal evidence in their defence. In a memorandum created at Butters's request, the Superintendent of the Commissariat Department wrote that a large proportion of the servants currently employed at the city's government-run hotels (servants who had *not* been a part of the Canberra domestic servant project) were evidently immigrants. He confirmed that, indeed, these immigrant servants had been hired by the methods recommended by the commission's critics. As to the relative 'quality and merit' of British and Australian servants, he indicated that in his opinion there was no difference. 'Unfortunately,' he wrote, 'our experience is that in busy seasons, there is not enough of either offering.' He recalled that in a recent busy period, when female servants could not be attained through any source, the shortage of servants had become so critical that the hotel management had been forced to resort to 'male labour'![49]

In a letter to the Secretary of the Department of Home and Territories, C.S. Daley of the Federal Capital Commission used the information concerning previous labour shortages to undermine newspaper representations of the commissioners as unpatriotic in their attempts to people Canberra with British women. He asserted that the published criticisms of the project were likely 'due to a want of appreciation of the conditions that exist in Canberra.' The insinuation by certain members of the press that the commission should have made use of the State Labour Bureau based in Sydney to supply Canberra with Australian servants merely indicated ignorance of the matter. According to Daley, 'the Commission has regularly obtained labor from the NSW State Labour Bureau, and the majority of those sent have been immigrants.' Furthermore, upon application to the bureau for more servants before the Christmas holidays, the commission was informed that 'no further girls could be sent until a certain immigration ship arrived.'[50] The commissioners were no less patriotic than any other Australian who desired to find a decent employee to do domestic work. In a small-town context like Canberra, Daley argued, domestic servants were, by necessity, immigrants.

As angry as the members of the commission were with the representations that journalists made of their work, even stronger feelings were evoked when they discovered that their efforts were being slandered by officers of the Ministry for Labour and Industry. According to Butters, these officers had informed news reporters that the importation of servants was not only unnecessary but also responsible for introducing substandard workers to Canberra. One newspaper article stated that the Department of Labour and Industry had been informed that 'some of the [British] girls [had] been found unsuitable for the work and their places [had] been filled by Australian girls from Sydney.'[51] Butters complained that '[the] difficulties of securing suitable labour at Canberra for domestic and hotel work are sufficient without it being aggravated by misstatements of this character by officers of the Department of Labour and Industry.' He closed his letter to the minister for that department with the hope that the trouble-making officers would be suitably reprimanded.[52]

The criticism that Butters and his commission received for their work on behalf of the servant-hiring population of Canberra was only one part of a larger, more broad-based negative response to the commission itself. By late 1927, people in the Canberra community who had no formal access to political or bureaucratic power had lost patience with the commission's heavy-handed authority and system of patronage. They had also come to understand that whenever a situation arose in which the interests of Canberra as a community were pitted against those of Canberra as the national capital, the Federal Capital Commission would find in favour of the capital. As Freeman Wyllie has noted, new and old residents of Canberra were brought together 'in opposition to an administration that had succeeded in building a city, but which had failed to meet the needs of the community that lived there.'[53] If the domestic-servant project is a reliable indicator, this reputation was gained in spite of the commissioners' efforts to the contrary. They saw the establishment of a contented community in Canberra as essential to the foundation of a capital city of which Australians could be proud.

If Canberra's citizens held the commission responsible for the problems of their community, outside the city the commission came under attack for the extent to which Canberra was privileged above all other Australian cities. Critics based in other states represented the commissioners as the official 'spenders' for an over-financed capital city. Certainly the commissioners' efforts on behalf of Canberra's servant-hiring population would have done nothing to undermine this perspective. Long-term inter-state and state-federal rivalries determined that the actions of the Federal Capital Commission would be jealously reviewed. Politicians and journalists elsewhere in Australia (especially in Sydney) were quick to point out instances of extravagance and unfair advantage for Canberra, and the very nature of the Federal Capital Commission decided that it would become a symbol of the abuse of government power.[54] As a result, some of the authority that the commission had been given in its early career was stripped away by higher government officials. Thus, when the members of the commission tried again to import domestic servants for the use of Canberra residents later in 1927, they were informed by the Development and Migration Commission that they no longer had that authority. Rather, they would have to requisition the domestic servants through the federal bureaucracy in the same manner as all other states. Furthermore, they were informed that in light of the fact that only half of the states' requisitions for domestic-servant immigrants tended to be filled, the commission should not expect to have all of their requirements met.[55]

The members of the Federal Capital Commission refused to accept their loss of power. Eight months later, the commission tried once again to exercise its authority when Lady Butters and Mrs Potts (the wife of Canberra's chief engineer) decided that they required several English servants.[56] The request that Lady Butters's requisition be 'expedited' was firmly rebuffed by higher authorities. The secretary for the commission was informed that the matter had been discussed with the manager of the State Labour Exchange, who suggested that 'in the first place Sir John Butters and Mrs. Potts be advised to apply to him for suitable help.'[57] The commissioners appear to have made no further attempts to use their own means to obtain immigrant domestics.

The Federal Capital Commission, which was only supposed to exist for five years anyway, began to fall apart at about this time. With the onset of the Depression, the commission's budget was reduced, while the commissioners were expected to deal with an ever-increasing number of Canberra's problems. In October 1929 Butters and his family left

Canberra, exasperated and feeling ill-used. With Butters's departure from Canberra, the force behind the state-directed servant project disappeared.

Australia's capital city was designed to be the home of the country's leading politicians and bureaucrats, and the site for interaction with visiting foreign dignitaries. Its creators were conscious that, as Australia's political meeting place, Canberra would be constantly in the public eye. Canberra was unlike other 'instant' towns in that it was designed to be a political showpiece. Because it was built from scratch, the city offered the people who worked on its development a rare opportunity: they were not hampered by any pre-existing (European) physical or social environment. The capital city's architects were charged with the responsibility of creating a city of which Australians could be proud. Its planners had great ambitions for Canberra. They were determined that it would be a world-class 'Garden City' – an ideal urban environment.

Influential members of the male community of capital-city designers recognized that, although this city would be a quintessentially public place, the existence of a healthy, supportive domestic sphere would be essential to its social and bureaucratic effectiveness. Not only was the domestic sphere the site at which the men of the city would be daily regenerated into productive state employees, it was also the context in which important political socializing would be carried out. The commissioners' recognition of the significance of domestic work to the smooth running of the capital city resulted in an attempt to ensure that the appropriate quantity and quality of female labour was available in Canberra. Because of their belief in its importance, the commissioners were unwilling to leave control of domestic labour to women alone. They attempted to ensure that Canberra's homes would be properly run by taking upon themselves the job of supplying suitable household workers and overseeing domestic labour relations. The project that resulted was both consistent with the Australian government's increased responsibility for emigrant care during this period, and inconsistent with the general lack of enthusiasm with which immigration projects were actually embraced by government bodies in Australia. The commissioners tried hard to make domestic service in Canberra a more desirable occupation without investing it with any more power. Likewise, they attempted to make Canberra employers more satisfied with the quality of the service they received from domestics without allowing them the traditional rights of control over the employer's side of the contract.

In the case of the domestic-servant project, the fact that representatives of the state took control of matters usually considered better left to women's voluntary societies seems to have caused no trouble. Rather, it was the fact that the servants were immigrants that caused a stir. Whereas the commissioners had assumed that the value of British domestics to the capital city would be self-evident – that it would be understood that their 'Britishness' could only add positively to Canberra's cultured image – other Australians asserted that the imported domestics should be seen only as foreigners, and that their importation represented a lack of appropriate nationalist sentiment in Canberra's administrators. Suspicious of these government officials' politics, observers worried that Australians were being passed over in favour of British immigrants in the commission's search for servants of a 'superior type.' The determination of the wives of key members of the commission to secure for themselves English domestic servants added validity to the concerns of those critical of the commissioners.

The Canberra domestic-servant project was unprecedented in the extent to which a federal government involved itself in trying to solve a local-level domestic-servant problem. For close to a century, Australian governments had disregarded the requests of philanthropists and reformers that the state take on some of the responsibility for the immigration and aftercare of female domestic servants along the lines set out by the Federal Capital Commission. As a rule, federal and state governments preferred to leave this sort of work to private organizations, even if that meant providing them with some government funding. The Canberra domestic-servant project was the exception to this rule for several reasons: the symbolic and political importance of Australia's capital city determined that Canberra's various crises would receive more notice than would those of other Australian cities; its emergence as an 'instant' city meant that there was no local pool of labour for its servant-hiring population (whatever labour was available in the closest neighbouring towns was considered either inadequate or inappropriate by the commission); and because Australia's capital city was given its own Territory, there were none of the usual state-federal jurisdiction problems that plagued other attempts to create comprehensive immigration projects. When the commissioners decided that the provision of qualified domestic labourers was essential to the establishment of a showpiece capital city, domesticating the capital's homes became a government priority.

The Federal Capital Commission's domestic-servant project was designed to solve the problem of Canberra's chronic shortage of servants. Drawing upon an understanding of colonial domestic-servant shortages that originated with British female emigration promoters, Butters and his co-commissioners looked to British immigration to answer the capital city's needs. They had intended that British domestic servants would arrive in Canberra in periodic waves according to demand. As it turned out, the women who arrived in February of 1927 were the first and last such group. In reality, the commission's project did little more than meet the short-term needs of those prospective employers who were in Canberra before the mass migration of public servants was undertaken. In spite of early signs of success in terms of access to funding and recruits, the project suffered an early demise. It never came close to matching its designers' ambitions.

In its construction and in its premature end, the Canberra domestic-servant project provides a wealth of interesting material for analysis relating to contests about Australia's national identity and the use that was made of women and their domestic labour in these contests. This case study highlights ways in which Canberra's emergent identity was fought over in terms that relied upon gendered and classed images of culture and civilization. At the same time, as with most of the work performed by the female emigrators discussed earlier in this book, the fact of Aboriginal people's presence in and around Canberra's development was studiously ignored. The contest here was clearly between opposing white parties; cultural imperialism was depicted in these documents in terms of British impositions on white Australians. The region's Aboriginal population was literally written out of the larger socio-political picture.

In his introduction to *Inventing Australia: Images and Identity, 1688–1980*, Richard White reminds us that '[when] we look at ideas about national identity, we need to ask, not whether they are true or false, but what their function is, whose creation they are, and whose interests they serve.'[58] In the various representations of immigrant domestic workers and their place in the building of the nation's capital, women's rights, duties, and natures were publicly explored and debated in order to support opposing visions of the Australian nation and its capital city. In the representations of the servant problem in Canberra that appeared in the *Imperial Colonist*, single British women emigrated to destinations within the dominions with a mandate to shore up overburdened settled women, while positively influencing the level of civilization of their new communities. The implications of these representations have been explored in earlier chapters of this book. Within the Australian context, aspects of the female imperialists' perspective were taken up and promoted by the members of the Federal Capital Commission, who drew upon the SOSBW for inspiration, guidance, and support. Likewise, the arguments used by female emigration promoters to support their work were adopted by these men as they tried to convince other government officials, members of the public, and the press that the project was necessary for Canberra's successful evolution into a respectable, highly civilized community. In all these respects, the decades of careful work of women in Britain and the dominions had clearly paid off. Men charged with creating a showpiece capital city had been convinced that British females could solve their domestic labour problems, and their template for how these women's migration should occur was adopted as a matter of course. But the shift from women's voluntary efforts to state-directed management of these matters effectively undermined the female-centred system that had been put in place by previous generations of female emigrators.

Images of good, hardworking Australian housewives and mothers, overwhelmed by their domestic responsibilities because no 'help' was available, were highlighted in the arguments put forward by Butters and his co-commissioners. As the people who would transform the 'Bush Capital' into the nation's parliamentary 'home,' this class of women was deserving of special efforts to facilitate their work. After his early references to the need for a 'superior type' of domestic for Canberra, Butters stopped suggesting that British women were particularly appropriate for the nation's capital city. But the assumption that British women represented quality continued to hang over the Canberra domestic-servant project in spite of the commissioners' careful silence on the subject. As criticisms of the project mounted, the commissioners placed more and more emphasis upon their assertion that Australian women would have been hired if only they had been available; that it was the absence of Australians that led the commissioners to look to immigrants to fill the gap.[59]

In the commissioners' justifications of their domestic-servant project, the needs of respectable Australian housewives were foregrounded, while the British immigrants were presented as invaluable assets to the community. The critics of the Canberra project painted a completely different picture of the women involved in this dispute. In their discussions about domestic labour in Canberra, oppositional politicians, government workers, and journalists foregrounded the disservice done to Australian 'girls' by the importation of 'foreign' labour. In the critics' renditions of this story, not only were Australian women denied their right to the jobs being offered in the new city, but they were also denied the opportunity to help create the capital city's identity. In a telling statement, an article in the *Argus* noted that 'alarm and indignation' had been raised by 'the importation of 24 domestics to wait upon the Duke and Duchess at Canberra.'[60] The article referred to critics who worried that Canberra's most influential visiting dignitaries would not get a chance to witness Australian women's domestic skills because British women had taken their place. In the important political context of Australia's capital city, Australia ought to be represented by Australians.

The arguments between the Federal Capital Commission and its critics about Canberra's domestic labour needs rested upon opposing views about which Australian women's interests ought to take precedence – those of employers or those of labourers – and upon differing understandings of the place of British immigrant women in Australia. These differences were underscored by alternative visions of the nation and its place within the British Empire, which in turn reflected the changing history of managed British female migration. In neither case was there any question about the fact that Australia ought to be a 'white' nation. The struggle revolved around what sort of a white nation it would be. Whereas the commissioners embraced an Australian national identity that drew heavily upon British traditions, manners, and associations, the more nativist perspective of the domestic-servant project's critics highlighted Australia's need for independence from British influence. Historians who have explored the evolution of Australia's national identity have shown how Australians have struggled over the relationship between Australian nationhood and the country's imperial connections.[61] In the early decades of the twentieth century, male promoters of both types of white Australian identity coexisted, sharing power, authority, and the rights to official representations of the nation. By the end of the Second World War, an Australian identity that had largely broken free from its British ties had gained ascendancy. In the arguments between members of the commission and their critics over the importation of British domestic servants may be seen one example of this contest being worked out.

In the tradition of Australian nativist nationalism, the ruling English elite and their culture were treated as suspiciously effeminate.[62] As a group of men who embraced British ties and British culture, the commissioners' masculinity would likely have been considered suspect by their critics. Yet the Canberra commissioners and their opponents had in common their determination to keep control of the city and its identity in the hands of men. Their ideas about what the nation was, and what it ought to be, might have differed. But in neither case were the opinions of women who were central to this situation sought or recorded. Both groups of men publicly championed the rights of specific women, and valorized women's work. But although the women they fought for were the central actors in the various scenarios created around the Canberra domestic-servant project – as migrants, as domestics, as employers, as disappointed, unemployed women – their perspectives on the commission's activities were given no voice.

Conclusion

Over the course of the second half of the nineteenth century, Britons embraced the empire and imperialism with increasing enthusiasm. At the turn of the century, propaganda associated with the Anglo-Boer War was added to the already substantial body of pro-empire cultural production to whip up a frenzy of imperial celebration. The British Empire was central to Britons', and especially English people's, understandings of themselves and their place within the larger world. Yet the changes that occurred within the British Empire over the late nineteenth and early twentieth centuries were deeply troubling for fervent imperialists. Between the mid-1800s and the onset of the Great Depression of the 1930s, Britons witnessed the transition of most of the British Empire's white settler societies, as well as most of Ireland, to independent nations. Canada, New Zealand, Australia, and South Africa evolved from communities that could still legitimately be referred to as colonies in that they relied upon Britain for funding, defence, and political guidance, to political entities that celebrated, as central to their new identities, their independence from British control. During this period, colonized peoples throughout the empire rebelled, physically and intellectually, against imperial domination, undermining the confidence of liberal imperialists in various aspects of the imperial project. And, in the face of economic competition from other nations (especially the United States of America and Germany), Britons could no longer boast of their world-leader status – a fact that was clearly highlighted by the international stockpiling of arms and by England's participation in the scramble for Africa at the turn of the century.

The disparity between British imperialists' enthusiasm for, and confidence in, the empire, on the one hand, and the reality of Britain's not-so-slow decline as an imperial force, on the other, produced both anxiety and an outpouring of intense creativity. The emigrators studied here exhibited both of these responses to the problem of Britain's imperial situation. As British women who were interested in the overseas development of the British Empire, and as Canadian and Australian women (often self-proclaimed anglophiles) who desired to see their nations firmly embedded within the British Empire, the emigrators sought to create their versions of the ideal empire through carefully managed British female migration. By inserting large numbers of appropriately acculturated women into colonial spaces, the emigrators imagined that they were ensuring the growth of the 'right' sort of socio-political attitudes within colonial populations. In the words of Mrs Chapin (a regular contributor to the *Imperial Colonist*), 'the ideal that lies at the back of emigration – or the motive for emigration – determines the character of the nation which emigration creates.'[1] In other words, if imperially minded female emigrators could alter the course of Canadian and Australian immigration to conform more closely to their own understandings of these destinations' needs, they would be fundamentally altering both the natures of those societies and the health of the British Empire for the foreseeable future.

In the years around the turn of the twentieth century, the international network of imperial female emigrators was at the height of its influence and power. Confident of their own strategic importance within Britain's imperial system, the emigrators published article after article about the success of their colonizing work. The idea of empire projected by female emigration promoters was reflected in a paper presented by Mrs Chapin at a Girls' Friendly Society conference in 1906 that was subsequently published in the Society's *Associates' Journal* and in the *Imperial Colonist*, along with a glowing introduction by the *Imperial Colonist*'s editor, Lady Knightley of Fawsley. In this paper Chapin argued that the imperialist impulse dominating Britain's relations with its colonies at the turn of the century was one of 'imperious maternity.' She noted that Britain's imperialism had evolved from a paternalistic (domineering) style of governance, through fraternal governance (which had not worked very well, as was evidenced by the secession of the American colonies from the empire), to a form of governance inspired by maternalism. 'A mother serves what she creates, and this England is trying to do,' she wrote.[2] '[England] has helped Australia to find herself, and Australia answers, in the words of Kipling[:] "the crown of our crowning is that we lay our crown at your feet!"' Likewise, England was 'helping

Canada to find herself,' and in so doing was 'binding her to England by unbreakable bonds – bonds of voluntary allegiance and love.'[3] As the creators and disseminators of an imperial ideology that emphasized cultural imperialism rather than raw force, and as the women who would manage the implementation of that cultural imperialism, the members of female emigration societies imagined themselves as key players within the new imperial order.

The female imperialists also envisioned a role of critical importance for emigrant women. After all, it would be these emigrants who would put cultural imperialism into practice. In spite of the absence of overt discussions of race in the emigrators' work, it is clear that their visions of a transformed, feminized empire were informed by a well-defined sense of gendered class and race relations. The British emigrators' assumptions regarding the significance of the emigrants' feminine Britishness (or preferably, in most cases, Englishness) in raising the colonies' levels of civilization were central to their work and to their writing. The cultural superiority of British women over all other groups was asserted forcefully and persistently. Chapin was typical of female emigrators in her assertion that British female emigrants were a key factor in this new, more effective form of imperialism. It was their role to 'be the bearers of the torch that kindles and lightens.'[4] As the *Imperial Colonist*'s editor noted in her endorsement of Chapin's article, the central argument of this piece was that 'They who serve truly reign' – clearly, a message designed to catch the attention of the hundreds of single women who would become domestic servants upon their arrival overseas.

The British emigrators used the fact that people around the world came to the defence of Britain in the First World War as evidence that their version of empire-building work was paying off. In an article published in 1916 on the sacrifices made by expatriate men and women in South America for the sake of Britain, an emigrator noted that attachments to Britain were 'deep-rooted and sincere,' and that they had been shown, 'not only by the men sacrificing lucrative positions to volunteer to fight under the old flag, but by generous gifts in money and kind sent for Red Cross work among our brave soldiers and sailors.' The reason for this continued attachment to the motherland, even outside the official bounds of the British Empire, was clear: 'This spirit, deep-rooted as it is, would perhaps die out were it not that wherever there is a community of British residents they are kept in touch with British ideals by the bonds of intercourse established by many great organizations in England that have branches and representatives in all parts of the world.'[5] In the opinion of the emigrators, the British Women's Emigration Association and the South African Colonisation Society were foremost among such organizations.

The emigrators' ability to publish for a full quarter of a century a substantial monthly journal, the *Imperial Colonist*, entirely dedicated to reviewing the intersections of British empire building and female migration highlights the enthusiasm that the emigrators' project generated. The demise of this journal in 1927 marks the end of an era of British women's efforts to control female emigration in the name of the empire. In her history of the *Imperial Colonist*, Lady Cecil chose to read the end of the journal positively: '[This journal] has fulfilled its purpose. For a quarter of a century the little magazine has met a need, and the very fact that it is no longer wanted is a proof that its work is accomplished.'[6] The 'whole programme' promoted in the *Imperial Colonist* 'has been carried out, and although much remains to be done before the system is complete, the broad principles of selection, protection and aftercare which were then the monopoly of a few Societies, are now accepted by the Government and those responsible for migration.' According to Cecil, the necessity of the improvements that had been made to the management of single female migration had been 'constantly urged upon the Government and private bodies' during the journal's existence.[7] 'It is with great satisfaction,' Cecil wrote, 'that those of us who started the *Imperial Colonist*, who are still giving time and energy to this absorbing problem of migration, are handing on the task of publication to the Government.'[8]

The female imperialists' sense of confidence at the beginning of the twentieth century was born of their managerial and ideological successes. But their organizations' position of strength could not long survive the First World War. As a result of the sweeping social and political changes brought on by the war, the female emigrators' relationships with emigrants and with the state were transformed. The British public had come to assume that emigration would now be managed by the state.[9] The emigrators could no longer base their claims for public support on the assumption that governments could not or would not manage imperial migration efficiently. The transformed culture of femininity and gender relations in the post-war period also undermined the emigrators' efforts to assert the need for single women's protection and care by older, more experienced women. Moreover, by the 1920s British imperialism had lost its mass appeal. The argument that the interests of the colonies ought to be prioritized over those of Britain – an argument that the emigrators had often used to support their own agendas in the nineteenth century – had evolved logically into support for assertions that Canadians and Australians ought to have control over their own immigration matters. Canadian and Australian women, working under the direction of state bureaucrats, supplanted British emigrators in the management of female migration.

Lady Cecil's reflections upon the closure of the *Imperial Colonist* also underscore the central instability of the ideology painstakingly constructed by female emigrators around imperial female migration in the late nineteenth and early twentieth centuries. The radical potential embodied in the female imperialist project was always vulnerable to the contradictions inherent in the emigrators' work, and to the more mainstream power of male visions of migration and empire. Educated female emigrants were sent out to civilize the empire. But they were also encouraged to exploit the potential for upward mobility and occupational diversity that awaited cultured women who persevered in the new frontier. The emancipatory end of the spectrum of ideas developed in the female imperialist project fits well with the sense of empowerment that the middle class promoters themselves had experienced through their successes in organizing single female migration. The positive spin that Cecil put on the loss of the *Imperial Colonist* ignored some key aspects of the female imperialists' 'whole programme.' Under government direction, single female emigrants would continue to be treated as a special class of emigrant, in need of special care, and women would continue to provide this care as officially recognized agents and aids of the state. But there was little space in the post-war era for empowered female imperialists and their message that emigrant women – as individuals, not just as labourers and as prospective mothers – had special roles to play as the embodiment of empire in the formation and evolution of colonial societies.

In a recent historiographical review of women migrants as global and local agents, Christiane Harzig emphasizes that migration is 'a gendered process ... which reflects the different positions of women and men in society.'[10] As the case of the international migration of single British women during the late nineteenth and early twentieth centuries clearly demonstrates, interpreting migration's reflections offers significant challenges. British women's migration was an international process whereby labourers migrated from areas where their skills and abilities were undervalued (in one way or another) to locations where they thought their labour would be better rewarded. Certainly, for the single female migrant, economic opportunity was usually a key motivating factor behind her decision to move overseas. Likewise, for the Canadian and Australian governments that promoted and financially supported single female immigration, the immigrant's ability to gain paid labour was mainly what counted. But British female migrants signified much more than merely one particular category of migrating workers. The highly gendered nature of the work they were largely limited to performing, the specialized treatment that they received while in transit, the cultural status that both 'labelled' and empowered them – all these aspects of British female migration served to nuance and complicate their identities as migrant labourers. When the political climate within which these women were migrating is added to the mix, the single British female migrant becomes a fascinating object of historical analysis.

In *Civilising Subjects: Metropole and Colony in the English Imagination, 1830–1867*, Catherine Hall notes: 'Marking differences was a way of classifying, of categorising, of making hierarchies, of constructing boundaries for the body politic and the body social. Processes of differen-tiation, positioning men and women, colonisers and colonised, as if these divisions were natural, were constantly in the making, in conflicts of power.'[11] Although Hall's book explores the cultural underpinnings of England's domination of Jamaica, her observations are also useful for an analysis of relations between British imperialists and white colonial societies. In the work of the female emigrators, differences were marked between Britons and colonials; between English, Scots, and Irish; between men and women; between people of different classes; and between Britons and various categories of 'foreigners.' The process of marking and articulating these differences was key to female emigrators' quests for power in the field of empire emigration, and it was fundamental to their developing visions of the relationships among women, colonial societies, and empire.

The emigrators' work was not without its contradictions. Most striking, perhaps, is the discrepancy between the two identities that the emigrators constructed for the female emigrant. Safe-passage narratives were about protecting single women who were already emigrating in large numbers. These were women of the working class. Yet most of the emigrators' promotional writing aimed to motivate the emigration of women of a higher class. 'Educated' women were not easily convinced of the virtues of emigration, nor were they eagerly sought by the colonies. In order to marry their own visions of a feminized empire with the practical difficulties involved in stimulating the right sort of female emigration, the women who ran the British female emigration societies created a body of literature that contained a range of seemingly contradictory messages. Through their daily work with emigrants, and through their correspondence with others involved in managing female migration, the emigrators attempted to smooth over these contradictions as far as possible.

The female imperialists' sense of confidence at the beginning of the twentieth century was born of their managerial successes and the effectiveness of their propaganda. They manoeuvred themselves into positions of power through their effective exploitation of three areas of concern about female migration. First, in Britain and in the colonies in the nineteenth century, members of the public believed that migration required better management. Government bodies were often unwilling or poorly equipped to manage the basic aspects of mass migration, let alone the finer details of properly orchestrated female migration. Female emigration societies established a clear agenda to create a well-oiled, efficient system of imperial migration, and they were untiring in publicizing their own abilities to transform migration chaos into order. Second, the emigrators exploited contemporary moral panics about women's sexual vulnerability. The general perception that railways and ocean travel were particularly problematic for women's physical and social safety became the basis for the emigrators' campaign for their own empowerment as protectors of female virtue. Third, these middle- and upper-class women made strategic use of the late-nineteenth-century passion for imperialism. They adopted and nurtured arguments about how the emigration of single women would be of benefit to both Britain and the colonies. These three areas of public concern became points of entry through which emigration promoters gradually constructed a sophisticated and compelling vision of female migration.

The emigrators who worked with single women were not a completely homogenous group of British imperialists. A range of motivations impelled them to do this work, and they were able to tap into a range of social and political associations to forward their projects. Some of the emigrators were permanently based in British locales, while others were Canadian or Australian citizens. Depending upon their location, these emigrators experienced completely different contexts within which they endeavoured to perform their emigration work. As Michele Langfield has noted, 'Australian officials hoped that financial support and rigorous selection would lead to both increased immigration and a better class of immigrant; Canada, however, viewed the assisted immigrant as lacking in independence and initiative.' On the other hand, 'In the early twentieth century, Canada was more sympathetic than Australia to the work of non-government organizations since they performed a role, especially in reception and aftercare, which would otherwise fall to a reluctant government.' Yet in the period after the First World War, 'Australians were much more enthusiastic about the Empire Settlement Act' than were Canadians.[12] As this book has shown, the respect that these female emigrators received from members of the public and from government officials also differed according to locale and historical juncture.

At the beginning of the period covered in this study, the women who promoted and facilitated the emigration of single women were based overwhelmingly in Britain. But by the end of the nineteenth century, women throughout the colonies had committed themselves to this work. Tensions between women who worked together to promote the emigration of British women were manifestly evident where the emigrators were of different nationalities. But although they differed in many respects, the attitudes and sympathies of imperially minded women in Canada and Australia were closer to those of British female imperialists than to those of colonial government officials. As female philanthropists and social reformers, these women were more appreciative of British women's concerns about female emigrants' welfare than were male government officials, who tended to become concerned about such issues only when they threatened to become the focus of a public scandal.

In a recent article that reviews the history of female migration, James Hammerton emphasizes that the simple dichotomy between emigrators who were feminist reformers in the 1860s and 1870s and the next generation of emigrators, who were philanthropists motivated by more conservative, anti-feminist agendas,[13] has been complicated by revisionist readings of the gender politics of the late nineteenth and early twentieth centuries.[14] The activities of Victorian and Edwardian women that had been labelled 'conservative' by historians because they promoted women's traditional rights, social purity, and British imperialism have been reassessed, resulting in much broader understandings of the potentially radical nature of women's work for women.[15] The automatic association of pro-suffrage activity with feminism that used to serve as a useful political guide has been effectively undermined in recent scholarship, although there is no agreement among historians of women as to how early feminism ought to be defined. As Julia Bush has noted, 'The formation of women's imperialist associations was not designed deliberately to challenge existing gender divisions, whether in Britain or in the

Empire.'[16] As this book has shown, the emigrators' agenda of feminizing the empire had the potential for incorporating more liberating possibilities than those intended by the majority of female emigration society members. Although most of the female-emigration work of the late nineteenth and early twentieth centuries was designed to maintain the status quo in terms of gender relations, it is inappropriate to dismiss the emigrators' work as simply conservative and unabatedly oppressive.

As historians of other women's voluntary efforts have found, the transition to government control was not necessarily empowering for women. The women who ran the female emigration societies had long sought the moral sanction and financial backing of the state, and they had yearned for the added power that state recognition would provide. Although wary of committing themselves to a relationship with the state that would not serve their purposes, the emigrators publicly welcomed government overtures when it became obvious that some sort of union was inevitable. When union was achieved, in spite of their efforts to maintain control, the emigrators experienced a loss of self-direction. The new relationships that the female emigration societies formed with the British and dominion governments in the aftermath of the First World War were not on the terms that their members had desired. The co-optation of female emigrators' voluntary labour by government bodies in the post-war period is ironic in light of emigrators' earlier efforts to place themselves at the centre of imperial migration by taking upon themselves men's traditional roles as protectors of women and as experts on imperial matters.

Notes

Introduction

1 Ishbel Aberdeen, 'Prefatory Note,' National Council of Women of Canada, *Women of Canada: Their Life and Work* (Ottawa: Government of Canada, 1900), iii.
2 G. Julia Drummond, 'Introductory,' ibid., 4.
3 Ibid.
4 A large body of literature makes this point. See, for example, the essays in Marlene Epp et al., eds, *Sisters or Strangers? Immigrant, Ethnic, and Racialized Women in Canadian History* (Toronto: University of Toronto Press, 2004); A. James Hammerton, 'Gender and Migration,' in Philippa Levine, ed., *Gender and Empire* (Toronto: Oxford University Press, 2004); and Fiona Paisley, *Loving Protection? Australian Feminism and Aboriginal Women's Rights, 1919–1939* (Victoria, Aust.: Melbourne University Press, 2000).
5 Marjory Harper's discussion of the complicated set of forces that were involved in an individual's decision to emigrate is particularly useful. See Marjory Harper, *Willing Exiles: Emigration from North-East Scotland*, vol. 1 (Aberdeen: Aberdeen University Press, 1988). For discussions of Irishwomen's motivations, which in some respects were different from those of women leaving England, Scotland, or Wales, see David Fitzpatrick, '"A Share of the Honeycomb": Education, Emigration and Irishwomen,' *Continuity and Change* 1:2 (1986): 217–34; and Pauline Jackson, 'Women in 19th Century Irish Emigration,' *International Migration Review* 18:4 (1984): 1004–21.
6 Jan Gothard, 'Wives or Workers? Single British Female Migration to Colonial Australia,' in Pamela Sharpe, ed., *Women, Gender and Labour Migration: Historical and Global Perspectives* (New York: Routledge, 2001), 158.
7 For a sample of articles that offer succinct historiographical discussions of

this literature, see Jane Haggis, 'Gendering Colonialism or Colonising Gender? Recent Women's Studies Approaches to White Women and the History of British Colonialism,' *Women's Studies International Forum* 13:1 (1990): 105–15; Ruth Roach Pierson, 'Introduction,' in Ruth Roach Pierson and Nupur Chaudhuri, eds, *Nation, Empire, Colony: Historicizing Gender and Race* (Bloomington: Indiana University Press, 1998); and Joan Sangster, 'Domesticating Girls: The Sexual Regulation of Aboriginal and Working-Class Girls in Twentieth-Century Canada,' in Katie Pickles and Myra Rutherdale, eds, *Contact Zones: Aboriginal and Settler Women in Canada's Colonial Past* (Vancouver: UBC Press, 2005).

8 Adele Perry, *On the Edge of Empire: Gender, Race, and the Making of British Columbia* (Toronto: University of Toronto Press, 2001); Ann McClintock, *Imperial Leather: Race, Gender and Sexuality in the Colonial Contest* (New York: Routledge, 1995); Antoinette Burton, *Burdens of History: British Feminists, Indian Women, and Imperial Culture, 1865–1915* (Chapel Hill: University of North Carolina Press, 1994); Margaret Strobel, *European Women and the Second British Empire* (Indianapolis: Indiana University Press, 1991); Mary Louise Pratt, *Imperial Eyes: Travel Writing and Transculturation* (New York: Routledge, 1992); Ruth Frankenberg, *White Women, Race Matters: The Social Construction of Whiteness* (Minneapolis: University of Minnesota Press, 1993); and Patricia Grimshaw, Marilyn Lake, Ann McGrath, and Marian Quartly, *Creating a Nation, 1788–1990* (Ringwood, Vict.: Penguin Books, 1996).

9 Antoinette Burton, Keynote Address: 'Archive Stories: Gender and the Making of Imperial and Colonial Histories,' unpublished paper presented to the Canadian Historical Association, Winnipeg, 4 June 2004; and see various reviews of David Cannadine, *Ornamentalism: How the British Saw Their Empire* (Toronto: Penguin Books, 2001), especially Geoff Eley, 'Beneath the Skin, or: How to Forget about the Empire without Really Trying,' *Journal of Colonialism and Colonial History* 3:1 (2002).

10 James Hammerton, *Emigrant Gentlewomen: Genteel Poverty and Female Emigration, 1830–1914* (London: Croom Helm, 1979).

11 Marilyn Barber, *Immigrant Domestic Servants in Canada* (Ottawa: Canadian Historical Association, 1991); Julia Bush, *Edwardian Ladies and Imperial Power* (New York: Leicester University Press, 2000); Emma Curtin, 'Gentility Afloat: Gentlewomen's Diaries and the Voyage to Australia, 1830–80,' *Australian Historical Studies* 26:105 (1995): 634–52; Joy Damousi, 'Chaos and Order: Gender, Space and Sexuality on Female Convict Ships,' *Australian Historical Studies* 26:104 (1995): 351–72; Damousi, *Depraved and Disorderly: Female Convicts, Sexuality and Gender in Colonial Australia* (New York: Cambridge University Press, 1997); Marion Diamond, *Emigration and Empire: The Life of Maria S. Rye* (New York: Garland Publications, 1999); Lisa Gaudet, 'The Empire Is

Woman's Sphere: Organized Female Imperialism in Canada, 1880s–1920s,'
PhD thesis, Carleton University, 2001; Janice Gothard, '"The Healthy,
Wholesome British Domestic Girl": Single Female Migration and the Empire
Settlement Act, 1922–1930,' in Stephen Constantine, ed., *Emigrants and
Empire: British Settlement in the Dominions between the Wars* (Manchester:
Manchester University Press, 1990); Gothard, *Blue China: Single Female Migra-
tion to Colonial Australia* (Melbourne: Melbourne University Press, 2001);
Gothard, '"Pity the Poor Immigrant": Assisted Single Female Migration to
Colonial Australia,' in Eric Richards, ed., *Poor Australian Immigrants in the
Nineteenth Century (Visible Immigrants,* vol. 2) (Canberra: Highland Press,
1991); Gothard, '"Radically Unsound and Mischievous": Female Migration to
Tasmania, 1856–1863,' *Australian Historical Studies* 23:93 (October 1989):
386–404; Gothard, 'Space, Authority and the Female Emigrant Afloat,' *Aus-
tralian Historical Studies* 12 (April 1999): 96–115; Paula Hamilton, '"No Irish
Need Apply": Prejudice as a Factor in the Development of Immigration Pol-
icy in New South Wales and Victoria, 1840–1870,' PhD thesis, University of
New South Wales, 1981; Hamilton, 'The "Servant Class": Poor Female Migra-
tion to Australia in the Nineteenth Century,' in Richards, ed., *Poor Australian
Immigrants in the Nineteenth Century*; Margaret Kiddle, *Caroline Chisholm* (1957;
Carlton, Vict.: Melbourne University Press, 1990); Rita Kranidis, ed., *Imperial
Objects: Essays on Victorian Women's Emigration and the Unauthorized Imperial
Experience* (New York: Twayne Publishers, 1998); Kranidis, *The Victorian Spinster and Colonial Emigration: Contested Subjects* (New York: St Martin's Press,
1999); Angela McCarthy, '"A Good Idea of Colonial Life": Personal Letters
and Irish Migration to New Zealand,' *New Zealand Journal of History* 35:1
(2001): 1–21; Charlotte MacDonald, *A Woman of Good Character: Single Women
as Immigrant Settlers in Nineteenth-Century New Zealand* (Wellington, NZ:
Bridget Williams Books, 1990); Norma J. Milton, 'Essential Servants: Immigrant Domestics on the Canadian Prairies, 1885–1930,' in Susan Armitage
and Elizabeth Jameson, eds, *The Women's West* (London: University of Okla-
homa Press, 1987); Adele Perry, '"Oh I'm Just Sick of the Faces of Men":
Gender Imbalance, Race, Sexuality, and Sociability in Nineteenth Century
British Columbia' *B.C. Studies* 105–6 (1995): 27–43; Katie Pickles, 'Empire
Settlement and Single British Women as New Zealand Domestic Servants
during the 1920s,' *New Zealand Journal of History* 35:1 (2001): 22–44; Pickles,
'Exhibiting Canada: Empire, Migration and the 1928 English Schoolgirl
Tour,' *Gender, Place and Culture* 7:1 (2000): 81–96; Marian M. Press, 'Advising
Women Emigrants to Canada: The Ideology of the Nineteenth and Twenti-
eth Century British Female Emigration Movement,' MA thesis. Ontario Institute for Studies in Education, 1989; Barbara Roberts, 'Ladies, Women and
the State: Managing Female Migration,' in Roxana Ng et al., eds, *Community*

Organization and the Canadian State (Toronto: Garamond Press, 1990); Elizabeth Rushen, *Single and Free: Female Migration to Australia, 1833–1837* (Melbourne: Australian Scholarly Publications, 2003); Cecillie Swaisland, *Servants and Gentlewomen to the Golden Land: The Emigration of Single Women from Britain to Southern Africa, 1820–1939* (Providence, RI: Berg, 1993); Elizabeth Thompson, *The Pioneer Woman: A Canadian Character Type* (Montreal and Kingston: McGill-Queen's University Press, 1991).

12 Julia Bush notes the continued central importance of James Hammerton's book to any study of British female emigration in her introduction to *Edwardian Ladies and Imperial Power*, 10.

13 This theme was central to Hammerton's *Emigrant Gentlewomen*. For two different approaches to the study of agency and power as related to female migration, see Bush's *Edwardian Ladies and Imperial Power* on emigrators and Gothard's *Blue China* on emigrants.

14 Hammerton's *Emigrant Gentlewomen* is a study of organized female migration to all colonial destinations. But Hammerton was not particularly concerned about being comparative in his analysis. In spite of the fact that Rita Kranidis's *The Victorian Spinster and Colonial Emigration* explores the subject of single women's migration throughout the British Empire, her work lacks a comparative framework to the extent that colonial destinations are not differentiated, and frequently go unnamed in the text. Julia Bush's study is about British female imperialists, but she does pay some attention to their relationships with the dominions. Janice Gothard indicates an interest in the possible benefits of studying the attitudes and actions of women and men in multiple imperial contexts – although the colonies in her study are all Australian. Michele Langfield has begun to work on a major Canadian-Australian comparative history of female migration. See Michele Langfield, '"A Chance to Bloom": Female Migration and Salvationists in Australia and Canada, 1890s–1939,' *Australian Feminist Studies* 17:39 (2002): 287–303; and Langfield, 'Gender Blind? Australian Immigration Policy and Practice, 1901–1930,' *Journal of Australian Studies* 79 (2003).

15 Christiane Harzig, 'Women Migrants as Global and Local Agents: New Research Strategies on Gender and Migration,' in Pamela Sharpe, ed., *Women, Gender and Labour Migration: Historical and Global Perspectives* (New York: Routledge, 2001), 16.

16 Donna R. Gabaccia, *Italy's Many Diasporas* (Seattle: University of Washington Press, 2000).

17 Marjory Harper, *Beyond the Broad Atlantic: Emigration from North-East Scotland*, vol. 2 (Aberdeen: Aberdeen University Press, 1988), 286 (table 1). As Harper notes, the figures provided by the BWEA were inconsistent in that those provided for individual years did not always add up to the estimates they

provided for several years' worth of emigration. See ibid., p. 287 n 4. Hammerton estimates that in total 156,606 women emigrated to the colonies between 1899 and 1911. Hammerton, *Emigrant Gentlewomen*, 177. See also Kranidis, *Imperial Objects*, 2.

18 The Australian federal government was very reticent to commit itself to providing qualified matrons for *all* ships carrying groups of female emigrants. The members of the Society for the Oversea Settlement of British Women celebrated Australia's capitulation in this matter with a victorious announcement in their *Annual Report* for 1926 (see p. 38).

19 For an interesting variety of approaches to this subject, see Judith Allen, *Rose Scott: Vision and Revision in Feminism* (New York: Oxford University Press, 1994); Jane Lewis, *Women and Social Action in Victorian and Edwardian England* (Aldershot, Eng.: Edward Elgar, 1991); Leila J. Rupp, *Worlds of Women: The Making of an International Women's Movement* (Princeton, NJ: Princeton University Press, 1997); and Seth Koven and Sonya Michel, eds, *Mothers of a New World: Maternalist Politics and the Origins of Welfare States* (New York: Routledge, 1993).

20 James Hammerton, '"Out of Their Natural Station": Empire and Empowerment in the Emigration of Lower Middle-Class Women,' in Rita Kranidis, ed., *Imperial Objects: Victoria Women's Emigration and the Unauthorized Imperial Experience* (New York: Twayne Publishers, 1998), 145. Here, Hammerton is referring to Julia Bush's argument along these lines in '"The Right Sort of Woman": Female Emigrators and Emigration to the British Empire, 1890–1910,' *Women's History Review* 3:3 (1994): 385–409.

21 For recent examples, see the essays collected in Pickles and Rutherdale, eds, *Contact Zones*.

22 Andrew Thompson's study of the meaning of empire to Britons is very useful in this respect. It shows how the empire's white populations, rather than the empire's colonized peoples, tended to dominate British imperialists' attention. Andrew S. Thompson, *Imperial Britain: The Empire in British Politics, c. 1800–1932* (New York: Longman, 2000). Stephen Howe emphasizes this point in his review of Thompson's book in *20th Century British History* 13:2 (2002): 208–10.

23 For a brief period at the middle of the nineteenth century the Colonial Office was relatively engaged with the management of migration to Australia. For a discussion of the involvement of the Colonial Office, local British poor-law authorities, voluntary orgainizations, and Australian government bodies in promoting, assisting, and overseeing Australian immigration during this period, see Robin F. Haines, *Emigration and the Labouring Poor: Australian Recruitment and Ireland, 1831–60* (New York: St Martin's Press, 1997).

24 This pattern of the absorption of women's voluntary labour into state-

controlled programs, and the related professionalization of women's social work, may be found in a wide range of fields. Angela Woollacott provides a good summary of this process in 'From Moral to Professional Authority: Secularism, Social Work, and Middle-Class Women's Self-Construction in World War I Britain,' *Journal of Women's History* 10:2 (Summer 1998): 85–111. See also Jane Lewis, 'Gender, the Family and Women's Agency in the Building of "Welfare States": The British Case,' *Social History* 19:1 (January 1994): 37–55.

25 Specifically, I have examined the collected papers of the Female Middle-Class Emigration Society (1862–86), the Women's Emigration Society (1880–94), the Northern Branch, Women's Emigration Society (1882–1902), the British Women's Emigration Association (1884–1919), the Colonial Intelligence League (for Educated Women) (1911–19), the Joint Council of Women's Emigration Societies (1917–19), and the Society for the Oversea Settlement of British Women (1919–62). The original of these sources are housed at the Fawcett Library, in London, England. Microfilmed copies are also available at Library and Archives Canada in Ottawa (in MG 28), and at the Australian National Archives in Canberra.

26 Gothard, '"Pity the poor immigrant,"' 98.

Chapter 1: 'With This Sign I Conquer'

1 Mary Heath-Stubbs, *Friendship's Highway, Being the History of the Girls' Friendly Society, 1875–1925* (London: G.F.S. Central Office, 1926 [1925]), page facing 65.

2 Ibid., facing 71.

3 Ibid.

4 Ellen Joyce quoting the author of an article about the history of this symbol in 'Ventures within the Empire: To Women of the XX Century' (n.p., 1913), quoted in Heath-Stubbs, *Friendship's Highway*, 71. A copy of Joyce's article may be found at Library and Archives Canada (LAC), MG 28, I349 (Microfilm A-1199).

5 Joyce, 'Ventures within the Empire,' 19.

6 The papers of the Joint Council of Women's Emigration Societies from 1917 to 1919, together with the minutes of the Colonial Intelligence League's council meetings for this period, reveal the emigrators' disappointment concerning the terms under which they would be obliged to work with the government. See LAC, MG 28, I336 (Microfilm A-1055), Joint Council of Women's Emigration Societies; and LAC, MG 28, I336 (Microfilm A-1059), Colonial Intelligence League, Council Minutes.

7　It is interesting to note that simultaneously the management of child migration became a field of work that attracted a significant number of philanthropists and reformers – some of whom made this work their life mission. However, child migration work never became quite as dominated by women. For further discussion of this, see Kenneth Bagnell, *The Little Immigrants: The Orphans Who Came to Canada* (Toronto: Dundurn Press, 2001); Stephen Constantine, 'Children as Ancestors: Child Migrants and Identity in Canada,' *British Journal of Canadian Studies* 16 (2003): 150–9; and Joy Parr, *Labouring Children: British Immigrant Apprentices to Canada, 1869–1924* (Toronto: University of Toronto Press, 1994).

8　Julia Bush, *Edwardian Ladies and Imperial Power* (New York: Leicester University Press, 2000), 5.

9　Ibid., 17.

10　See Edwin C. Guillet, The Great Migration: The Atlantic Crossing by Sailing Ship, 1770–1860 (Toronto: University of Toronto Press, 1963 [1937]), chap. 3; Robin Haines, *Emigration and the Labouring Poor: Australian Recruitment in Britain and Ireland, 1831–1860* (London: Macmillan Press, 1997); and Frank Prochaska, *The Voluntary Impulse: Philanthropy in Modern Britain* (Boston: Faber, 1988).

11　Certainly, this is what colonials believed. According to Robin Haines, the London Emigration Committee was notable for its careful selection and protection of female emigrants in the 1830s. Haines writes that 'ironically, matching the colonial press's objections to the women's alleged depravity were the London Committee's fears that the selected women might be placed in moral danger on the voyage or on reaching their destination.' The London Emigration Committee saw themselves as 'guardians of the women's honour.' Robin Haines, '"The Idle and the Drunken Won't Do There": Poverty, the New Poor Law and Nineteenth-Century Government-assisted Emigration to Australia from the United Kingdom,' *Australian Historical Studies* 28:108 (April 1997): 6. See also Haines, *Emigration and the Labouring Poor.* For discussions about responses to the immigration of impoverished single women, see Janice Gothard, '"Pity the Poor Immigrant"': Assisted Single Female Migration to Colonial Australia,' in Richards, ed., *Poor Australian Immigrants* (see Introduction, n. 11, above); Gothard, '"Radically Unsound and Mischievous": Female Migration to Tasmania, 1856–1863,' *Australian Historical Studies* 23:93 (October 1989): 386–404; Margaret Kiddle, *Caroline Chisholm* (1957; Carlton, Vict.: Melbourne University Press, 1990); Una Monk, *New Horizons: A Hundred Years of Women's Migration* (London: Her Majesty's Stationary, 1963); and Barbara Roberts, 'Daughters of the Empire and

Mothers of the Race: Caroline Chisholm and Female Emigration in the British Empire,' *Atlantis* 1:2 (Spring 1976): 106–27.

12 This term, which has been used extensively by historians of immigration, was coined in 1849 by Edward Gibbons Wakefield, who was publicly critical of a system whereby the removal of emigrants, 'not by attraction but by repulsion, makes an impression in the neighbourhood that emigration is only fit for the refuse of the population.' Quoted in Cecillie Swaisland, *Servants and Gentlewomen to the Golden Land: The Emigration of Single Women from Britain to Southern Africa, 1820–1939* (Pietermartizberg, SA: University of Natal Press, 1993), 17.

13 See Suzann Buckley, 'British Female Emigration and Imperial Development: Experiments in Canada,' *Hecate* 3:2 (1977), especially 27–8; James Hammerton, *Emigrant Gentlewomen: Genteel Poverty and Female Emigration, 1830–1914* (London: Croom Helm, 1979), esp. 54–5; Gothard, '"Pity the Poor Immigrant"'; Gothard, 'Radically Unsound and Mischievous'; Margaret Kiddle, *Caroline Chisholm* (Carleton, Vict.: Melbourne University Press, 1957); and Roberts, 'Daughters of the Empire and Mothers of the Race.' In Australia this image of female immigrants as corrupting influences was heightened by public scandals relating to the shipboard activities of female convicts. See Joy Damousi, *Depraved and Disorderly: Female Convicts, Sexuality and Gender in Colonial Australia* (New York: Cambridge University Press, 1997); and Jan Gothard, *Blue China: Single Female Migration to Colonial Australia* (Melbourne: Melbourne University Press, 2001).

14 This is emphasized in Hammerton, *Emigrant Gentlewomen.*

15 As Deborah Oxley and Eric Richards point out, 'Government intervention was crucial in determining the supply of women' to the Australian colonies during the nineteenth century. Deborah Oxley and Eric Richards, 'Convict and Free Immigrant Women before 1851,' in James Jupp, ed., *The Australian People: An Encyclopaedia of the Nation, Its People and Their Origins* (New York: Cambridge University Press, 2001), 30. This continued to be the case through the 1920s for Australia and New Zealand. For discussions of the New Zealand government's sponsorship of female immigrants, see Charlotte Macdonald, *A Woman of Good Character* (Wellington, NZ: Bridget Williams Books, 1990); and Katie Pickles, 'Empire Settlement and Single British Women as New Zealand Domestic Servants during the 1920s,' *New Zealand Journal of History* 35:1 (2001): 22–44.

16 Irish single female emigrants were an exception to this rule. Especially in the second half of the nineteenth century, relatively large percentages of Irish emigrants were single women. For a discussion of this subject, see David Fitzpatrick, '"A Share of the Honeycomb": Education, Emigration and Irish-

women,' *Continuity and Change* 1:2 (1986): 217–34; and Pauline Jackson, 'Women in 19th Century Irish Emigration,' *International Migration Review* 18:4 (1984): 1004–21.

17 Some Australian governments handed over the recruitment and chaperonage of female immigrants to these female emigrators completely. The immigration form that the Canadian government used for female immigrants from the mid-1890s was designed by the British Women's Emigration Association. See Una Monk, *New Horizons: A Hundred Years of Women's Migration* (London: Her Majesty's Stationary Office, 1963); and G.F. Plant, *SOSBW: A Survey of Voluntary Effort in Women's Empire Migration* (London: HMSO, 1950).

18 Caroline Chisholm is the best known of these philanthropists, but there were also a number of other people working at improving female migration at this time. See Haines, '"The Idle and the Drunken Won't Do There"'; Hammerton, *Emigrant Gentlewomen*, chap. 4; and Macdonald, *A Woman of Good Character*, 8.

19 For discussions of Caroline Chisholm's work, see Hammerton, *Emigrant Gentlewomen*, 99–103; Kiddle, *Caroline Chisholm*; and Roberts, 'Daughters of the Empire and Mothers of the Race.'

20 For discussion of Rye's work with emigrant women, see Marion Diamond, *Emigration and Empire: The Life of Maria S. Rye* (New York: Garland Publication, 1999); Diamond, 'Maria Rye's Journey: Metropolitan and Colonial Perceptions of Female Emigration,' in Rita Kranidis, ed., *Imperial Objects: Essays on Victorian Women's Emigration and the Unauthorized Imperial Experience* (New York: Twayne Publishers, 1998); Hammerton, *Emigrant Gentlewomen*, chap. 5; and Macdonald, *A Woman of Good Character*. Maria Rye later became famous for her emigration of children to Canada. See Parr, *Labouring Children;* and Nupur Chaudhuri, '"Who Will Help the Girls?": Maria Rye and Victorian Juvenile Emigration to Canada, 1869–1895,' in Kranidis, ed., *Imperial Objects*.

21 'Charity,' as used here, should be understood as different from 'philanthropy.' Over the course of the nineteenth century, philanthropic work (which combined the donation of money and/or goods with efforts to reform the recipient) largely replaced charity (which did not require reform, and was understood by middle-class reformers to be antithetical to social reform).

22 Quoted in Kiddle, 107.

23 Another organization that helped to make female emigration more respectable was the British Ladies' Female Emigrant Society, founded in 1849. The members of this society visited emigrants upon their departure, provided appropriate materials for the female emigrants' diversion during the jour-

ney, and, most importantly, supplied ships carrying single women with carefully selected matrons. See Maria Rye, 'Emigrant-Ship Matrons,' *The Englishwoman's Journal* 5:25 (1 March 1860): 24–36.

24 See Hammerton, *Emigrant Gentlewomen*, chap. 5.

25 See Maria Rye, 'Emigration of Educated Women,' paper read at the Social Science Congress in Dublin, 1861 (reprinted in the *Englishwoman's Journal*). See also J.E. Lewin, 'Female Middle Class Emigration,' paper read at the Social Science Congress in October 1863.

26 The relationship between female emigration societies and female imperialism is the focus of Julia Bush's discussion of emigration in *Edwardian Ladies and Imperial Power*.

27 Ibid.

28 In the *Imperial Colonist*, the alarm that British women were desperately needed in South Africa to help 'raise' the country's cultural tone was regularly sounded. See Katherine Pease, 'Experiences of an English Worker in South Africa,' *Imperial Colonist* 2:1 (January 1903): 3–4, continued in 2:2 (February 1903): 20–1; and Johnson, 'Domestic Helps in Natal,' *Imperial Colonist* 2:4 (April 1903): 42–4. See also Brian Blakely, 'Women and Imperialism: The Colonial Office and Female Emigration to South Africa, 1901–1910,' *Albion* 13:2 (1981): 131–49; Swaisland, *Servants and Gentlewomen to the Golden Land;* and J.J. Van-Helten and Keith Williams, '"The Crying Need of South Africa": The Emigration of Single British Women to the Transvaal, 1901–10,' *Journal of Southern African Studies* 10:1 (1983): 17–38.

29 Supporters of the SACS included Alfred Milner, Joseph Chamberlain, Alice Balfour, Adelina Brassey, Alicia Cecil, Gwendolin Cecil, Susan Grosvenor, Victoria Grosvenor, Mary Hervey, Louisa Knightley, Katherine Lyttleton, Susan Malmesbury, Laura Ridding, and Maud Selborne.

30 For more on this, see Bush, *Edwardian Ladies and Imperial Power*.

31 Caroline Chisholm left Australia in 1866 for the last time. She died in 1877. For a discussion of the life of Chisholm's Family Colonisation and Loan Society, see Kiddle, *Caroline Chisholm*.

32 Jane Lewin retired from her position as honorary secretary in 1881. Her commentary in the *Female Middle-Class Emigration Society, Annual Report for 1862–1872* makes clear her frustration at having to carry the burden of the society's management almost completely by herself. See also Hammerton's discussion of Jane Lewin's role in the Female Middle-Class Emigration Society in *Emigrant Gentlewomen*, chap. 5.

33 The Women's Emigration Society (WES) was founded in 1880 and dissolved in 1894. The Northern Branch, Women's Emigration Society, was founded in 1882. It changed its name to the Colonial Emigration Society in 1883, and

disbanded in 1902. Neither of these societies competed very effectively with the BWEA.

34 The BWEA capitalized on the ill fortune in the mid-1880s of the WES, which had managed to secure the patronage of Princess Mary Adelaide and Princess Louise. After key working members left the WES amid acrimonious debates relating to control, the BWEA drew away most of its royal supporters.

35 For example, they shared members with the Girls' Friendly Society, the Young Women's Christian Association, the Travellers' Aid Society, the National Vigilance Association, the various British and dominion national councils of women, and a range of church organizations. See Julia Bush, *Edwardian Ladies and Imperial Power*, for a discussion of the overlap in membership between various women's imperialist organizations.

36 See Hammerton, *Emigrant Gentlewomen*, chaps. 4 and 5.

37 Prochaska makes a similar point about the involvement of upper-class philanthropists in multiple causes in *The Voluntary Impulse*.

38 For brief discussions of Ellen Joyce's life and work, see Ellen Joyce, 'Thirty Years of Girls' Friendly Society Imperial Work,' a paper read at the GFS Imperial Conference at York, 17 July 1912; *Imperial Colonist* 6:75 (March 1908): 1–2; her obituaries in *Imperial Colonist* 22:262 (June 1924): 101–2 and 22:264 (July 1924): 130–2; Monk, *New Horizons;* and Bush, *Edwardian Ladies and Imperial Power*, 219.

39 For biographical information about Adelaide Ross, see her obituary in the *Imperial Colonist* 13:161 (June 1915): 94–5; Adelaide Ross, *Memoir of Alexander J. Ross* (London: W. Isbiter Ltd, 1888); and Monk, *New Horizons*. For Grace Lefroy, see *Imperial Colonist* 25:2 (January 1927): 6.

40 For example, Emily Worth Bromfield began her emigration work with Ellen Joyce for the Winchester Emigration Society in 1883, and only resigned her position as honorary secretary for the BWEA when she became ill in 1913. See 'A Very Faithful Worker' in *Imperial Colonist* 11:134 (March 1913): 38; and her obituary in *Imperial Colonist* 11:140 (August 1913): 121. E.L. Blanchard worked at female emigration – as a promoter, manager, and voluntary matron – for at least 35 years. See Monk, *New Horizons*, 7–13.

41 Joyce's style of management is commented upon in Ross's loose, handwritten reflections on the early history of the BWEA in her scrapbooks, copies of which may be found at LAC, MG 28, I336 (Microfilm A-1056).

42 The scrapbooks in which Ross kept articles and notes concerning imperial migration – mainly during the nineteenth century – are a testament to her commitment to this work.

43 Lefroy is the focus of some discussion in Monk, *New Horizons* (see pp. 15, 22–3, 55, 89, 121–2, 129, and 171). She is mentioned once in passing in Bush,

Edwardian Ladies and Imperial Power, and does not feature in the index of Hammerton's *Emigrant Gentlewomen*.

44 It is interesting to note that Joyce and Ross differed on the issue of women's suffrage. See appendix 2, 'Female Imperialist Networks,' in Bush, *Edwardian Ladies and Imperial Power*, 214–5.

45 *Imperial Colonist* 7:86 (February 1909): 9.

46 Lefroy was only in her twenties when she joined the BWEA, so whatever experience she had would have been significantly less than that of a woman like Joyce, who was 52 when she headed up the GFS emigration department in 1882.

47 *Imperial Colonist* 22:264 (July 1924): 130–2.

48 For example, she joined forces with other female philanthropists in founding the East London Nursing Society in 1868.

49 Joyce's position within the GFS was particularly useful. See Lisa Chilton, 'Migrants in Montreal: Managing British Female Immigrants at the Turn of the Twentieth Century,' *British Journal of Canadian Studies* 16:1 (2003): 59–70; and chapter 5 of this book.

50 See Ross's obituary in *Imperial Colonist* 13:161 (June 1915): 95.

51 When the society's patrons tried to impose their own vision of managed female migration, the middle-class women who had actually worked with the emigrants left the society. See Fawcett Library (FL), 'The Women's Emigration Society,' in *Catalogue 1: Female Emigration Societies*; and Monk: *New Horizons*, 10–12.

52 *British Women's Emigration Association, Annual Report, 1896–1897* (n.p., [1897]), 11.

53 The Girls' Friendly Society was an organization that worked at improving the morals and attitudes of working-class girls and young women. See Brian Harrison, 'For Church, Queen and Family: The Girls' Friendly Society, 1874–1920,' *Past and Present* 61: 107–38; and Mary Heath-Stubbs, *Friendship's Highway: Being the History of the Girls' Friendly Society, 1875–1925* (London: GFS Central Office, 1926). I do not think that Ross was a member of the GFS, but she was clear about her admiration of the society's methods.

54 *British Women's Emigration Association: Annual Report, 1888* (n.p., [1888]), 5.

55 *British Women's Emigration Association: Annual Report, 1896–1897* (n.p., [1897]), 11.

56 LAC, MG 17, B9 (Microfilm A-1899), Society for Promoting Christian Knowledge, Emigration Committee Minutes, 17 December 1896.

57 See chap 5, 'Welcoming Women,' for information on reception work in Montreal.

58 See Blakely, 'Women and Imperialism.'

59 Ross made this perspective clear to a philanthropically minded correspondent who desired to assist someone of her acquaintance who had 'fallen' to
emigrate. The correspondent insisted that the woman in question was
reformed, and that she was otherwise a worthy case for support. The correspondent also emphasized that the prospective emigrant would benefit
immeasurably from emigration. Ross responded with a definitive 'no.' See
Ross, 'Scrapbook,' 55.

60 For an Australian example, see Ellen Joyce, 'Thirty Years of Girls' Friendly
Society Imperial Work,' paper delivered at the GFS Imperial Conference at
York, 17 July 1912, 2–3; and Gothard's discussion of this same case in *Blue
China*, 198–9. For a Canadian example, see the support of the BWEA and
affiliated women's organisations for the work of Georgina Binnie-Clarke,
who campaigned for changes to Canada's homesteading laws, in the *Imperial
Colonist*.

61 Although Lefroy does not seem to have published much of her own writing,
she collected letters from emigrants that were then inserted in the societies'
journals, annual reports, and other promotional publications. Even after her
official retirement from the position of honorary secretary for the Joint
Council of Women's Emigration Societies in 1919, Lefroy continued to work
as the sub-editor of the *Imperial Colonist* until her health would no longer per-
mit it, in 1923. Joyce wrote the 'Emigration Notes,' which consisted of
employment announcements, shipping arrangements, and other bits and
pieces of migration information, for the *Imperial Colonist*, and acted as the
GFS's emigration correspondent for several decades.

62 Joyce and Ross both wrote articles and made public speeches about female
emigration; however, the avid self-promotion of Joyce has ensured that her
writing has been better preserved. Her articles included 18 essays on matters
ranging from 'Responsibility of the Church with Regard to Emigration'
(1885), to 'Openings for Educated Women in Canada,' to a 'Report on Agriculture and Colonization' for Ottawa (1890). These Joyce collected for the
use of other people working in the field. A copy of this collection was presented to the president of the GFS, and may be found at LAC, MG 28, I349
(Microfilm A-1199).

63 For example, Grace Lefroy was known to give emigrants gifts of fresh flowers
at their departure from London, and Adelaide Ross collected little gifts and
prizes to be given out by the matron on board ship. See Monk, *New Horizons*,
55.

64 In the nineteenth century, British women working alone often made an
income as immigration agents (i.e., they promoted and organized the emigration of individuals, families, and groups for remuneration from the colo-

nial governments). Monk refers to a number of such cases in *New Horizons*. Elise von Koerber, who worked as an agent for the Canadian government in Europe during the 1870s and early 1880s presents a fascinating case study along these lines (my thanks to Angelika Sauer for information about von Koerber). By the turn of the century, it was unusual for women not affiliated with major organizations to do this work.

65 Joint Council of Women's Emigration Societies, Minutes, 5 November 1918. Miss Wileman had been a known entity for some time by this point. In 1910 Ellen Joyce requested that an Anglican minister who was about to embark on a fact-finding tour of Canada for the church find out what he could about Miss Wileman and her work relating to the management of Canadian immigration. See LAC, MG 17, B9 (Microfilm A-1900), SPCK, Emigration Committee Minutes, 15 December 1910, 'Report of the Rev. H. E. Elwell's Visit to Canada.' Joyce's request was likely in response to the complaints of Mary Agnes FitzGibbon, a leading figure in Canadian reception work, concerning Wileman's misrepresentation of Canadian conditions to emigrants. See Barbara Roberts, '"A Work of Empire": Canadian Reformers and British Female Immigration,' in Linda Kealey, ed., *A Not Unreasonable Claim: Women and Reform in Canada, 1880s–1920s* (Toronto: Women's Press, 1979), 197.

66 See FL, 'IV: Joint Council of Women's Emigration Societies 1917–1919,' in *Catalogue 1: Female Emigration Societies.*

67 Ross, Scrapbook, Ellen Joyce to Adelaide Ross, 16 December 1914. Apparently Joyce was considered especially skilled at evaluating how best to promote the interests of the societies in public and private correspondence. See, for example, the Joint Council of Women's Emigration Societies, Minutes, 8 October 1917, in which Miss Vernon indicates that the rough draft of a circular that had been drawn up by the Joint Council had been revised after it had been shown to Mrs Joyce, because Joyce felt that it came across too negatively.

68 Bush's chap 2, 'Society Lifestyles,' in *Edwardian Ladies and Imperial Power*, is particularly useful for understanding the class-specific contributions of these women's social status to the female emigration societies.

69 See Anthony Howe, *The Cotton Masters, 1830–1860* (New York: Oxford University Press, 1984); Leonore Davidoff and Catherine Hall, *Family Fortunes: Men and Women of the English Middle Class, 1780–1850* (London: Hutchinson, 1987); R.J. Morris, *Class, Sect and Party: The Making of the British Middle Class, Leeds, 1820–1850* (Manchester: Manchester University Press, 1990); and Theodore Koditschek, *Class Formation and Urban-Industrial Society in Bradford, 1750–1850* (Cambridge: Cambridge University Press, 1990).

70 See, for example, Elizabeth Elbourne, 'Indigenous Peoples and Imperial

Networks in the Early Nineteenth Century: The Politics of Knowledge,' in Phillip Buckner and R. Douglas Francis, eds, *Rediscovering the British World* (Calgary: University of Calgary Press, 2005), 59–85.

71 F.K. Prochaska, *Royal Bounty: The Making of a Welfare Monarchy* (New Haven: Yale University Press, 1995), 72.

72 Davidoff and Hall, *Family Fortunes;* Christine Stansell, *City of Women: Sex and Class in New York, 1789–1860* (New York: Knopf, 1986); Ellen Ross, *Love and Toil: Motherhood in Outcast London, 1870–1918* (New York: Oxford University Press, 1993); Lori Ginzberg, *Women and the Work of Benevolence: Morality, Politics, and Class in the Nineteenth-Century United States* (New Haven: Yale University Press, 1990); Penny Russell, *A Wish of Distinction: Colonial Gentility and Femininity* (Carlton, Vict.: Melbourne University Press, 1994); and Mariana Valverde, *The Age of Light, Soap, and Water: Moral Reform in English Canada, 1885–1925* (Toronto: McClelland and Stewart, 1991).

73 See Monk, *New Horizons,* 135.

74 Linda Gordon and Ellen Ross offer good examples of this approach in their studies of working-class people's interaction with philanthropists and social workers. See Linda Gordon, *Heroes of the Own Lives: The Politics and History of Family Violence: Boston 1880–1960* (New York: Penguin, 1989); and Ellen Ross, *Love and Toil: Motherhood in Outcast London, 1870–1918* (New York: Oxford University Press, 1993).

75 Prochaska, *Royal Bounty,* 35.

76 Ibid., 65.

77 Brian Harrison, *Peaceable Kingdom: Stability and Change in Modern Britain* (Oxford: Clarendon Press, 1982), 227. See also Geoffrey Finlayson's discussion of Shaftesbury in *Citizen, State, and Social Welfare in Britain, 1830–1990* (Oxford: Oxford University Press, 1994), 53.

78 Davidoff and Hall, *Family Fortunes,* 20–2.

79 The CIL's Princess Patricia Ranch in British Columbia is perhaps the best example. For discussion of this institution, see Andrew Yarmie, '"I had always wanted to farm": The Quest for Independence by British Female Emigrants at the Princess Patricia Ranch, Vernon, British Columbia, 1912–1920,' *British Journal of Canadian Studies* 16:1 (2003): 102–25.

80 See Bush, chap 2, 'Society Lifestyles,' in *Edwardian Ladies and Imperial Power.*

81 See Adelaide Ross's rough notes in her scrapbook, LAC, MG 28, I336 (A-1056). Joyce's dominance of the BWEA and the GFS's emigration department for at least a couple of decades illustrates the extent to which elite women were willing to let a middle-class woman of exceptional ability dictate how their societies would function.

82 See Bush, *Edwardian Ladies and Imperial Power.*

2: Safe Passage

1 Fawcett Library (FL), 4/TAS, box 201, *Travellers' Aid Society, Annual Report, 1905.*
2 *Travellers' Aid Society, Annual Report, 1905.*
3 Joanne Meyerowitz has defined this character as the 'woman adrift.' According to Meyerowitz, '[the] more sympathetic writers, often middle-class women, considered wage-earning women the victims of a ruthless urban and industrial society ... In popular romance fiction and in reform literature, authors constructed a discourse that portrayed "women adrift" as pure and passive orphans threatened with sexual danger.' Joanne Meyerowitz, *Women Adrift: Independent Wage Earners in Chicago, 1880–1930* (Chicago: University of Chicago Press, 1998), xix.
4 The only exception is the figure of the procuress – an image very much in line with that painted by William Stead in 'The Maiden Tribute of Babylon.' See Judith Walkowitz, *City of Dreadful Delight: Narratives of Sexual Danger in Late-Victorian London* (Chicago: University of Chicago Press, 1992).
5 The good sense and gallantry of train porters and other railway officials who alerted TAS women to the presence of stray girls was regularly applauded in the TAS's annual reports. See, for example, *Travellers' Aid Society, Annual Report, 1896,* 11; *Travellers' Aid Society, Annual Report, 1897,* 12; and *Travellers' Aid Society, Annual Report, 1899,* 15.
6 In the case of the emigration societies, the GFS, and the YWCA, some men held positions as patrons and, occasionally, as advisers. In the case of the TAS, a higher proportion of the members were male, although men usually played minor roles in the day-to-day management of the organization. These organizations differed from the National Vigilance Association, in which men played a very important role. See Edward J. Bristow, *Vice and Vigilance: Purity Movements in Britain since 1700* (Totowa, NJ: Rowman and Littlefield, 1978).
7 See, for example, Ellen Joyce, *Warning Signals for Young Women Travellers,* Library and Archives Canada (LAC), MG 28, I349 (Microfilm A-1199).
8 Elaine Showalter, *Sexual Anarchy: Gender and Culture at the Fin de Siècle* (New York: Viking Penguin, 1990), 3. See also Bristow, *Vice and Vigilance;* and Walkowitz, *City of Dreadful Delight.*
9 Walkowitz, *City of Dreadful Delight,* 2.
10 Catherine Stimpson, 'Preface' to Walkowitz, *City of Dreadful Delight,* x.
11 For studies of other voluntary work by women during this period that relied upon similar self-promotions, see Gisela Bock and Pat Thane, eds, *Maternity and Gender Policies: Women and the Rise of the European Welfare States, 1880s–*

1950s (New York: Routledge, 1994); Seth Koven and Sonya Michel, eds, *Mothers of a New World: Maternalist Politics and the Origins of Welfare States* (New York: Routledge, 1993); Molly Ladd-Taylor, *Mother Work: Women, Child Welfare, and the State, 1890–1930* (Urbana: University of Illinois Press, 1994); Jane Lewis, 'Gender, the Family and Women's Agency in the Building of "Welfare States": The British Case,' *Social History* 19:1 (January 1994): 37–55; Jane Lewis, *The Politics of Motherhood: Child and Maternal Welfare in England, 1900–1939* (London: Croom Helm, 1980); and Angela Woollacott, 'From Moral to Professional Authority: Secularism, Social Work, and Middle-Class Women's Self-Construction in World War I Britain,' *Journal of Women's History* 10:2 (Summer 1998): 85–111.

12 I use the term 'maternalist' here to denote these women's assumption of a matriarchal, familial model for their protection work with younger women of a lower class. I do not mean that this maternalism was necessarily feminist.

13 The relationship between maternalism and women's efforts to reform society and the state has been the focus of numerous studies and much scholarly debate. The following recently published works are key texts on this subject: Bock and Thane, eds, *Maternity and Gender Policies*; Nancy Christie, *Engendering the State: Family, Work, and Welfare in Canada* (Toronto: University of Toronto Press, 2000); Lori D. Ginzberg, *Women and the Work of Benevolence: Morality, Politics, and Class in the Nineteenth-Century United States* (New Haven: Yale University Press, 1990); Koven and Michel, eds, *Mothers of a New World*; Ladd-Taylor, *Mother Work*.

14 See Lewis, 'Gender, the Family and Women's Agency in the Building of "Welfare States"'; and Woollacott, 'From Moral to Professional Authority.'

15 See the *British Women's Emigration Association: Annual Report, 1896–1897* (n.p., [1897]), 11.

16 Woollacott makes this point particularly well in 'From Moral to Professional Authority.'

17 Ibid., 103.

18 For extensive discussion of this subject in a Canadian context, see Karen Dubinsky, *Improper Advances: Rape and Heterosexual Conflict in Ontario, 1880–1929* (Chicago: University of Chicago Press, 1993).

19 See Walkowitz, *City of Dreadful Delight*.

20 Carol Dyehouse, *Feminism and the Family in England, 1880–1939* (New York: Basil Blackwell, 1989); Sheila Jeffreys, *The Spinster and Her Enemies: Feminism and Sexuality, 1880–1930* (Boston: Pandora Press, 1985); Sally Ledger, *The New Woman: Fiction and Feminism at the Fin de Siècle* (New York: Manchester University Press, 1997); Showalter, *Sexual Anarchy*.

21 For a sample of the range of female migrants during this period, see James

Hammerton, *Emigrant Gentlewomen: Genteel Poverty and Female Emigration, 1830–1914* (London: Croom Helm, 1979); Charlotte MacDonald, *A Woman of Good Character: Single Women as Immigrant Settlers in Nineteenth-Century New Zealand* (Wellington, NZ: Bridget Williams Books, 1990); and Joy Parr, *Labouring Children: British Immigrant Apprentices to Canada, 1869–1924* (Toronto: University of Toronto Press, 1994).

22 *Travellers' Aid Society, Annual Report, 1894.*

23 Lady B.C. Grey, *Friendly Work*, November 1885, 163 (italics in original).

24 In theory, the TAS and the GFS did not promote emigration. However, under the influence of Ellen Joyce, imperial migration became a significant part of the GFS's work for the empire around the turn of the century. See Mary Heath-Stubbs, 'O'er Land and Sea,' chapter 9 in *Friendship's Highway: Being the History of the Girls' Friendly Society, 1875–1925* (London: GFS Central Office, 1926).

25 *Friendly Work*, February 1884, 29 (emphases as in original).

26 See, for example, 'How Not to Do It,' *Imperial Colonist* 6:81 (September 1908): 9. In this article the editor relates a series of stories about the foolishness and inefficiencies of would-be female emigrants.

27 For a particularly thorough example, see *Imperial Colonist* 12:151 (August 1914): 138.

28 See, for example, the new immigrant quoted by Anne Mercier in 'The GFS in the Far West,' *Friendly Work*, September 1902: 142.

29 Ethel Hudson, a woman who had purportedly 'travelled alone a good deal' in the past, noted that 'the aid and protection of the Society [for Oversea Settlement of British Women] is splendid for anyone travelling alone ... One has the protection it gives and many advantages that one could not have if alone.' The advantages of protected travel that Hudson had personally experienced included the fact that she was 'never lost sight of' and that she was able to save £10 by travelling colonist or third class, 'which is almost impossible for a young woman alone.' Ethel Hudson, quoted in *Imperial Colonist* 22:268 (December 1924): 240. A similar argument comes from a woman quoted in *Friendly Work*, September 1894: 156.

30 *Imperial Colonist* 9:105 (February 1911): 252–3.

31 See Ray Strachey, *The Cause: A Short History of the Women's Movement in Great Britain* (Port Washington, NY: Kermikat Press, 1969 [1928]).

32 See Arthur Marwick, *Women at War, 1914–1918* (London: Fontana Paperbacks, 1977); and Martin Pugh, *Women and the Women's Movement in Britain, 1914–1959* (Houndsmills, UK: Macmillan, 1992).

33 *Imperial Colonist* 18:222 (September 1920): 143.

34 *Travellers' Aid Society, Annual Report, 1886.*

35 The TAS noted that women working for white-slave-trade organizations were potentially a serious problem, as they were able to impersonate the society's members and their paid female helpers and thus could lure young women with the image of safety. However, the safe-passage narratives seldom highlighted female villains. In light of the role of the procuress in Stead's 'Maiden Tribute,' this omission is noteworthy.

36 See *Travellers' Aid Society, Annual Report, 1896*, 11; and *Travellers' Aid Society, Annual Report, 1897*, 15.

37 *Imperial Colonist* 9:115 (July 1911): 330.

38 'Mormon Activity' and 'Mormon Recruiting in Switzerland,' in *Imperial Colonist* 10:132 (December 1912): 199. As late as the 1920s, Mormons were still considered a cause for alarm in this magazine. See *Imperial Colonist* 20:235 (March 1922): 35.

39 Brian Blakely discusses an interesting example of the evolving nature of the relations between the British state and female emigration societies in 'Women and Imperialism: The Colonial Office and Female Emigration to South Africa, 1901–1910,' *Albion* 13:2 (Summer 1981): 131–49.

40 Maria S. Rye, 'Emigrant-Ship Matrons,' *Englishwomen's Journal* 5:25 (1 March 1860): 25.

41 Ibid., 27 and 33–4.

42 Ibid., 36.

43 Ibid., 34.

44 These women were quite conscious that they were working as a part of a team of reformers, and that they could not present ideas that were not sanctioned by the group as a whole. For examples of cases where individuals stepped out of line and were disciplined accordingly, see LAC, MG 28, I336, A-1056, Scrapbook, Ellen Joyce to Adelaide Ross; James Hammerton's discussion of the suffrage activities of a BWEA member in *Emigrant Gentlewomen*, 150 and n.10 on 179; and the debacle concerning Miss Philimore's period as the editor of the *Imperial Colonist*, cited in FL, 'VIII: The Imperial Colonist,' in *Catalogue 1: Female Emigration Societies*.

45 For example, when the BWEA and the Society for Oversea Settlement of British women became enraged about government reception arrangements for single women in Queensland in the early twentieth century, their anger was only given proper vent in unpublished letters. Published criticisms of the Queensland government's handling of the affair are absent from these organizations' journal (the *Imperial Colonist*), replaced only by recommendations that young women avoid Queensland as a destination until more suitable reception arrangements had been put into place. Julia Bush provides a good example of the difference between the TAS's published criticism of Austra-

lian reception facilities and their private correspondence with Australian officials on the same subject. See *Edwardian Ladies and Imperial Power* (New York: Leicester University Press, 2000), 67.

46 *Girls' Quarterly* (January 1900): 19–20.

47 *Imperial Colonist* 9:109 (January 1911): 235.

48 *Travellers' Aid Society, Annual Report, 1902.*

49 For another example, see *Travellers' Aid Society, Annual Report, 1903*, 25.

50 For references to girls who were not met by family members or friends, see *Travellers' Aid Society, Annual Report, 1886*, 3; *Travellers' Aid Society, Annual Report, 1902*, 39; *Travellers' Aid Society, Annual Report, 1904*, 45; *Travellers' Aid Society, Annual Report, 1907*, section entitled 'Vancouver.'

51 *Imperial Colonist* 7:90 (June 1909): 84.

52 Ibid., 84–5.

53 Articles about the journey across the ocean or across Canada were regularly featured in the *Imperial Colonist*. See, for example, Grace Lefroy's article about her trip across Canada with an escorted party of young women in *Imperial Colonist* 6:75 (March 1908): 5–9.

54 *Imperial Colonist* 7:90 (June 1909): 84. The opinions of upper-class and upper-middle-class women concerning the quality of the travel arrangements for emigrants differed from their opinions about these sorts of arrangements when faced with the prospect of having to travel 'emigrant class' themselves. See LAC, MG 28, I245, vol. 33, International Council of Women (Canada Council), Emily Cummings to Lady Aberdeen, 18 January 1909.

55 *Friendly Work*, April 1885: 52.

56 *Travellers' Aid Society, Annual Report, 1886*. Throughout the TAS annual reports there are references to the fact that the railway porters had been thoroughly educated by the TAS in their safe-passage duties.

57 The history of the GFS is riddled with debates about the lengths to which the organization ought to go to in order to ensure that its image as a society of 'virtuous' girls would not be sullied. See Brian Harrison, 'For Church, Queen and Family: The Girls' Friendly Society, 1874–1920,' *Past and Present* 61 (November 1973): 107–38.

58 *Friendly Work*, February 1884: 29.

59 The fact that this pamphlet was circulated far and wide is indicated by a note of thanks and praise sent to Lefroy upon its receipt by the West Australian Women's National Council. The Council clearly intended to distribute Joyce's pamphlet further themselves. See *Imperial Colonist* 13: 156 (January 1915): 2.

60 Joyce, *Warning Signals.*

61 See Emma Curtin, 'Gentility Afloat: Gentlewomen's Diaries and the Voyage

to Australia, 1830–80,' *Australian Historical Studies* 26:105 (1995): 634–52; and Jan Gothard, 'Space, Authority and the Female Emigrant Afloat,' *Australian Historical Studies* 12 (April 1999): 96–115.

62 The *Imperial Colonist* advertised the departures of ships on a monthly basis, and the names and credentials of matrons were regularly noted in these announcements. Similar advertisements also appeared in the GFS journals *Friendly Work* and *Girls' Quarterly*, though on a less regular basis. Particularly accomplished matrons were highly prized by the organizations that employed them, and their comings and goings were well publicized. In fact, there were cases of bitter arguments between societies about who had the right to add emigrants to matrons' groups. See LAC, MG 17, B9 (Microfilm A-1900), Society for Promoting Christian Knowledge [hereafter SPCK], Minutes of the Emigration Committee, 25 February 1897, in which the committee discusses complaints filed by the Church Emigration Society about the BWEA's heavy-handed approach to controlling ships' matrons.

63 Joy Damousi's study of convict women who were sent to Australia clearly outlines the basis of the nineteenth-century stigma that was attached to sea travel for women. See Damousi, 'Chaos and Order: Gender, Space and Sexuality on Female Convict Ships,' *Australian Historical Studies* 26:104 (1995): 351–72; and Damousi, *Depraved and Disorderly: Female Convicts, Sexuality and Gender in Colonial Australia* (New York: Cambridge University Press, 1997).

64 *Imperial Colonist* 20:234 (February 1922): 18.

65 Ibid., 19.

66 In the 1840s ship matrons were employed by the British and colonial governments, but in the opinions of the women who desired to reform migration, these matrons were accorded little respect and poor remuneration. See Hammerton, *Emigrant Gentlewomen*, chap. 4; Una Monk, *New Horizons: A Hundred Years of Women's Migration* (London: HMSO, 1963), chap. 3; and Rye, 'Emigrant-Ship Matrons.' When governments again routinely provided matrons for emigrant ships in the twentieth century, the women's organizations set themselves up as critical observers, carefully monitoring the authority and respect that the matrons received and reporting on all abuses of the system.

67 BWEA pamphlet, quoted in SPCK, Minutes of Emigration Committee, 25 February 1897.

68 For a typical description of a ship matron, see *Friendly Work*, June 1884:88.

69 Complaints received about the matron or her charges from the ship captain, surgeon, minister, or any other passenger could seriously damage her relationship with her employers. For example, the disobedience of a party of

girls en route to Canada cost their matron, Mrs Francis, her job. SPCK, Minutes of the Ladies' Emigration Committee Meeting, 27 October 1899.

70 As one article in the *Imperial Colonist* put it, the ship matron served as 'a visible guarantee for safe-conduct during the voyage,' and as such her appearance was 'usually hailed with welcome by the relatives of the departing emigrants.' *Imperial Colonist* 20:234 (February 1922): 18.

71 Some of the letters from emigrants that were published in the organizations' journals reveal a high degree of consciousness about the matrons' ideal public persona. See, for example, *Imperial Colonist* 8:105 (September 1910), 139–40.

72 The Queen Charlotte's Coronation Hostel in Vancouver was an extreme example of a hostel run along these principles. Designed to receive middle-class women only, this hostel was truly supposed to be a home away from home. For a small fee, young women who had been received there as immigrants were welcome to come back, to be nursed by the matron and her staff while sick. See Marilyn Barber, 'The Gentlewomen of Queen Mary's Coronation Hostel,' in Barbara K. Latham and Roberta J. Pazdro, eds, *Not Just Pin Money: Selected Essays on the History of Women's Work in British Columbia* (Victoria: Camosun College, 1984).

73 See, for example, *Travellers' Aid Society, Annual Report, 1894*; ibid., *1911*, 47; and ibid., *1912*, 49.

74 Ibid., *1887*.

75 *Imperial Colonist* 1:6 (June 1902): 51–2 and 6:84 (December 1908): 11.

76 FL, 4/TAS, box 201, Travellers' Aid Society, Minutes of the Executive Committee, 19 December 1890.

77 Not all of these qualities were equally represented in the portraits of individual women. Some portraits clearly aimed to emphasize the regal standing of the emigrator (as in that of Lady Knightley in *Imperial Colonist* 11:142 [November 1913]: 175), others emphasized their maternal respectability (see, for example, that of Ellen Joyce in *Imperial Colonist* 22:263 [July 1924]: 131), while some were clearly designed to offset representations in the popular press of these same women as unattractive in appearance and in personality (see, e.g., the illustration of Mrs Chaloner Chute in *Friendly Work*, August 1913: 115).

78 Ellen Joyce, 'In Memorium. Louisa Mary, Baroness Knightley of Fawsley (Lady of the Grace of the Order of St. John of Jerusalem).' This was circulated within the GFS and published in *Imperial Colonist* 11:142 (November 1913): 176–82.

79 Ibid., 177.

80 Ibid., 178.

81 Ibid., 181.
82 Ibid., 182.
83 Ibid., 177.
84 Ibid., 180.
85 See, for example, *Friendly Work*, May 1912: 76.
86 *GFS Associates' Journal and Advertiser*, August 1885: 134.
87 Mrs Townsend, 'The Girls FS,' *Friendly Work*, November 1885: 166.
88 *Travellers' Aid Society, Annual Report, 1887.*
89 The women who desired to provide safe passage were very conscious of this resistance. See, for example, Lady Knightley of Fawsley's 'Preface' to Ellen Joyce's *Letter to Young Women on Leaving England* (Winchester: Warren and Son Ltd, 1913); and Joyce, *Warning Signals*, 2–3.
90 For figures relating to the female emigration societies, see the Introduction. In 1896 alone, the Travellers' Aid Society claimed to have aided 2003 individuals, 855 of whom had been met by appointment. In 1907 they indicated they had aided 5113 individuals. See *Travellers' Aid Society, Annual Report, 1896*; ibid., *1907*.
91 Archives of the Girls' Friendly Society, Dorothy Harris, letter to the GFS, uncatalogued.
92 See *Imperial Colonist* 10:123 (March 1912): 38 and 10:127 (July 1912): 121–4.

3: 'Grit and Grace'

1 Kathleen Saunders, 'Home Helps,' *Imperial Colonist* 6:61 (January 1907): 5.
2 Ibid. The poll tax on Chinese immigrants was in fact $500 by 1907.
3 Ellen Joyce, 'Emigration Notices,' *Imperial Colonist* 6:67 (July 1907): 11.
4 Elizabeth Elbourne provides a useful longer-term context for this work in 'Indigenous Peoples and Imperial Networks in the Early Nineteenth Century: The Politics of Knowledge,' in Phillip Buckner and R. Douglas Francis, eds, *Rediscovering the British World* (Calgary: University of Calgary Press, 2005), especially 59–60.
5 For discussions of the empire and masculinity, see Anna Davin's review article 'Historical Masculinities: Regulation, Fantasy and Empire,' *Gender and History* 9:1 (April 1997): 135–8; Susan L. Blake, 'A Woman's Trek: What Difference Does Gender Make?' in Nupur Chaudhuri and Margaret Strobel, eds, *Western Women and Imperialism: Complicity and Resistance* (Bloomington and Indianapolis: Indiana University Press, 1992); Joseph Bristow, *Empire Boys: Adventures in a Man's World* (London: HarperCollins Academic, 1991); and Graham Dawson, *Soldier Heroes: British Adventure, Empire, and the Imagining of Masculinities* (London: Routledge, 1994).

6 Anne M. Windholz, 'An Emigrant and a Gentleman: Imperial Masculinity, British Magazines, and the Colony That Got Away,' *Victorian Studies* 42:4 (Summer 1999/2000), 631.

7 See also Patrick A. Dunae, 'Boy's Literature and the Idea of Empire, 1870–1914,' *Victorian Studies* 24:1 (Autumn 1980): 105–22.

8 Anne McClintock, *Imperial Leather: Race, Gender and Sexuality in the Colonial Contest* (New York: Routledge, 1995), 4.

9 See Introduction, note 8.

10 Mary Procida provides an interesting discussion of this in *Married to the Empire: Gender, Politics and Imperialism in India, 1883–1947* (Manchester: Manchester University Press, 2002). See also Dea Birkett, *Spinsters Abroad: Victorian Lady Explorers* (Cambridge, Mass.: Basil Blackwell, 1989); Blake, 'A Woman's Trek'; and Penny Russell, 'The Allure of the Nile: Jane Franklin's Voyage to the Second Cataract, 1834,' *Gender and History* 9:2 (1997): 222–41.

11 Adele Perry, *On the Edge of Empire: Gender, Race, and the Making of British Columbia, 1849–1871* (Toronto: University of Toronto Press, 2001), 79.

12 Dominic Alessio shows that the 'white' colonies were frequently gendered female in symbolic representations, in part in an effort to convince prospective immigrants of these societies' civilized status. Dominic David Alessio, 'Domesticating "the Heart of the Wild": Female Personifications of the Colonies, 1886–1940,' *Women's History Review* 6:2 (1997): 239–69.

13 See Marilyn Lake, 'Australian Frontier Feminism and the Marauding White Man,' in Clare Midgley, ed., *Gender and Imperialism* (New York: Manchester University Press, 1998); and Perry, *On the Edge of Empire.*

14 Brian Blakely's study of the differences between the attitudes of the women involved in female emigration work and the male bureaucrats and politicians who wished to see an increase in female migration to South Africa in the early part of the twentieth century is instructive in this respect. See Brian Blakely, 'Women and Imperialism: The Colonial Office and Female Emigration to South Africa, 1901–1910,' *Albion* 13:2 (1981): 131–49.

15 I use the term 'female imperialists' to refer to the emigrators in the same way that the term is used by Julia Bush – to designate women who worked together within women-run organizations to promote a particularly women-centred version of imperialism, with the understanding that 'female imperialist' is not the same as 'imperial feminist.' As Bush notes, only a small proportion of the female imperialists who were involved in the female emigration societies would have espoused feminist views. See Julia Bush, *Edwardian Ladies and Imperial Power* (New York: Leicester University Press, 2000), 179. I have used the term female imperialist rather than maternal imperialist because, although women's understandings of their 'maternal nature' was

important in their work, it was not the only discourse used in their promotion of imperial migration for women. Their safe-passage literature featured the emigrators and their paid assistants solidly in the role of mother to the emigrant daughter, and discussions about the importance of emigrant women's futures as mothers of the race were regularly published in the *Imperial Colonist*. But the emigration societies' promotion of imperial migration to single women was more frequently presented as an opportunity to gain independence than to become a wife and mother. The term 'maternal imperialism' is used by Barbara N. Ramusack in 'Cultural Missionaries, Maternal Imperialists, Feminist Allies: British Women Activists in India, 1865–1945,' in Chaudhuri and Strobel, eds, *Western Women and Imperialism*. See also Antoinette Burton, 'The White Woman's Burden: British Feminists and "The Indian Woman," 1865–1915,' ibid., 144.

16 See chapter 10, 'Imperialism, the Women's Movement and the Vote,' in Bush, *Edwardian Ladies and Imperial Power*.

17 Mrs Skinner, 'In British Columbia,' *Imperial Colonist* 2:4 (April 1903): 41.

18 See, for example, John Mackenzie, *Propaganda and Empire: The Manipulation of British Public Opinion* (Manchester: Manchester University Press, 1984); and Mark Moss, *Manliness and Militarism: Educating Young Boys in Ontario for War* (Toronto: Oxford University Press, 2001), chap. 4.

19 See Birkett, *Spinsters Abroad*.

20 Articles in the *Imperial Colonist* about the need for more British women in South Africa sometimes contained a note of moral panic about what would happen to British men in South Africa who did not have British female partners. See, for example, *Imperial Colonist* 9:111 (March 1911): 266–7. For a discussion about this issue for the British Columbian context half a century earlier, see Perry, *On the Edge of Empire*.

21 This policy is emphasized in the BWEA's annual reports. See, for example, *United British Women's Emigration Association, Annual Report, 1888* [n.p.], 5. See Blakely, 'Women and Imperialism,' for a discussion of how this policy limited their ability to effectively send out large numbers of emigrants.

22 Adelaide Ross, *Emigration for Women* (London, 1886), 312.

23 As Julia Bush has shown for the BWEA, the SACS, and related imperial organizations, these societies and their leaders were unshakeably Anglo-centric. See chapter 6: 'Imperial Sisterhood?' in Bush, *Edwardian Ladies and Imperial Power*.

24 For a particularly clear statement in this regard, see Ellen Joyce, 'Openings for Educated Women in Canada,' 2, Library and Archives Canada (LAC), MG 28, I349 (Microfilm A-1199).

25 Irish migration tended more towards North America than to Australia. By

1871 the Irish had become the largest ethnic group in English Canada, with 24.3% of the population of Irish origin, and only 20.3% and 15.8% of the population being respectively English and Scottish. David A. Wilson, *The Irish in Canada* (Ottawa: Canadian Historical Association, 1989), 9–11. Australia's ethnic composition was very different, in that the English-originated population dominated numerically. In 1881 15.9% of Australians had been born in England (as opposed to claiming English origins) as opposed to 4.3% and 9.4% born in Scotland and Ireland respectively. See James Jupp, *The English in Australia* (New York: Cambridge University Press, 2004).

26 Marilyn Barber, *Immigrant Domestic Servants in Canada* (Ottawa: Canadian Historical Association, 1991), 5.

27 Maria Rye, 'Emigration of Educated Women,' paper read at the Social Science Congress in Dublin, 1861, 12. This paper was also published in the *Englishwoman's Journal* and as a pamphlet by Emily Faithful and Co.

28 Rye quoted in Perry, *On the Edge of Empire*, 151. Similarly antagonistic sentiments towards single female Irish immigrants were made public in Canada and in Australia. Paula Hamilton focuses on this issue at some length in 'The "Servant Class": Poor Female Migration to Australia in the Nineteenth Century,' in Eric Richards, ed., *Poor Australian Immigrants in the Nineteenth Century* (*Visible Immigrants*, vol. 2) (Canberra: Highland Press, 1991). Rye's attitude about Scottish female emigrants does not seem to have been as commonly stated.

29 For South Africa, see Blakely, 'Women and Imperialism'; and Jean Jacques Van-Helten and Keith Williams, '"The Crying Need of South Africa": The Emigration of Single British Women to the Transvaal, 1901–10,' *Journal of Southern African Studies* 10:1 (October 1983): 17–38. For an example of the female imperialists' statements of concern about European immigrants, see *Imperial Colonist* 6:67 (July 1907): 11.

30 Bush, *Edwardian Ladies and Imperial Power*, 163.

31 Rye, 'Emigration of Educated Women,' 7–9.

32 See Ellen Joyce, 'British Women's Emigration Association: Objects,' LAC, MG 28, I349 (Microfilm A-1199); *Imperial Colonist* 4:38 (February 1905): 21; and *Imperial Colonist* 4:46 (October 1905): 113. This policy was the result of a combination of factors, including the fact that the association's subscribers would not support the emigration of much-needed servants.

33 *Colonial Intelligence League (for Educated Women), First Annual Report, 1911.*

34 Vancouver City Archives (VCA), Queen Mary's Coronation Hostel (QMCH), box 55, vol. 1, file 1, Helen Ferguson to Mrs Fitzgibbon, 4 December 1912.

35 VCA, QMCH, box 55, vol. 1, file 1, Caroline Grosvenor to Mrs FitzGibbon, 7 August 1913.

36 An agreement was signed at some point in 1914. See VCA, QMCH, box 55, vol. 1, file 1, 'Memorandum of Agreement.'

37 Ellen Joyce, 'Imperial Aspect of the GFS,' 5. See also Joyce, 'The Joyce Hostel for Gentlewomen.' Both papers may be located at LAC, MG 28, I349 (Microfilm A-1199).

38 For discussions of the trend away from domestic service as an occupation for working-class women, see Margaret Anderson, 'Good Strong Girls: Colonial Women and Work,' in Kay Saunders and Raymond Evans, eds, *Gender Relations in Australia: Domination and Negotiation* (Sydney: Harcourt Brace, 1992), 231–6; Marilyn Barber, 'The Women Ontario Welcomed: Immigrant Domestics for Ontario Homes, 1870–1930,' *Ontario History* 72:3 (1980); Raymond Evans and Kay Saunders, 'No Place Like Home: The Evolution of the Australian Housewife,' in Evans and Saunders, eds, *Gender Relations in Australia,* 182–3; Pamela Horn, *The Rise and Fall of the Victorian Servant* (New York: St Martin's Press, 1975); Beverley Kingston, *My Wife, My Daughter, and Poor Mary Ann: Women and Work in Australia* (Melbourne: Nelson, 1975), chap. 3; and Genevieve Leslie, 'Domestic Service in Canada, 1880–1920,' in Janice Acton, Penny Goldsmith, and Bonnie Shephard, eds, *Women at Work: Ontario 1850–1930* (Toronto: Canadian Women's Educational Press, 1974).

39 Correspondence on this subject was initiated by the FMCES in the 1860s, by the CIL before the First World War, and by the SOSBW in the period immediately after the war.

40 See Susan Jackel, intro. to Georgina Binnie-Clark, *Wheat and Woman* (Toronto: University of Toronto Press, 1979); and Michele Langfield, 'Gender Blind? Australian Immigration Policy and Practice, 1901–1930,' *Journal of Australian Studies* 79 (2003).

41 Labour organizations had different understandings of their communities' needs from those of Liberal or Conservative governments, or big business. Conflict around the issue of immigrant labourers was thus a standard theme in labour politics during the late nineteenth and early twentieth centuries. See David Goutor, 'The Walls of Solidarity: The Mainstream Canadian Labour Movement and Immigration Policy, 1872 to the Early 1930s,' PhD thesis, University of Toronto, 2003; Michael Roe, *Australia, Britain, and Migration, 1915–1940* (New York: Cambridge University Press, 1995).

42 See Valerie Knowles, *Strangers at Our Gates: Canadian Immigration and Immigration Policy, 1540–1990* (Toronto: Dundurn Press, 1992); Michele Langfield, '"The Ideal Immigrant": Immigration to Victoria between Federation and the First World War,' *Australian Studies* (UK) 8 (June 1994): 1–14; Roe, *Australia, Britain, and Migration;* and Reg Whitaker, *Canadian Immigration Policy Since Confederation* (Ottawa: Canadian Historical Association, 1991).

43 It is ironic that the emigrators had such a hard time convincing government bodies and employers in the dominions that they ought to sponsor the immigration of more of their selected, educated single women to do domestic service. In both Canada and Australia creative schemes were constantly in the works to solve the servant shortage problem through immigration. In Canada and Australia there are large bodies of literature available on this subject. See, for example, Sedef Arat-Koc, 'From "Mothers of the Nation" to Migrant Workers: Immigration Policies and Domestic Workers in Canadian History,' in Veronica Strong-Boag, Mona Gleason, and Adele Perry, eds, *Rethinking Canada: The Promise of Women's History*, 4th ed. (Toronto: Oxford University Press, 2002); and B.W. Higman, 'Testing the Boundaries of White Australia: Domestic Servants and Immigration Policy, 1901–45,' *Immigrants and Minorities* 22:1 (March 2003): 1–21.

44 Robin Haines, *Emigration and the Labouring Poor: Australian Recruitment in Britain and Ireland, 1831–1860* (London: Macmillan Press, 1997); and Robin Haines, '"The Idle and the Drunken Won't Do There": Poverty, the New Poor Law and Nineteenth-Century Government-Assisted Emigration to Australia from the United Kingdom,' *Australian Historical Studies* 28:108 (April 1997).

45 Hamilton, quoting government officials, 'The "Servant Class,"' 130.

46 For further discussion about Australians' scepticism regarding British emigrators' motives, see Jan Gothard, 'Wives or Workers? Single British Female Migration to Colonial Australia,' in Pamela Sharpe, ed., *Women, Gender and Labour Migration: Historical and Global Perspectives* (New York: Routledge, 2001).

47 See Perry, *On the Edge of Empire*, 153. See also correspondence concerning colonials' attitudes about the immigration of educated women to Australia in Fawcett Library (FL), 1/FME, 2/1-2, FMCES, Letterbooks 1 and 2.

48 See Marion Diamond, 'Maria Rye's Journey: Metropolitan and Colonial Perceptions of Female Emigration,' in Rita Kranidis, ed., *Imperial Objects: Essays on Victorian Women's Emigration and the Unauthorized Imperial Experience* (New York: Twayne Publishers, 1998); and Barber, 'The Women Ontario Welcomed.'

49 See Australian Archives (AA), Australian Capital Territory (ACT), series A458, item A154/14, for examples of Australian lobby groups; and see LAC, RG 76, vol. 284, file 250923 (Microfilm C-7833) for an example of a Saskatchewan-based Canadian lobby group.

50 *Imperial Colonist* 3:35 (November 1904): 127.

51 See for example, *Imperial Colonist* 3:32 (August 1912): 134–5 and 4:41 (May 1905): 57.

52 *Imperial Colonist* 3:32 (August 1904): 86.

53 See, for example, the June and November issues of the *Imperial Colonist* of 1904 (pages 69 and 126 respectively), in which the monthly salaries that domestic workers might expect were listed as follows: mother's help, $12–$15; nurse-housemaids, $15; lady helps, $15; servants, $20; cooks, $20–$25.

54 *Imperial Colonist* 6:74 (February 1908): 9–10.

55 See, for example, *Imperial Colonist* 7:87 (March 1909): 37–8 and 41.

56 *Imperial Colonist* 9:115 (July 1911): 338. The thoughts of this British traveller had been influenced by Miss Fitzgibbon, a leading Toronto philanthropist and social reformer, who ran Toronto's women's hostel for immigrants.

57 See *Imperial Colonist* 9:109 (January 1911): 226–7; 'Commission's Report,' *Imperial Colonist* 18:214 (January 1920): 6; and a pamphlet produced by the Society for Oversea Settlement of British Women, *Handbook for Women who are Thinking of Settling Overseas* (n.p., 1923).

58 See *Imperial Colonist* 9:108 (February 1911): 244.

59 According to the emigrators, British Columbia was a particularly good destination for educated home helps. It was thus regularly promoted to this class of women above all other locations.

60 For discussions of the negative reactions of colonial communities to extended programs of immigration of educated women, see Marion Diamond, *Emigration and Empire: The Life of Maria S. Rye* (New York: Garland Publishing, 1999); and chapter 6, '"Fair Ones of a Purer Caste": Bringing White Women to British Columbia,' in Perry, *On the Edge of Empire.*

61 For a particularly 'heavy' example of this sort of argument, see 'Waste Women' in *Imperial Colonist* 11:133 (February 1913): 27–8. More representative is the article in *Imperial Colonist* 3:31 (July 1904): 73.

62 See Hammerton, *Emigrant Gentlewomen,* chap. 4.

63 See Maria Rye's 'Emigration of Educated Women.'

64 William Rathbone Greg, 'Why Are Women Redundant?' *National Review* 28 (April 1862): 434–60.

65 For further discussions of these debates, see chapter 3, 'Solutions for Surplus Women,' in Diamond, *Emigration and Empire*; chapter 5, 'Feminism and Female Emigration, 1861–1886,' in Hammerton, *Emigrant Gentlewomen;* and Rita Kranidis, *The Victorian Spinster and Colonial Emigration: Contested Subjects* (New York: St Martin's Press, 1999).

66 The theme of the redundant gentlewoman features prominently in Marilyn Barber, 'The Gentlewomen of Queen Mary's Coronation Hostel,' in Barbara K. Latham and Roberta J. Pazdro, eds, *Not Just Pin Money: Selected Essays on the History of Women's Work in British Columbia* (Victoria: Camosun College, 1984); Diamond, *Emigration and Empire*; Hammerton (esp. chap. 1, 'The Problem of

the Distressed Gentlewoman'); and Kranidis, *The Victorian Spinster and Colonial Emigration.*

67 For two very different approaches to this subject, see Kranidis, *The Victorian Spinster and Colonial Emigration*; and Adele Perry, '"Oh I'm Just Sick of the Faces of Men": Gender Imbalance, Race, Sexuality, and Sociability in Nineteenth Century British Columbia,' *B.C. Studies* 105–6 (1995): 27–43.

68 Perry, *On the Edge of Empire*, 151.

69 See FL, FMCES, 1/FME, 2/1-2, Letterbooks.

70 Carmen Faymonville, '"Waste Not, Want Not": Even Redundant Women Have Their Uses,' in Rita Kranidis, ed., *Imperial Objects: Essays on Victorian Women's Emigration and the Unauthorized Imperial Experience* (New York: Twayne, 1998), 66.

71 Michele Langfield, 'Gender Blind? Australian Immigration Policy and Practice, 1901–1930,' *Journal of Australian Studies* 79 (2003): 143–52.

72 Katie Pickles, 'Empire Settlement and Single British Women as New Zealand Domestic Servants during the 1920s,' *New Zealand Journal of History* 35:1 (2001): 22–4.

73 Carol Dyehouse, *Feminism and the Family in England, 1880–1939* (New York: Basil Blackwell, 1989); Sheila Jeffreys, *The Spinster and Her Enemies: Feminism and Sexuality, 1880–1930* (Boston: Pandora Press, 1985); Sally Ledger, *The New Woman: Fiction and Feminism at the Fin de Siècle* (New York: Manchester University Press, 1997); Elaine Showalter, ed., *Daughters of Decadence: Women Writers of the Fin de Siècle* (London: Virago Press, Ltd, 1993); Elaine Showalter, *Sexual Anarchy: Gender and Culture at the Fin de Siècle* (New York: Viking Penguin, 1990).

74 This quote comes from an article on the National Guild of Housecraft in *Imperial Colonist* 13:156 (January 1915): 13. For a discussion of 'The Rationalization of Housework' during the nineteenth century, see chapter 5 in Leonore Davidoff, *Worlds Between: Historical Perspectives on Gender and Class* (Cambridge: Polity Press, 1995).

75 Joyce, 'Openings for Educated Women in Canada,' 2.

76 Elizabeth Thompson, *The Pioneer Woman: A Canadian Character Type* (Montreal and Kingston: McGill-Queen's University Press, 1991), 4.

77 Ibid.

78 See Susanna Moodie, *Roughing It in the Bush or Forest Life in Canada* (Toronto: McClelland and Stewart, 1962 [1852]).

79 Thompson, *The Pioneer Woman*, 31.

80 Ibid., 45.

81 Ibid., 13–14. Thompson argues that 'in her creation of the pioneer lady, Traill had few, if any literary precedents' (16).

82 Catharine Parr Traill, cited in Thompson, *The Pioneer Woman*, 51.

83 See, for example, the discussion in the CIL Minutes, 23 February 1910, about questionnaires sent out to the National Councils of Women in the dominions asking about work opportunities for women. LAC, MG 28, I336 (Microfilm A-1059).

84 *The Colonial Intelligence League, First Annual Report, 1911*, 8.

85 Ibid.

86 Ibid., 10–11.

87 Diamond, *Emigration and Empire*, 81.

88 *The Colonial Intelligence League, First Annual Report, 1911*, 11.

89 *Imperial Colonist* 3:34 (October 1904): 117.

90 *The Colonial Intelligence League, Third Annual Report, 1913*, 11.

91 *Imperial Colonist* 7:86 (February 1909): 26.

92 Ibid. 7:87 (March 1909): 42.

93 G. Binnie-Clarke, 'Are Educated Women Wanted in Canada,' *Imperial Colonist* 8:98 (February 1910): 23.

94 Mrs Skinner, 'In British Columbia,' *Imperial Colonist* 3:30 (June 1904): 67.

95 Mrs Alfred Watt, 'Farm Homes in Canada,' *Imperial Colonist* 13:159 (April 1915): 61.

96 My argument here contrasts with that of other historians of female migration. There has been a consensus in studies of female emigration societies of the late Victorian years and early twentieth century that these organizations were single-minded in their efforts to direct single women into domestic work. A recent example of this argument may be found in Michele Langfield, 'A Chance to Bloom,' where she likens the work of the BWEA to that of the Salvation Army and Dr Barnardo's Homes in this respect.

97 *Imperial Colonist* 8:100 (April 1910): 51.

98 Ibid. In 'The Imperial Aspect of the GFS,' Ellen Joyce writes that she looks upon 'Home Help work as the stepping-stone of opportunity' for single women (6).

99 M. Montgomery-Campbell, 'Ca-na-da. A Contradiction in Terms,' *Imperial Colonist* 2:2 (February 1903): 18.

100 Bush, *Edwardian Ladies and Imperial Power*, 156–9.

101 See Hammerton, *Emigrant Gentlewomen*; Diamond, *Emigration and Empire*, 86; and Perry, *On the Edge of Empire*, chap. 6.

102 See, for example, *Imperial Colonist* 9:113 (May 1911): 307 and 9:116 (August 1911): 346; and Ellen Joyce, 'Ventures within the Empire: To Women of the XX Century' (n.p., 1913). In Joyce's article may be found an excellent example of the 'scarcity model' argument that is explored in Perry, 'Oh I'm Just Sick of the Faces of Men.'

103 *Imperial Colonist* 7:86 (February 1909): 23–4.

104 *Imperial Colonist* 7:88 (April 1909): 52.

105 See, for example, 'Educated Girls in Winnipeg,' *Imperial Colonist* 23:3 (March 1925): 46–8.

106 For example, Georgina Binnie-Clark used the female emigration network to help stir up support for her campaign to allow women homesteaders in Canada to receive free land (160 acres) on the same terms as men. See Susan Jackel, Introduction to Georgina Binnie-Clark, *Wheat and Woman* (Toronto: University of Toronto Press, 1979), xx–xxxi. See also Lisa Chilton, 'Land and Imperial Adventure: Promoting Emigration to the Young Single Woman,' unpublished paper presented at the Canadian Historical Association conference, Winnipeg, June 2004.

107 Andrew Yarmie provides an excellent discussion of the CIL's work along these lines in '"I Had Always Wanted to Farm": The Quest for Independence by British Female Emigrants at the Princess Patricia Ranch, Vernon, British Columbia, 1912–1920,' *British Journal of Canadian Studies* 16:1 (2003): 102–25.

108 E.L. Chicanot, 'Some Canadian Women Pioneers,' *Imperial Colonist* 23:9 (September 1925): 177–9. This article is continued in the October 1925 edition of the *Imperial Colonist*. See also the April 1910 edition of the *Imperial Colonist*, which contains several articles on farming for women in the colonies.

109 See, for example, Marjorie Mitchell, 'Down Under: My First Job in Australia,' *Imperial Colonist* 24:9 (September 1926): 183–5.

110 *Imperial Colonist* 5:52 (April 1906): 47.

111 Joyce, 'Ventures within the Empire,' 3.

112 Joyce, 'Openings for Educated Women in Canada,' 2.

113 Lady Knightley of Fawsley, preface to Ellen Joyce, *Letter to Young Women on Leaving England*, 7th ed. (Winchester: Warren and Son, Ltd, 1913).

114 Every issue of the *Imperial Colonist* advertised specific destinations in its section entitled 'Emigration notices.' Those destinations that failed to make it into this section were often absent for specific reasons. Periodically, destinations were explicitly singled out in this section for criticism. Most of the time, however, criticism in the 'Emigration notices' was reserved for destinations such as the United States and South America, which were discouraged on the grounds of safety and imperial pride.

115 See, for example, *Imperial Colonist*, 6:63 (March 1907): 11, and its issues for March, April, and August 1909.

116 Joyce, 'Ventures within the Empire,' 10.

117 Thus, 'The party of 11 superior women who went out [to western Canada] last year have all done well, excepting one who valued herself too highly

and had to find her level, where she remains.' There was not much sympathy for women with inflated egos. *Imperial Colonist* 2:6 (June 1903): 70. See also *Imperial Colonist* 5:54 (June 1906): 83–4; and Joyce, 'Ventures within the Empire,' 12.

118 *Imperial Colonist* 7:88 (April 1909): 52.

119 *Society for the Oversea Settlement of British Women, Annual Report, 1923*, 15–16. See also *Imperial Colonist* 2:4 (April 1903): 45, 6:62 (February 1907): 7.

120 For examples of this argument, see *Imperial Colonist* 6:62 (February 1907): 7; 7:87 (March 1909): 41; 7:88 (April 1909): 52–3; 7:92 (August 1909): 121; and 7:95 (November 1909): 188–9.

121 Hammerton, *Emigrant Gentlewomen* (especially chapters 5 and 6).

122 Bush, *Edwardian Ladies and Imperial Power*, 179.

123 Ibid., 175.

124 Rita Kranidis, Introduction to *Imperial Objects: Essays on Victorian Women's Emigration and the Unauthorized Imperial Experience* (New York: Twayne Publishers, 1998), 14.

4: Letters 'Home'

1 *Imperial Colonist* 8:107 (November 1910): 181–2.

2 Ibid., 181.

3 Ibid.

4 Una Monk, *New Horizons: A Hundred Years of Women's Migration* (London: Her Majesty's Stationary Office, 1963); and G.F. Plant, *SOSBW: A Survey of Voluntary Effort in Women's Empire Migration* (London: HMSO, 1950).

5 For example, see discussions of this problem in the introductions to Jan Gothard, *Blue China: Single Female Migration to Colonial Australia* (Melbourne: Melbourne University Press, 2001) and to Jean Barman, *Sojourning Sisters: The Lives and Letters of Jessie and Annie McQueen* (Toronto: University of Toronto Press, 2003).

6 One rich set of unpublished letters to the emigrators who worked through the Female Middle-Class Emigration Society (FMCES) does exist. They were copied out into letterbooks by Jane Lewin, and are now stored at the Fawcett Library (FL), 1/FME, 2-1. They have been drawn upon extensively by historians writing about female emigration, and are part of the reason why for so long historians' interest was directed largely at middle-class emigrants.

7 Historians of migration are increasingly returning to published emigrants' letters as a potentially rich set of sources. For historiographical reviews of

the use of published immigrant letters by historians, see David A. Gerber, 'The Immigrant Letter between Positivism and Populism: The Uses of Immigrant Personal Correspondence in Twentieth-Century American Scholarship,' *Journal of American Ethnic History* 16:4 (Summer 1997); and Bill Jones, 'Immigrant Letters in the Periodical Press in Late Nineteenth-Century Wales,' in Bruce S. Elliott, David A. Gerber, and Suzanne M. Sinke, eds, *Letters across Borders: The Epistolary Practices of International Migrants* (Basingstoke: Palgrave, 2006).

8 Gothard, *Blue China,* 17

9 For examples, see Gothard, *Blue China*; Paula Hamilton, 'The "Servant Class": Poor Female Migration to Australia in the Nineteenth Century,' in Eric Richards, ed., *Poor Australian Immigrants in the Nineteenth Century* (*Visible Immigrants,* vol. 2) (Canberra: Highland Press, 1991); and Barbara Roberts, 'Ladies, Women and the State: Managing Female Migration,' in Roxana Ng et al., eds, *Community Organization and the Canadian State* (Toronto: Garamond Press, 1990).

10 Ellen Joyce and Grace Lefroy corresponded with thousands of emigrants and prospective emigrants over their careers. This correspondence does not appear to have been saved. Joyce also kept an album of photos that emigrants sent back to her of themselves after they had settled. These photos have likewise not been archived with the other female emigration society documents at the Fawcett Library in London.

11 *Imperial Colonist* 8:100 (April 1910): 58.

12 Eleven members of the party travelled in second-class accommodation; 61 travelled third class. *Imperial Colonist* 8:100 (April 1910): 58.

13 A couple of examples of letters that were clearly solicited: 'Letter from a former Student of Stoke Prior Training College' and 'Canada for the Teacher,' *Imperial Colonist* 9:115 (July 1911): 334–6.

14 'A Business Opening in Vancouver,' *Imperial Colonist* 11:133 (January 1913): 227–8.

15 'Farm for Sale in Saskatchewan,' *Imperial Colonist* 19:227 (July 1921): 91. For a sample of other business ventures that were advertised in this way, see *Imperial Colonist* 2:12 (December 1903): 140–1 and 10:131 (November 1912): 190–1.

16 It is not evident in the literature whether or not Mrs Horsfall was a British emigrant. Most of the colonial correspondents wishing to advertise their businesses clearly identified themselves as BWEA migrants.

17 *Imperial Colonist* 9:115 (July 1911): 339.

18 *Imperial Colonist* 8:107 (November 1910): 182.

19 Ibid., 181.

20 For a particularly interesting example of an effort to elicit help for a charitable cause, see a nurse's request for financial assistance to set up a nursing home in South Africa, *Imperial Colonist* 10:131 (November 1912): 100–10

21 Details concerning financial donations were not provided in the societies' publications – even when the donations were made to the hostels of small communities' churches. The omission was likely an effort to protect the editor and donors from an onslaught of requests for more of the same. However, donations were noted in the hostels' annual reports.

22 'A Pathetic Appeal,' *Imperial Colonist* 6:82 (October 1908): 9 (emphasis in original).

23 *Imperial Colonist* 6:83 (November 1908): 10.

24 Ibid., 14:174 (July 1916): 102.

25 Ibid., 19:232 (December 1921): 60.

26 Ibid., 18:28 (July 1919): 105.

27 Girls' Friendly Society Archives, 2/217, copy of letter dated 27/8/1933, from Mrs Rebecca Podmole to Lady Bertha Dawkins.

28 *Imperial Colonist* 23:9 (September 1925): 174.

29 Ibid., 14:174 (July 1916): 103; 23:9 (September 1925): 175.

30 Ibid., 23:9 (September 1925): 175. A similar point is made in 'Australian Women and "S.O.S.B.W. Settlers,"' *Imperial Colonist* 25:1 (January 1927): 3–4.

31 Since the journey in March, Black had overseen the migration of at least one other group of women to Canada. On 9 June Black had set sail with Miss Rintoul, another matron, and 146 second- and third-class emigrants. In this instance, Black had travelled to Vancouver with any women who were going that far. Whether she stayed on in BC until Glanville met her in Vancouver on the morning of 23 September or made yet another trip as chaperone in the interim, is unclear. *Imperial Colonist* 8:102 (June 1910): 91.

32 Ibid., 8:107 (November 1910): 182.

33 Emigrants' responses to ship matrons are discussed in chapter 5, 'Gliding Over the Waves,' in Gothard, *Blue China*; Hamilton, 'The "Servant Class"'; Emma Curtin, 'Gentility Afloat: Gentlewomen's Diaries and the Voyage to Australia, 1830–80,' *Australian Historical Studies* 26:105 (1995): 634–52; and James Hammerton, *Emigrant Gentlewomen: Genteel Poverty and Female Emigration, 1830–1914* (London: Croom Helm, 1979).

34 *Imperial Colonist* 8:105 (September 1910): 139–40.

35 Ibid., 1:5 (May 1902): 44.

36 Indications of affection for the emigrators were likewise prominent in many of the letters that emigrants sent back to Jane Lewin, Maria Rye, and other members of the FMCES. See FL, 1/FME, Letterbooks, 2-1.

37 *Imperial Colonist* 8:107 (November 1910): 187–8.

38 Ibid.
39 Gothard, *Blue China*, 4–7.
40 *Imperial Colonist* 6:65 (May 1907): 9–10.
41 See, for example, Barbara Roberts, 'Ladies, Women and the State: Managing Female Migration,' in Roxana Ng et al., eds, *Community Organization and the Canadian State* (Toronto: Garamond Press, 1990); and Gothard, *Blue China*.
42 FL, 1/FME, Letterbooks, 2-1.
43 FMCES letters clearly illustrate this point. Two of the organization's key 'receivers' turned out to be less willing to volunteer their services for the FMCES cause than the British-based emigrators had imagined. See references to Mrs Baker, Mrs Dillon, and Mrs à Beckett, as well as Mrs à Beckett's letter of protest (22 December 1864) in FL, 1/FME, Letterbooks, 2-1.
44 See the articles and introduction in Seth Koven and Sonya Michel, eds, *Mothers of a New World: Maternalist Politics and the Origins of Welfare States* (New York: Routledge, 1993); Leila Rupp, 'Constructing Internationalism: The Case of Transnational Women's Organisations, 1888–1945,' *American Historical Review* 99:5 (December 1994): 1571–1600; Rupp, *Worlds of Women: The Making of an International Women's Movement* (Princeton, NJ: Princeton University Press, 1997); Angela Woollacott, 'From Moral to Professional Authority: Secularism, Social Work, and Middle-Class Women's Self-Construction in World War I Britain,' *Journal of Women's History* 10:2 (Summer): 85–111; and Jane Lewis, 'Gender, the Family and Women's Agency in the Building of "Welfare States": The British Case,' *Social History* 19:1 (January 1994): 37–55.
45 Likewise, historians have debated the extent to which female reformers influenced the creation of social-welfare programs that emerged in the first half of the twentieth century. See Lewis's commentary on all these issues in 'Gender, the Family and Women's Agency in the Building of "Welfare States,"' 38–41.
46 'From a Nursery Governess in Winnipeg,' *Imperial Colonist* 18:218 (May 1920): 79–80.
47 Gothard, *Blue China*.
48 Angela Woollacott, '"All This Is the Empire, I Told Myself": Australian Women's Voyages "Home" and the Articulation of Colonial Whiteness,' *American Historical Review* 102:4 (1997): 1004.

5: Welcoming Women

1 For a small sample of works that explore this subject for Canada and Australia, see Carl Berger, *The Sense of Power: Studies in the Ideas of Canadian Imperialism, 1867–1914* (Toronto: University of Toronto Press, 1970); Mark Moss,

Manliness and Militarism: Educating Young Boys in Ontario for War (Toronto: Oxford University Press, 2001); David Carter and Gillian Whitlock, eds, *Images of Australia* (St Lucia: University of Queensland Press, 1992); and Patricia Grimshaw, Marilyn Lake, Ann McGrath, and Marian Quartly, eds, *Creating a Nation, 1788–1990* (Toronto: Penguin, 1996).

2 Louis Wain, 'Canada's Deathtrap. Further Warnings to Canadian Emigrants,' *John Bull* 10 (December 1910): 924.

3 Library and Archives Canada (LAC), Record Group (RG) 76, vol. 42, file 1070, part 4.

4 LAC, RG 76, vol. 42, file 1070.

5 'Englishmen Express Indignation over Libellous Attack on Man in Canada,' *Ottawa Free Press*, 13 January 1911.

6 See, for example, Christine Stansell, *City of Women: Sex and Class in New York, 1789–1860* (New York: Knopf, 1986); Carolyn Strange, *Toronto's Girl Problem: The Perils and Pleasures of the City, 1880–1930* (Toronto: University of Toronto Press, 1995); and Judith Walkowitz, *City of Dreadful Delight: Narratives of Sexual Danger in Late-Victorian London* (Chicago: University of Chicago Press, 1992).

7 Historians of Australian immigration have emphasized the gendered nature of respectability, especially in relation to the journey overseas. The Australian and British press regularly pointed to the long ocean voyage as a testing ground, if not a corrupting agent, of women's respectability. See Emma Curtin, 'Gentility Afloat: Gentlewomen's Diaries and the Voyage to Australia, 1830–80,' *Australian Historical Studies* 26:105 (1995): 634–52; Joy Damousi, 'Chaos and Order: Gender, Space and Sexuality on Female Convict Ships,' *Australian Historical Studies* 26:104 (1995): 351–72; Damousi, *Depraved and Disorderly: Female Convicts, Sexuality and Gender in Colonial Australia* (New York: Cambridge University Press, 1997); and Jan Gothard, 'Space, Authority and the Female Emigrant Afloat,' *Australian Historical Studies* 12 (April 1999): 96–115.

8 Mariana Valverde, *The Age of Light, Soap, and Water: Moral Reform in English Canada, 1885–1925* (Toronto: McClelland and Stewart, 1991), 128. See similar arguments made in Marilyn Barber, 'The Women Ontario Welcomed: Immigrant Domestics for Ontario Homes, 1870–1930,' *Ontario History* 72:3 (1980); Janice Gothard, '"Pity the Poor Immigrant": Assisted Single Female Migration to Colonial Australia,' in Eric Richards, ed., *Poor Australian Immigrants in the Nineteenth Century* (*Visible Immigrants*, vol. 2) (Canberra: Highland Press, 1991); and Barbara Roberts, '"A Work of Empire": Canadian Reformers and British Female Immigration,' in Linda Kealey, ed., *A Not Unreasonable Claim: Women and Reform in Canada, 1880s–1920s* (Toronto: Women's Press, 1979).

9 Although the focus of Katie Pickles's article 'Exhibiting Canada: Empire, Migration and the 1928 English Schoolgirl Tour' is not female immigrants, it provides an interesting analysis of the attempts of British and Canadian female imperialists to simultaneously manipulate images of young British women for a Canadian audience, and images of Canada for a female British audience. As Pickles's puts it, 'A focus on the schoolgirls themselves shows how the girls were positioned to transmit an image of Canada to Britain, while themselves being on display so as to set an example to which Canadians should aspire' (81). The schoolgirls' tour was designed and managed by the SOSBW and the Imperial Order Daughters of the Empire. Katie Pickles, 'Exhibiting Canada: Empire, Migration and the 1928 English Schoolgirl Tour,' *Gender, Place and Culture* 7:1 (2000): 81–96.

10 Marilyn Lake, 'Australian Frontier Feminism and the Marauding White Man,' in Clare Midgley, ed., *Gender and Imperialism* (New York: Manchester University Press, 1998); Walkowitz, *City of Dreadful Delight*; Strange, *Toronto's Girl Problem*; Stansell, *City of Women*; Karen Dubinsky, *Improper Advances: Rape and Heterosexual Conflict in Ontario, 1880–1929* (Chicago: University of Chicago Press, 1993); Adele Perry, *On the Edge of Empire: Gender, Race, and the Making of British Columbia, 1849–1871* (Toronto: University of Toronto Press, 2001).

11 Lady Ishbel Aberdeen was explicit on this point in her introduction to *Women of Canada: Their Life and Work* (Ottawa: Government of Canada, 1900), iv.

12 An interesting parallel may be seen in the efforts of Australian women to replace white men as the protectors of Aboriginal women. In this case too, women in Australia looked to female activists in Britain for support. See Alison Holland, 'The Campaign for Women Protectors: Gender, Race and Frontier between the Wars,' *Australian Feminist Studies* 16:34 (2001): 27–42; and Fiona Paisley, *Loving Protection? Australian Feminism and Aboriginal Women's Rights, 1919–1939* (Melbourne: Melbourne University Press, 2000).

13 See Michele Langfield, 'Attitudes to European Immigration to Australia in the Early Twentieth Century'; Langfield, '"White Aliens": The Control of European Immigration to Australia 1920–30,' *Journal of Intercultural Studies* 12:2 (1991): 1–14; Roberts, '"A Work of Empire"'; Michael Roe, *Australia, Britain, and Migration, 1915–1940* (New York: Cambridge University Press, 1995); and Valverde, *The Age of Light, Soap, and Water*.

14 David Jacques Goutor, 'The Walls of Solidarity: The Mainstream Canadian Labour Movement and Immigration Policy, 1872 to the Early 1930s,' PhD thesis, University of Toronto, 2004.

15 As John Atchison notes, although this was the dominant public opinion in

both countries, Australia was much more willing to let this opinion determine how immigration policies would be formulated in the period before the Great Depression. John Atchison, 'Patterns of Australian and Canadian Immigration 1900–1983,' *International Migration* (Netherlands) 22:1 (1984): 4–8. Ann Curthoys raises interesting questions about the extent to which all Australians shared the belief that Britons made the best immigrants in her article 'History and Identity,' in Wayne Hudson and Geoffrey Bolton, eds, *Creating Australia: Changing Australian History* (St Leonards, NSW: Allen and Unwin, 1997).

16 *Seventh Annual Report of the British Immigration League of Australia (New South Wales Branch)*, 2.

17 A. Martin, 'Public Policy before Federation,' in James Jupp, ed., *The Australian People: An Encyclopaedia of the Nation, Its People and Their Origins* (Sydney: Angus and Robertson, 1988), 74. See Goutor, 'The Walls of Solidarity,' for a similar discussion of Canadian immigration politics.

18 An exception was the case of Queensland in the early 1890s, where, according to the *Annual Report* of the British Women's Emigration Association for 1891–1892, the assisted immigration of domestics was suspended because 'the working man will not vote expenditure to provide servants for the richer classes.'

19 For example, see LAC, RG 76, vol. 317, file 306064; and Australian Archives (AA), Australian Capital Territory (ACT), Series A1, item 1932/7386.

20 LAC, RG 76, vol. 317, file 306064, *Toronto World*, 12/4/14, 'Australia Hard After Emigrants. Canada's Chief Competitor Displaying Indiscriminate Zeal' (newspaper clipping).

21 Marilyn Barber, 'Sunny Ontario for British Girls, 1900–1930,' in Jean Burnet, ed., *Looking Into My Sister's Eyes: An Exploration in Women's History* (Toronto: Multicultural History Society of Ontario, 1986), 162.

22 See, for examples, AA, ACT, A461/8, Y349/1/5, 'Immigration Encouragement. Early Schemes. Correspondence with States – Tasmania'; and Queensland State Archives (QSA), Brisbane, PRE/122, 'Correspondence re Immigration of Domestics.'

23 Women in rural areas formed lobby groups to encourage governments and emigration societies to favour them over city dwellers when directing the flow of female emigrants. Most notable of these was the Country Women's Association of Australia. See Country Women's Association, *The Silver Years* (Sydney, 1947); Pam Roberts, 'Tea, Scones and a Willing Ear: The Country Women's Association of Victoria, 1928–1934,' *Lilith* 1 (Winter 1984): 23–30; and Elizabeth Kenworthy Teather, 'The Country Women's Association of New South Wales in the 1920s and 1930s as a Counter-revolutionary Organi-

sation,' *Journal of Australian Studies* 41 (June 1994): 67–78. See also the 'Domestic Immigration Society of New South Wales,' AA, ACT, Series A458; item A154/14; and the 'Women's British Immigration League of Saskatchewan,' LAC, RG 76, vol. 284, file 250923, reel C-7833.

24 Discussion of this aspect is particularly good in Marjory Harper, *Beyond the Broad Atlantic: Emigration from North-East Scotland*, vol. 2 (Aberdeen: Aberdeen University Press, 1988).

25 See ibid., and Angela McCarthy, '"A Good Idea of Colonial Life": Personal Letters and Irish Migration to New Zealand,' *New Zealand Journal of History* 35:1 (2001): 1–21.

26 This continued to be the case even after reception and aftercare were taken up wholeheartedly by government bodies in the 1920s, and receptions in various cities were supposed to be standardized and monitored. For example, in the early 1920s, the GFS made it clear to the women who ran the SOSBW that when GFS girls were sent out from their organizations, with no particular destination in mind, they 'should be recommended and advised to go to places where there are G.F.S. Correspondents and G.F.S. Lodges or Hostels. That Canada and New Zealand are the two Dominions to which G.F.S. Members should be recommended to go and in the Commonwealth of Australia, to Perth Western Australia, Sydney New South Wales, Adelaide South Australia, Melbourne Victoria.' Girls' Friendly Society Archives, 2/263, 'Details of Arrangements as to Procedure with Regard to Travellers Sent by the Society for the Settlement of British Women.'

27 See, for example, Margaret Kiddle, *Caroline Chisholm* (Carleton, Vict.: Melbourne University Press, 1957); and Barbara Roberts, 'Daughters of the Empire and Mothers of the Race: Caroline Chisholm and Female Emigration in the British Empire,' *Atlantis* 1:2 (Spring 1976).

28 Canadian Institute for Historical Micro-reproductions (CIHM) 43383, 'Female Emigration'; and CIHM 43383, *Annual Report of the Female Protection Society, 1855–1856* (Toronto: [n.p.], 1856). A more successful attempt to establish a committee to receive single female immigrants was made in Melbourne in 1856. However, like the Toronto organization, the Melbourne committee of ladies had a hard time funding any special reception projects. See State Library of Victoria, MS 12124, MSS Store Bay 52, 'Governesses' Institute and Melbourne Home.'

29 See Perry, *On the Edge of Empire*, 153.

30 The FMCES received numerous complaints about its misrepresentation of the help that female migrants could expect from correspondents in Sydney. See Fawcett Library (FL), 1/FME, 2-1, FMCES Letterbook #1.

31 For example, representatives of the Salvation Army travelled around the

empire inspecting facilities for immigrant reception. See Harper, *Beyond the Broad Atlantic*, 209–20.

32 In the tradition of Maria Rye, who spent a couple of years in Australia and New Zealand to gain a better understanding of local conditions for immigrant women, an endless procession of British women set off for the colonies, funded personally or by the societies within which they worked. These women's movements are recorded in the minutes of the BWEA, the GFS, the South African Colonisation Society, and the Colonial Intelligence League and in the *Imperial Colonist.*

33 Harper, *Beyond the Broad Atlantic*, 251. See also Harper's discussion of Annie McPherson's emigration of children to Canada. McPherson's good friend, Ellen Bilborough, and two sisters, Rachel Merry and Louisa Birt, moved to Canada to run receiving homes for McPherson's emigrants. See Harper, *Beyond the Broad Atlantic*, 185–6.

34 Roberts, '"A Work of Empire,"' 195.

35 *Girls Home of Welcome Association, Winnipeg, Manitoba, 1st Annual Report, 1898*, 10.

36 *The Women's National Immigration Society, Annual Report for 1898*, 11.

37 Vancouver gained its version of Miss Fowler in 1911 in the form of Mrs Mary Agnes FitzGibbon (not to be confused with Miss FitzGibbon of the Toronto Women's Hostel), who established the Queen Mary's Coronation Hostel for Gentlewomen. See Marilyn Barber, 'The Gentlewomen of Queen Mary's Coronation Hostel,' in Barbara K. Latham and Roberta J. Pazdro, eds, *Not Just Pin Money: Selected Essays on the History of Women's Work in British Columbia* (Victoria: Camosun College, 1984).

38 Una Monk, *New Horizons: A Hundred Years of Women's Migration* (London: Her Majesty's Stationary Office, 1963), 123.

39 Leaton College was a school established by women associated with the BWEA specifically to train women in colonial domestic and farm work.

40 Monk, *New Horizons*, 123.

41 Georgina Binnie-Clarke was both the author of two books on life as an Englishwoman farming on the Prairies and an activist for reforms to the Canadian homesteading acts so that single women might take up farms on the same terms as men. See Susan Jackel, introduction to Georgina Binnie-Clark, *Wheat and Woman* (Toronto: University of Toronto Press, 1979). Binnie-Clarke's activities and writings were duly noted in the *Imperial Colonist*, and she seems to have established a good working relationship with some members of the BWEA.

42 *British Women's Emigration Association, Annual Report, 1897–1899*, 9.

43 Ibid., *1896–1897*, 15.

44 *Imperial Colonist* 23:3 (March 1925): 46

45 *British Women's Emigration Association, Annual Report, 1892–1893*, 10.

46 Ibid.

47 For discussions of the politics and work of the GFS, see Ellen Joyce, 'The Imperial Aspect of G.F.S. Emigration,' LAC, MG 28, I349 (Microfilm A-1199); Mary Heath-Stubbs, *Friendship's Highway: Being the History of the Girls' Friendly Society, 1875–1925* (London: GFS, 1926); and Brian Harrison, 'For Church, Queen and Family: The Girls' Friendly Society 1874–1920,' *Past and Present* 61: 107–38.

48 Stubbs, *Friendship's Highway*, 70–1. The GFS was much more successful in Australia than in Canada. By the First World War, the GFS had thriving branches, dedicated reception committees, and GFS-affiliated hostels in all of Australia's port cities.

49 New South Wales State Archives (NSWA), City 9/6174, George Wise to Mrs Alexander Gordon, May 1884; Alexander Stuart to Wise, 26 May 1884; Alexander Stuart to Sir Paul, 30 June 1884.

50 LAC, MG 28, I349 (Microfilm A-1188), Minutes of the Colonial and Emigration Committee of the GFS, 12 June 1884.

51 Jan Gothard also reviews this case in *Blue China: Single Female Migration to Colonial Australia* (Melbourne: Melbourne University Press, 2001), 180–7.

52 See NSWA, City 9/6174, correspondence from Alexander Stuart to Sir Paul, 30 June 1884; and to George Wise, Agent of Immigration, during June 1885.

53 NSWA, City 9/6174, 'The GFS and the Hiring-Room' (undated newspaper clipping, letter to the editor of the *Herald*).

54 It appears that Daley purposely disregarded his superior's intentions that the GFS's wishes be accommodated in this matter. See NSWA, City 9/6174, correspondence among Daley, Wise, and Stuart.

55 See, NSWA, City 9/6174, correspondence between George Wise, Immigration Agent, and Mrs Alexander Gordon during April and May 1885.

56 NSWA, City 9/6174, clipping from the *Herald*, 11 April 1885.

57 See NSWA, City 9/6174, 'Newspaper Clippings: Girls' Friendly Society, March and April, 1885.'

58 See NSWA, City 9/6174 (untitled newspaper clipping). Gothard's analysis of this type of response and its role in the management of the labour market is compelling. She writes: 'According to the press, immigrant women were in fact the ultimate winners in the domestic servant market place ... It was a false image. Through the two tied strategies of isolating new arrivals and forcing them to compete for employment at the government-controlled hiring day, the reception process served both to exclude immigrant domestics from knowledge of the prevailing price of domestic labour and prevented

them [from] competing effectively in the local employment market.' Goth-ard, *Blue China*, 187.

59 Janice Gothard provides some valuable context for this issue, writing that in the 1880s the comparatively high cost of getting to NSW determined that 'women with no contacts in the colony chose to avoid the more expensive destination.' As a result, few women 'offered themselves for hire at the emigrant hiring depot.' Gothard, '"Pity the Poor Immigrant,"' 111. Within this context, it is not surprising that the activities of the GFS resulted in a scandal.

60 According to Gothard, the New South Wales government's practices in this respect were no different from those of other Australian colonies. See Gothard, '"Pity the Poor Immigrant,"' 115.

61 NSWA, City 9/6174, 'Hiring of Immigrants.'

62 The case of the WPIS hostel for single women in Montreal has also been reviewed by Barbara Roberts, in 'Sex, Politics and Religion: Controversies in Female Immigration Reform Work in Montreal, 1881–1919,' *Atlantis* 6:1 (1980). Roberts's discussion focuses upon the more local context of this case.

63 See ibid., 7.

64 Princess Louise also supported British organizations doing similar work, including the British Women's Emigration Association.

65 The WPIS annual reports reveal that by the early 1890s more than half of the immigrant women managed by this society were en route to destinations in the West. In 1898 the society further emphasized its national agenda by changing its name to the Women's National Immigration Society.

66 For further discussion of the Anglican church's imperialist work in Canada, see Myra Rutherdale, *Women and the White Man's God: Gender and Race in the Canadian Mission Field* (Vancouver: UBC Press, 2002).

67 Further details of the conflict between the Montreal Anglicans and the WNIS may be found in Roberts, 'Sex, Politics and Religion.'

68 Ibid., 28–9.

69 Archives of the Society for Promoting Christian Knowledge, *The Story of the SPCK* (n.p., n.d.).

70 *United British Women's Emigration Association, Annual Report*, 1891–2.

71 LAC, MG 17, B9, Society for Promoting Christian Knowledge [hereafter SPCK], Emigration Committee Minutes, 19 December 1895.

72 Renaud, quoted in SPCK, Emigration Committee Minutes, 22 October 1896.

73 See SPCK, Emigration Committee Minutes, 19 December 1895, 22 April 1896, and 25 June 1896.

74 Ellen Joyce, quoted in SPCK, Emigration Committee Minutes, 22 April 1896.

75 This is a point that Joyce believed had been proved by the way Renaud had treated the affair of Mary Weston. See Joyce, quoted in SPCK, Emigration Committee Minutes, 17 December 1896.

76 Joyce quoted in SPCK, Emigration Committee Minutes, 19 December 1895.

77 Joyce, quoted ibid.

78 For example, in a letter to the SPCK Joyce noted: 'I am conscious that I have more information bearing upon the subject than anyone else in England can have, because it is my business and duty to know how well my girls have been treated and cared for.' Quoted in SPCK, Emigration Committee Minutes, 19 December 1895.

79 See LAC, MG28, I336, British Women's Emigration Association [hereafter BWEA], Minutes of Council Meetings, 24 February 1897, 11 March 1897, and 6 April 1897.

80 Quoted in SPCK, Emigration Committee Minutes, 22 April 1896.

81 See SPCK, Emigration Committee Minutes, 22 April 1896.

82 BWEA, Minutes of Council Meetings, 6 April 1897.

83 SPCK, Emigration Committee Minutes, 17 February 1898.

84 Ibid., 17 December 1896.

85 Ibid., 25 December 1897. Fanshawe had a hard time letting this matter rest. Early in 1898 he published his opinions about Joyce's practice of sending girls to a home that was not approved by the Montreal bishop in the *Guardian*. Naturally, Joyce replied. See SPCK, Emigration Committee Minutes, 17 February 1898.

86 SPCK, Emigration Committee Minutes, 25 December 1897; BWEA, Minutes of a Special Meeting of Council, 11 March 1897.

87 BWEA, Minutes of Council Meetings, 11 March 1897 (italics mine).

88 BWEA, Minutes of Council Meetings, 6 April 1897.

89 'Emigration Notice,' *Friendly Work*, May 1890: 80.

90 FL, *United British Women's Emigration Association, Annual Report, 1889*, 13.

91 For examples of BWEA statements of confidence in the work of the WNIS, see the *United British Women's Emigration Association, Annual Report* for 1891–2, and for 1895–6.

92 I have examined this case in further detail in Lisa Chilton, 'Migrants in Montreal: Managing British Female Immigrants at the Turn of the Twentieth Century,' *British Journal of Canadian Studies* 16:1 (2003): 59–70.

93 QSA, Brisbane, PRE/122, 'Correspondence re Immigration of Domestics,' letter from H.M. James, Assistant Government Matron, Australia House, London, [November or December 1926].

94 QSA, PRE/122, Letter from H.M. James.

95 Ibid.

96 In fact, complaints of a strikingly similar nature were made during the late nineteenth century too. See Gothard, *Blue China*, esp. 169–71.

97 See QSA, PRE/1221, 'Correspondence re Immigration of Domestics,' David Garland to Under Secretary, Chief Secretary's Department, 19 April 1927; L.E. Grierson Brown, President Women's Committee, memorandum entitled 'New Settlers' League of Australia, Queensland Division,' received 1 May 1927; Fleming to Ferry, 6 July 1927; Abell to Ferry, 13 July 1927; Ferry to Fleming, 18 July 1927; Abell to Undersecretary, Chief Secretary's Department, 17 August 1927; David Garland to Ferry, 9 September 1927.

98 Representatives from the BWEA, the Girls' Friendly Society, the Travellers Aid Society, the Victoria League Settlers' Welcome Committee, the South African Colonization Society, the National Vigilance Society, the Self Help Society, the Central Emigration Board, the Society for Promoting Christian Knowledge Church Emigration Society, and the Young Women's Christian Association attended the meeting.

99 'Reception Overseas,' *Imperial Colonist* 8:108 (December 1910): 201.

100 Ibid., 203.

101 FL, 1/SOS/1/1, box 3/6, Joint Council of Women's Emigration Societies, Minutes, 8 October 1917. This official protest was not unprecedented. See Julia Bush, *Edwardian Ladies and Imperial Power* (New York: Leicester University Press, 2000), 67.

102 It is interesting to note that in the female emigrators' complaints about the Brisbane depot, the depot's matron was immune from attack. If anything, she seems to have been the focus of these women's support and sympathy.

103 *Australian Dictionary of Biography*, vol. 10, *1891–1939* (Melbourne: Melbourne University Press, 1986), 432–5.

104 FL, SOSBW, Minutes of the Australian Sub-Committee, 2 November 1922.

105 See the minutes of the meeting between the NSL representatives and Senator Wilson on 20 August 1923 regarding female migration. AA, ACT, series A461/8, item G349/1/6.

106 Lady Masson, quoted in 'The New Settlers' League and Its Problems,' *Imperial Colonist* 24:9 (September 1926): 187.

107 Bush, *Edwardian Ladies and Imperial Power*, 101.

108 See, for example, the rivalry between the Canadian Imperial Order Daughters of the Empire and the British-based Victoria League. This is discussed in Bush, *Edwardian Ladies and Imperial Power*, chap. 6.

109 See Valverde, 'Racial Purity, Sexual Purity, and Immigration Policy,' chapter 5 in *The Age of Light, Soap, and Water*, and Barbara Roberts, *Whence They Came: Deportation from Canada, 1900–1935* (Ottawa: University of Ottawa Press, 1988), for a discussion of the work of Ethel West and others regard-

ing deportation. For British responses to the deportation of single women, see Monk, *New Horizons*, 135.

110 As the example of M.E. Chomley illustrates, women became more evident as representatives of the dominion governments *and* of the British government in the post-war period. Chomley worked with the Australian Red Cross in England during the war. When the war was over, she decided to stay on in England to work in the British government's Society for the Oversea Settlement of British Women, where she dealt with issues relating to female emigration to Australia. For Chomley's work with the Australian Red Cross, see Jay Winter, *Sites of Memory, Sites of Mourning: The Great War in European Cultural History* (New York: Cambridge University Press, 1995), 43.

111 The establishment of the New Settlers' League and the Canadian Council of Immigration of Women went a long way to improve the relations between government bodies and women's organizations. For information about the NSL in Australia, see Michael Roe, *Australia, Britain, and Migration, 1915–1940: A Study of Desperate Hopes* (New York: Cambridge University Press, 1995), chap. 10. For information about the Canadian Council of Immigration of Women, see Marilyn Barber, *Immigrant Domestic Servants in Canada* (Ottawa: Canadian Historical Association, 1991); Roberts, 'Sex, Politics and Religion,' 34–5; and Valverde, *The Age of Light, Soap, and Water*, 125–8.

6: Domesticating Canberra

1 Quoted in Lionel Wigmore, *Canberra: History of Australia's National Capital* (Canberra: Dalton Publishing Co., 1963), 58.

2 Roger Pegrum, 'Canberra: The Bush Capital,' in Pamela Stratham, ed., *The Origins of Australia's Capital Cities* (New York: Cambridge University Press, 1989), 337.

3 This term was regularly used to describe Canberra in its early years. See Pegrum, 'Canberra'; Jim Gibbney, *Canberra, 1913–1953* (Canberra: AGPS Press, 1988); and Godfrey Linge, 'Butters' Drive,' *Sunday Timestyle* (supplement to *Canberra Times*), 14 October 1979.

4 According to Donald Leslie Johnson, Canberra is internationally unique because 'it was a world competition nurtured to materialization'; 'because it was a synthesis of current advanced ideas contemporary with its initial design'; and 'because it was a city *ab initio* and a federal seat of government ... Few cities have such distinctions: only Washington D.C., and Brazilia come to mind when one considers modern times.' Johnson, *Can-*

berra and Walter Burley Griffin (Melbourne: Oxford University Press, 1980), 1. For discussions of the designers' intentions in creating Canberra, see Gibbney, *Canberra*; Pegrum, 'Canberra'; Freeman Wyllie, 'The Community Spirit – 'Intangible but All Important': Social Service Idealism in Canberra, 1925–1929,' *Canberra Historical Journal* 36 (September 1995): 7–17; and Robert Freestone, 'An Imperial Aspect: The Australian Town Planning Tour of 1914–15,' *Australian Journal of Politics and History* 44:2 (1998): 159–76.

5 Pegrum, 'Canberra,' 336.

6 Freeman Wyllie focuses upon the 'community' aspect of Canberra's creation in 'The Community Spirit.'

7 Gibbney, *Canberra*, 109.

8 Ibid., 130.

9 Linge, 'Butters' Drive,' 7.

10 Butters and his first assistant, Harrison, were both from England. See Gibbney, *Canberra*, 109.

11 Ibid., 123.

12 Ibid.

13 Ibid., 133–4.

14 Australian Archives (AA), Series A6266/1, item G1928/2290, J.H. Butters to G.F. Pearce, 25 March 1926.

15 Ibid.

16 For her Red Cross work, see Jay Winter, *Sites of Memory, Sites of Mourning: The Great War in European Cultural History* (New York: Cambridge University Press, 1995), 43.

17 AA, Series A6266/1, item G1928/2290, Butters to Pearce, 25 March 1926.

18 Aborigines did live in the Canberra area, although they are not mentioned in most histories of Canberra. (As part of the 'Journey of Healing' in May 2002, the Australian government announced it would erect signs indicating that the capital city had been built on the land of the Ngunawal people. See *Canberra Times*, Monday, 27 May 2002, 5. Thanks to Michele Langfield for this.) For information about the training and use of Aboriginal women for domestic service in Australia, see Joanne Scott and Raymond Evans, 'The Molding of Menials: The Making of the Aboriginal Female Domestic Servant in Early Twentieth Century Queensland,' *Hecate* 22 (1996): 140–57.

19 AA, Series A6266/1, item G1928/2290, Butters to Pearce, 25 March 1926. Certainly Butters was right in this. See Margaret Anderson, 'Good Strong Girls: Colonial Women and Work,' in Kay Saunders and Raymond Evans, eds, *Gender Relations in Australia: Domination and Negotiation* (Sydney: Harcourt Brace, 1992), 231–6; Evans and Saunders, 'No Place Like Home: The Evolution of the Australian Housewife,' ibid., 182–3; and Beverley Kingston,

My Wife, My Daughter, and Poor Mary Ann: Women and Work in Australia (Melbourne: Nelson, 1975), chap. 3.

20 AA, Series A6266/1, item G1928/2290, Butters to Pearce, 25 March 1926.

21 Ibid.

22 The emigrators would have been aware of contemporary discussions on this subject, such as C.V. Butler's *Domestic Service: An Enquiry by the Women's Industrial Council* (London: G. Bell and Sons Ltd, 1916). See Kingston, *My Wife, My Daughter, and Poor Mary Ann* for discussion on this subject for Australia.

23 For a discussion of some of the other projects taken on by the commission, see Wyllie, 'The Community Spirit.'

24 AA, Series A6266/1, item G1928/2290, Butters to Pearce, 25 March 1926.

25 The women who ran the SOSBW were delighted by the commission's plans for this hostel, which they singled out for applause in the *Imperial Colonist* 24:11 (November 1926): 225.

26 Servants' uniforms, wage rates, and hours allowed off work were all set out in detail in the club rules. See AA, Series A6266/1, file G1928/2290; and Series CP698/9, file 29.

27 AA, Series A6266/1, item G1928/2290, Pearce to Butters, 29 March 1926.

28 The number of domestic servants requisitioned by individual states was usually unmet, with about 50% of requisitions actually being filled most of the time. See AA, Series A461, item F349/2/1. See also AA, A461/9, item H349/1/6 part 1 for further information about the difficulties involved in requisitioning servants.

29 Discussion of the assignment of Miss Hawkins to this job may be found in AA, Series A6266/1, file G1928/2290.

30 See *Imperial Colonist* 24:11 (November 1926): 225 and 240.

31 Ibid., 24:5 (May 1926): 93–4.

32 Ibid., 24:11 (November 1926): 225.

33 Ibid.

34 Hawkins interviewed 100 women, out of which she selected 25. See AA, Series A6266/1, file G1928/2290, Hawkins to the Secretary of the Federal Capital Commission, 10 November 1926.

35 AA, Series A6266/1, file G1928/2290, Hawkins to the Secretary of the Federal Capital Commission, 2 December 1926.

36 Ibid., Hawkins to Federal Capital Commission, 10 November 1926.

37 Ibid., Doris T. Duffield to Mr Daley, 16 January 1927.

38 Ibid., C.S. Daley to Mrs Woodger, 31 December 1926.

39 Written requests for servants began as early as December 1926, and may be found throughout the file on the Canberra domestic-servant project. See AA, Series A6266/1, item G1928/2290.

40 AA, Series A6266/1, item G1928/2290, L.J. Hurley to Sec., FCC, 26 January 1927. For a description of the Melbourne reception committee's work with SOSBW immigrants at this time, see *Imperial Colonist* 25·1 (January 1927): 3–4.

41 AA, Series A6266/1, item G1928/2290, C.S. Daley to Deputy Director, Commonwealth Immigration Office, 14 February 1927. At a later date it appears that the commission lost two or three other women, 'who either fell for the glamour of Sydney or had become engaged to young men.' AA, Series A6266/1, item G1928/2290, J.H. Butters to J.M. Baddeley, 8 March 1927. The commissioners' decision to appoint a trustworthy matron to accompany the servants the whole way to Canberra was, in part, a response to fears that otherwise their immigrants would be 'stolen' en route. As was typical in such cases, the Canberra project also 'stole' servants who were headed to other destinations. See Hawkins's letter to the Secretary of the FCC, 24 January 1927, and correspondence concerning Ada Edwards in AA, Series A6266/1, item G1928/2290, 20 April 192; and 4 May 1927.

42 The image that the commissioners presented to other state officials and the press was conveniently superficial and uncomplicated. Obviously it was not in their best interests to search for, or record, cases of employer or employee dissatisfaction. An examination of different sources would likely show that, like everywhere else, servants and mistresses in Canberra continued to have their differences.

43 'Domestic Help. Solving Canberra's Problem,' *Canberra Times*, 3 February 1927. Apparently, the support that the editor of the *Canberra Times* gave to this project was unusual. By the end of 1927 this newspaper had become a mouthpiece for anti-commission sentiments originating in the Canberra community (see Gibbney, *Canberra*, 145).

44 See, for example, 'Domestics for Canberra: Why Girls Are Imported,' *Age* 4 February 1927. (All newspaper references may be found in AA, A659, item 1944/1/2690.)

45 'Domestics for Canberra.'

46 Similar complaints about the commission's decision to attract British rather than Australian domestic workers to Canberra were also registered outside of the press. See, for example, the formal complaint sent to Prime Minister Bruce by the Town Council of Waterloo, New South Wales. AA, Series A461/9, item H349/1/6.

47 Marilyn Lake, 'Mission Impossible: How Men Gave Birth to the Australian Nation – Nationalism, Gender and Other Seminal Acts,' *Gender and History* 4:3 (Autumn 1992), 306.

48 Ibid.

49 AA, Series A6266/1, item G1928/2290, Superintendent, Commissariat Department to Chief Commissioner, 5 February 1927.

50 Ibid., C.S. Daley to Secretary, Department of Home and Territories, 5 February 1927.

51 Butters refers here to an article in the *Evening News*, 25 February 1927. The article's header announced: 'Failed on Job. Canberra "Mary Anns." Sydney Girls Chosen.'

52 AA, Series A6266/1, item G1928/2290, Butters to J.M. Baddeley, 8 March 1927.

53 Wyllie, 'The Community Spirit,' 15. See also Linge, 'Butters' Drive,' 7.

54 This is discussed most thoroughly in Wyllie, 'The Community Spirit.'

55 AA, Series A6266/1, item G1928/2290, H. Farrands to C.S. Daley, 13 October 1927.

56 Ibid., Hawkins to Daley, 11 June 1928; and Daley to Davies, 14 June 1928.

57 Ibid., A.S. Davies to C.S. Daley, 26 June 1928.

58 Richard White, *Inventing Australia: Images and Identity, 1688–1980* (Sydney: George Allen and Unwin, 1987), viii.

59 See quoted commissioners in the *Canberra Times*, 3 February 1927.

60 *Argus*, 3 February 1927.

61 Joy Damousi and Marilyn Lake, Introduction, to Joy Damousi, ed., *Gender and War: Australians at War in the Twentieth Century*. (New York: Cambridge University Press, 1995), 2; White, *Inventing Australia*, 35; Lake, 'Mission Impossible,' 306.

62 White, *Inventing Australia*, 35.

Conclusion

1 Mrs Chapin, 'The Ethics of Emigration,' *Imperial Colonist* 2:8 (August 1903): 88

2 Ibid., 89.

3 Ibid., 90.

4 Ibid.

5 'British Ideals in South America,' *Imperial Colonist* 14:174 (July 1916): 103.

6 *Imperial Colonist* 25:4 (April 1927): 3.

7 Ibid., 4.

8 Ibid., 5.

9 This point is emphasized in a letter from the chairman of the Joint Council of Female Emigration Societies to Mr Macnaghten of the government's Oversea Settlement Committee. See Library and Archives Canada (LAC), MG 28, I349, (Microfilm A1055), 22 May 1919.

10 Christiane Harzig, 'Women Migrants as Global and Local Agents: New Research Strategies on Gender and Migration,' in Pamela Sharpe, ed., *Women, Gender and Labour Migration: Historical and Global Perspectives* (New York: Routledge, 2001), 15.

11 Catherine Hall, *Civilising Subjects: Metropole and Colony in the English Imagination, 1830–1867* (Cambridge: Polity Press, 2002), 17.

12 Michele Langfield, 'Voluntarism, Salvation, and Rescue: British Juvenile Migration to Australia and Canada, 1890–1939,' *Journal of Imperial and Commonwealth History* 32:2 (May 2004): 87.

13 This dichotomy was first fleshed out in chapter 5, 'Feminism and Female Emigration, 1861–1886,' in Hammerton, *Emigrant Gentlewomen: Genteel Poverty and Female Emigration, 1830–1914* (London: Croom Helm, 1979).

14 James Hammerton, '"Out of Their Natural Station": Empire and Empowerment in the Emigration of Lower Middle-Class Women,' in Rita Kranidis, ed., *Imperial Objects: Victorian Womens' Emigration and the Unauthorized Imperial Experience* (New York: Twayne Publishers, 1998), 144–9. Hammerton draws upon Julia Bush's analysis in *Edwardian Ladies and Imperial Power* (New York: Leicester University Press, 2000), in his discussion here.

15 This issue of how to interpret women's work for women has been the focus of extensive debate by historians of women over the past couple of decades. See Barbara Caine, *Victorian Feminists* (Oxford: Oxford University Press, 1992); Nancy Cott, *The Grounding of Modern Feminism* (New Haven: Yale University Press, 1987); Seth Koven and Sonya Michel, eds, *Mothers of a New World: Maternalist Politics and the Origins of Wefare States* (New York: Routledge, 1993); P. Levine, *Feminist Lives in Victorian England: Private Roles and Public Commitments* (Oxford: Basil Blackwell, 1990); Karen Offen, 'Contextualizing the Theory and Practice of Feminism in Nineteenth-Century Europe' in Renate Bridenthal, Susan Mosher Stuard, and Merry E. Weisner, eds, *Becoming Visible: Women in European History*, 3rd ed. (New York: Houghton Mifflin, 1998); and Jane Rendall, ed., *Equal or Different: Women's Politics, 1800–1914* (Oxford: Basil Blackwell, 1987).

16 Bush, *Edwardian Ladies and Imperial Power*, 3.

Index

STUDIES IN GENDER AND HISTORY

General editors: Franca Iacovetta and Karen Dubinsky